STILL WOMAN ENOUGH

LORETTA LYNN

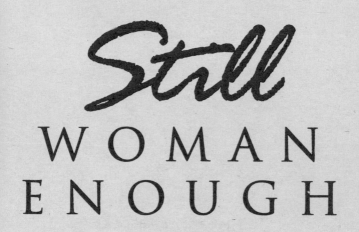

Still
WOMAN
ENOUGH

❧ A MEMOIR ❧

LORETTA LYNN
with Patsi Bale Cox

HYPERION

NEW YORK

Printed in the United States of America. For information address:
Hyperion, 77 W. 66th Street, New York, New York 10023-6298.

Mass Market ISBN: 0-7868-8987-X

Hyperion books are available for special promotions and
premiums.
For details, contact Hyperion Special Markets,
77 W. 66th Street, 11th floor, New York, New York 10023-6298,
or call 212-456-0133.

FIRST MASS MARKET EDITION

10 9 8 7 6 5 4 3 2 1

For my children,
Betty Sue, Ernest Ray, Cissie, Peggy,
and Patsy, and for Jack Benny, who lives in my heart.
You are the inspiration for everything that I do.
I love you all so much.

Your mother

❧ ACKNOWLEDGMENTS ❧

I WANT TO THANK DOO for the memories he has left me and for the children we had together. Those memories and our children will always be my ultimate treasure. Additionally, there have been so many people who have worked with me and helped me all these years that need to be thanked and are—I'll always love you.

This book has been important to me and harder to write than *Coal Miner's Daughter* since I have had such loss and tragedy since then. But it tells my story and it is my life.

Finally, I want to thank Pastor Arnold Murray for his friendship and, most specially, for his love and support.

Loretta Lynn

"MOMMY, WHY DO YOU TRY to talk like Sissy Spacek?"

One of my twin girls asked me that question after Sissy played me in the 1979 movie *Coal Miner's Daughter*. Most anyone reading this book would probably know that the movie was based on the autobiography I wrote in 1976. My twins, Peggy and Patsy, were little when they heard Sissy talk for the first time. That's why they didn't know who was tryin' to talk like who.

The movie won an Oscar for Sissy, and since I hand-picked her for the part, that award made me proud. What happened was this: When the Hollywood producers were trying to figure out who should play me, they showed me a bunch of pictures of actresses and asked me to pick one. As soon as I seen Sissy, I told 'em I didn't need to see no more pictures.

"That is the freckle-faced girl that looks just like I did, and she's the one I want," I said.

Not long after that meeting, I was on *The Tonight Show* and told Johnny Carson that Sissy Spacek was gonna play me in my life story. I didn't know nobody had talked to Sissy about it. Well, she happened to be watching the show that night and about fell off her chair. It took some talking, but I finally convinced her to take the part. Of course, I didn't know Sissy was fixin' to work me to death! She went on the road with me off and on for about a year during the late 1970s, studying me, and learning to talk the way I do. She went to the studio where Owen Bradley had produced so many of my hits and learned to sing the songs the way I sing them, too. After we worked together a good while, we went on the Opry and traded off verses of "Fist City." Most of the Opry regulars standing backstage couldn't tell who was singin' what. Owen also produced Sissy on the movie's soundtrack, and there was only one song on the album that I didn't think sounded as much like me. That song was "Coal Miner's Daughter," and it wasn't quite as good as the rest of them, even though she tried real hard on it. But as far as I'm concerned, she done a great job.

The subject of *Coal Miner's Daughter* came up again not long ago, when I was playing a show at the 2001 Strawberry Festival in Plant City, Florida. I hadn't played any shows since November when I had a knee injury, so I was surprised and tickled that we sold out the shows and set a festival attendance record. I was even more tickled to eat some of them ripe strawberries. If you never had any strawberries from that part of the world, you owe it to yourself to go get some of 'em. They're as sweet as any I ever had, and I have tasted a few strawberries.

The twins were appearing on the show, too, and we were sitting on the bus talking about their careers. I was threatening to fire their record company and their manager 'cause they missed the Disc Jockey Convention in Nashville. The twins were recording a new album, but I told 'em that it don't do you no good to make an album if you don't try to get the disc jockeys to play the music. I don't know how much I've learned in these forty years on the road, but that is one thing I know for a fact. Without the disc jockeys, an artist ain't got a chance. And when the deejays come to Nashville, you'd better be out shaking their hands. I know I was.

So I was thinking about the girls' careers, and about the five flats of ripe strawberries the festival organizers sent over to the bus, and how I ought to clean and freeze 'em before they had a chance to go bad. I was thinking back to when Doo and me moved to Washington state and how for quite a few years I'd been the fastest strawberry picker in the whole county. Then some old boy come in and started pickin' 'em faster than me, edging me down to the second fastest. The thing that made me mad was that he picked 'em dirty, with the stems on, while I picked 'em clean. His was just a filthy mess when he brought 'em in. Mine was almost ready to eat. But he still bumped me down to number two. Dirty sometimes wins over clean in this world, I am sorry to say.

But the girls weren't interested in my career as a field hand; they wanted to talk about *Coal Miner's Daughter*.

That movie was over twenty years old by then, but it might as well have been yesterday in Patsy's and Peggy's minds. This time they asked me something a lot more serious than whether I was talking like Sissy. They asked me why in the world I was writing another book.

" 'Cause I still got things to say," I answered.

I mean, just 'cause people liked your first record, it wouldn't mean you couldn't make another one, would it?

I reminded them that the first thing I regretted when I saw the first book in print was the fact I'd forgot to tell about my very first memory. Then the more I looked it over, the more things I realized I left out. I left out how bad I felt when my grandpa told me I wasn't pretty, and I left out the time Aunt Boyd almost accidentally killed me when she was showing Mommy how she planned to take a board after her husband's girlfriend. I also wanted to say a little more about how much I loved our cousin Lee Dollarhide even if he did escape from the penitentiary three times. Or maybe because of it.

There was people in the music business that I wished I'd said a little more about in *Coal Miner's Daughter*. People like Ernest Tubb, Conway Twitty, Cal Smith, Faron Young, Tammy Wynette, and Tanya Tucker. And I'll start at the beginning again, because in some cases there was stories that left out an important part. Like Paul Harvey says, *the rest of the story*.

Then my twins asked the question they was *really* interested in: was I gonna tell any bad stories about their daddy. They thought I'd said enough about the bad times in the first book. They thought people knew everything they needed to know about Doo and me.

"Everyone knows he drank too much and you two fought!" Patsy said.

"In the movie, you and Daddy kind of ride off into the sunset," Peggy chimed in. "Are you going to ruin that?"

Well, people almost never really ride off into no sunsets, so I tried to explain what it was I wanted to tell, why I felt like I needed to write another book after all these years. I loved Doolittle Lynn with all my heart. I loved him when he was sober and when he was drunk. I ain't sayin' I liked him when he was drunk, although to tell you the truth, once in a while Doo was easier to get along with after a swig or two. Other times he got plain mean, and I am gonna talk about some of those times. Maybe it will help someone who is living through the same illness.

If I hadn't loved him, I wouldn't have been able to stick it out. I tried to tell the girls that a lifetime with somebody means all the ups and downs, the times you fight and the times you hang on to each other for dear life.

I don't blame Doo for being an alcoholic. Shoot, it run in the Lynn family. His mama raised her child on a suck rag dipped in whiskey. That set him on a drinker's path early enough. Alcoholism is an awful disease, but I don't look down on folks for drinking. If I felt like taking a drink, I'd do it in a minute, because that's just the way I am. Luckily, I ain't had the urge.

While I was talking to the twins, I was reminded of something that Doo said to me not long before he died. He was in the hospital after they'd had to amputate his legs. He took my hand and squeezed it.

"I want to thank you for hanging in there with me all

these years, Loretta," he said. "If it hadn't been for you, I'd have probably ended up on skid row."

"Don't you say that, Doo. You'd 'a never let yourself get that low. You're a good worker and you'd have done fine anywhere," I said. And I meant it. Doo was a good man and a hard worker. But he was an alcoholic, and it affected our marriage all the way through. He was also a womanizer. Cheating husbands have been all over the news talk shows for a few years now. Lots of women say they don't understand why women stay with them dogs. My story is about one who did—me.

That night in Florida, the girls and me ended up cryin' and talkin' about the love of my life, their daddy, Oliver Venetta, or Doo, short for Doolittle Lynn. And to tell you the truth, I don't know that the girls still understand this, but even though I am gonna tell some bad stories, I am also gonna tell you a love story. It's one of the hardest love stories in the world. But it's got a soft side, too.

That's how Doo was. He could act just plain awful. But he could be an awful kind man. And he'd be the first one to tell me to tell it like it was. We had that conversation when I was writing *Coal Miner's Daughter*. Back then Doo said this: "Hell's fire, Loretta, just tell the story the way it happened. I've always said you should never try to cover up things. Look, we're not perfect. Let's not pretend we are."

Doo was right. He sure wasn't no perfect man. And I've always admitted that I can be mean as a snake. Yes, Doo hit me sometimes. And yes, I've been known to knock the fire out of him. I told him, "You hit me once and I'll hit you back twice." I broke my share of dishes throwin' 'em at him, too. Especially when we was up in Washington State.

Even though I made the movie people rewrite that script three times to get the "Hollywood" out of it, the movie did build a sort of myth around Doo and me and our marriage. And it was one that stuck with us. I can't tell you how many women would come up to me and talk about how it made them feel better about their marriages when they saw me and Doo—or, really, Sissy Spacek and Tommy Lee Jones—putting things back together in the movie.

But there was also a lot of women who got real mad at Doo and stayed mad. More than once, my girls have seen a woman walk right up to Doo, slap him in the face, and say, "How could you treat Loretta that way?" The twins say Doo was more startled and embarrassed than mad when it happened. On the other hand, lots of folks wanted to get to know Doo after the movie. Good old boys would bring their whiskey out to our campgrounds at Hurricane Mills, Tennessee, and want Doo to join them for a pop. Likely as not he did just that. Doo was a good old boy, too.

I sometimes think that the scene people remembered most from *Coal Miner's Daughter* was the one about the baloney. That was when Doo was teasing me about eating baloney, and said baloney "makes you horny." I didn't know what that meant. In the movie, they showed Sissy talking on the radio telling a disc jockey convention how eating baloney makes a person horny. The radio station manager had a fit, and told her she'd never be on his station again for using such awful language. Well, of course, that really did happen to me when I started out, and it's just one of the stories that folks laugh about to this day.

It makes me feel good to know that the book and the

movie touched people and that they got some laughs out of some of the stories. I was real proud of *Coal Miner's Daughter*, too, even though I ended up not making much money off it. The film ended up making over sixty-four million dollars in the United States, and no telling how much overseas. Don't that number make your head spin? I tried to find mine; I knew it was somewhere, but it hid from me and my share must have ran outta my pockets like water. All kinds of people had their fingers in that pot. I think I figured out at one point that after all the percentages were handed out, I was in the hole by five percent. That's just proof that it's a big jump between "figurin' on" and "gettin'." But that's all water under the bridge, and I ain't gonna dwell on it. Just remember this: when people talk money, write everything down.

Here's something you probably don't know: originally I didn't want no part of that book or movie. I began writing the book when I was only in my early thirties. I hadn't never done nothing with my life except sing and have babies, and I didn't think I had a life to talk about. But I'd had a bunch of number one songs, and my picture had been on the front of some magazines, like *Redbook* and *Newsweek*. So everybody kept hounding me to write a book, and I finally said I'd do it.

I had no idea that it would all be such a big success. People have told me that the movie is shown every day in the Smithsonian Institution in Washington, D.C., because it's about how a poor person, with little or no education, who works hard can go from rags to riches in the United States. It's the American dream, and it can't happen no place else but in our great country.

What I learned from *Coal Miner's Daughter* is that your stories become you, and you become your stories. And I believe folks love to hear about the back roads of this country.

But unlike Andy Griffith's Mayberry, Butcher Holler is real. Paintsville has a weekly newspaper, and it runs obituaries of folks in Johnson County, including Butcher Holler. It ain't unusual to read that somebody died in his late nineties.

You just ain't gonna read about somebody dying of stress-related disorders in Butcher Holler. Or work, either, unless you worked the mines. That's not saying it was an easy place to live. Life in Butcher Holler was peaceful, but the poverty there also made it a hard life. Life's most valuable lessons are often the most painful.

That's how it was when I was a little girl, and that's how it is today.

When I wrote *Coal Miner's Daughter*, I hadn't really been outta Butcher Holler all that many years. An awful lot has happened to me since then, and it ain't all been the riches side of the story.

I've lost twelve members of my immediate family and friends since Doo and me rode off into that sunset, including my mother, a son, my husband, two brothers, two aunts, and four uncles, along with my good friends Ernest Tubb, Conway Twitty, Tammy Wynette, and Owen Bradley. Most of 'em died within a four-year period of time.

People can say what they want to but nothing, nothing, can prepare you for the loss of a husband or child. One of the hardest things for me to talk about or think about is the day in 1984 when I learned that my son Jack had drowned in the Duck River out at our Hurricane Mills ranch. Jack was small, like my daddy, and he was an easy person to love. Do you know I can't remember one thing about Jack's funeral? The doctors said I was "traumatized" and that my forgetfulness was a "defense mechanism" against a nervous breakdown.

I think I had the nervous breakdown. I just didn't get no treatment for it.

When Patsy and Peggy and me got to talking about their daddy in Plant City, Florida, it got me to thinking about what a complicated man Doo was, and how he changed over the years. My older kids, Jack, Betty, Ernest Ray, and Cissie, had a much harder daddy than the twins did. Doo settled some over the years. Age and health problems will do that to you. It sorrows me that the older ones don't remember the same man 'that Patsy and Peggy recall. But I think if you talk to all the kids in a big family, most of 'em will have very different memories of their parents.

The years changed Doo, but there was some things about him that stayed the same. He was always a man who wanted to make good with something of his own—something more than helping me be a singer. He loved his family, no matter how he got to acting up. And he believed in me with every bit of his heart. Lots of women have asked me how in the world I stayed with a womanizin' alcoholic who could get violent like he sometimes did. There's so many reasons, starting with the way I was raised back in the hills. First, we never talked about alcoholics in the hills. They was just drinkin' men, and most people didn't hold that against 'em. More important, I was raised in the mountains of Kentucky in the 1940s and was taught to mind my man, whether he was a drinker or not. And I got taught that there wasn't no such thing as divorce among decent folks. If you married a man, you entered his life forever. There weren't no back doors—not even if he beat you, cheated on you, or mistreated your children. Back in the hills, they believed that when you make up your bed, you got to sleep in it. If you make it up bad, you'll end up wearin' the wrinkles. I only thought about leaving Doo one time, and I'll tell you about that later.

I married Doo when I wasn't but a child, and he was my life from that day on. But as important as my youth and upbringing was, there's something else that made me stick to Doo. He thought I was something special, more special than anybody else in the world, and never let me forget it. That belief would be hard to shove out the door. Doo was my security, my safety net. Maybe you will understand it when you finish reading what I got to say in this book. And just remember, I'm explainin', not excusin'.

Folks called him Doolittle as a joke 'cause they claimed he didn't do much work, but that ain't true. When Doo got diabetes, he lost two feet and two legs in five years, from 1991 until 1996, and even when he'd lost one leg he was still 'a tryin' to drive the tractor out at our ranch at Hurricane Mills. When he took bad, I almost never left his bedside. I slept in a chair, and I took showers at the hospitals he was in. I stayed out home whenever he was able to leave the hospital to be there. Doolittle Lynn was my husband; my soulmate from the time I was thirteen years old. He was my everything. When you lose everything, you are a lost person.

I got lost for quite a while after Doo died in 1996.

So many of my friends died right around that same time that I felt like my whole world was caving in. Except for family, I never loved no man more than Conway Twitty. I was sitting beside my husband's bedside in a Springfield, Missouri, hospital on June 4, 1993, when Conway was brought in that hospital's emergency room with a bleeding stomach. It liked to killed me when the doctor said he was dead. My wonderful friends Owen Bradley and Tammy Wynette are gone too. I've lost so many people that I feel numb.

Now, maybe somebody else can learn something from the things that have happened to me. I'm proud that I've been able to entertain some folks in my lifetime. Now, I'd like to inspire them. I'd like to uplift them.

So I'm writing another book, one about the twenty-five years that happened after the final credits for *Coal Miner's Daughter* rolled across the screen. For one thing, when I read my first book, or see the movie, I keep wishin' I'd told this or that story. Or I think about people who didn't get talked about as much as they should have been. Mainly, I've got the courage now to tell you some things I didn't tell completely in *Coal Miner's Daughter*.

I don't want this book to overlap too much with my first book. But sometimes it'll happen. I'll have to retell some stories for folks who haven't read the first book, just so things make sense. My maiden name will always be Webb, I'll always be from Butcher Holler, and my first hit song will always be "I'm a Honky Tonk Girl." And I'll always be a coal miner's daughter. Whenever I do a concert, I usually get past my second song when the fans start hollering for me to sing "Coal Miner's Daughter," a song that's entirely about life in Butcher Holler.

People will always want to see Johnny Cash wear black. They'll always want to see Jerry Lee Lewis play his piano standing up. And they'll always want to hear some of these same stories about Butcher Holler, especially if I remember something new about what happened this time around.

I'll tell some things I've never told before. I haven't always told everything I wanted to tell because various managers have advised against it, and because even though Doo said I should tell things like they happened, there was stories I left out because of him. Doo's gone now, and them managers ain't with me no more, so each time I tell a story in this book, I'm going to tell all I can think of this time around.

It's such a short length of time that you go from being a coal miner's daughter to being someone's mommy to being a grandma. It seems *awful* short when you're a mommy at fourteen and a grandma at twenty-nine. I've often said that at the age of fifteen, I felt like I was thirty-five, and at the age of thirty-five, I felt like I was fifteen. Having to grow up as fast as I did when I got married took something away from me. But it also gave me something: a hard-won strength. And through it all, I've tried to keep hanging on to the strength that comes from being able to say that after all was said and done, through good times and bad, I was still woman enough.

Loretta Lynn

One

A Series of Pictures That Come and Go in My Mind . . .

FLASHBULBS WAS POPPIN' and slick-looking young men was sticking microphones in folks' faces when we pulled up to Nashville's Bellemeade Theater. It turned out that they was waiting on me, but a limo carrying Mae Axton, who wrote "Heartbreak Hotel," and the Johnson Sisters, who was runnin' my fan club at the time, rolled up right in front of us and the photographers and reporters all jumped on 'em. When they couldn't figure out who the Johnsons and Mae was, they ran over to the limo carrying me and Doo and Mommy. "Loretta!" They was screamin' and makin' a big fuss. I got nervous and tried to pat my hair down a little, then checked out my clothes. I was just about to find out what it meant to be a movie star, even though you ain't been in a movie yourself. And that's about the time I figgered out that I was the worst-dressed person at the premiere of *Coal Miner's Daughter*.

For some reason, I didn't think about a movie premiere as being as fancy as a country music awards show, where you spend a lot of time looking for the right dress and getting your hair fixed. I wore this little old plain white dress, and my hair sure could have stood some work by a beauty operator.

My family must have understood it, because they all dressed up just fine. Doo wore a tuxedo, along with his cowboy hat and boots, of course. My oldest son, Jack, got dolled up in a white tux and top hat. Now, I have to admit, I laughed when I saw Jack all fancied up like that. He was a sight. There's a picture of him in them clothes in my museum at Hurricane Mills, and even now, as sad as I am over his death, when I look at it, the picture brings a smile to my face. Mommy wore bright lipstick and a sparkly dress. She looked beautiful that night, even though she'd already had a lung removed from cancer and wasn't feeling a bit good. She'd warned my brothers and sisters about any griping they might want to do after the movie, too. Mommy said if they didn't like something, they should just bite their tongues, and if they didn't she might smack their faces!

Doo would tell you that he'd got so worried they'd Hollywood up the story that he came to the premiere ready to pick the film to pieces. When he walked out he had to admit they done a good job. As he put it: "They hung close to the truth."

I also realized that I hadn't been paying attention to some other details, like where all my family was gonna sit, and ways to make them feel special at the premiere. I guess that's just one of them times I counted on managers and agents and other people working for me to take care of everything, when I should have been doin' it myself.

It seemed like every time I looked a different direction, some famous country star was 'a standin' there— Minnie Pearl, Roy Acuff, Ernest Tubb. Seeing my hero Ernest Tubb made me mad all over again because them Hollywood people didn't even want him in the movie. They never heard of him. I told them that Ernest had been the person who first introduced me on the Opry, and that scene had to be included. Ernest probably helped more people in the country music business than anyone else I know. Besides, I remembered how much I loved to hear Ernest singing on the radio when I was growing up, and how much our duets meant to me and to my career. But it was still a fight when it came to Ernest, because some of them people acted downright rude around him. They showed him no respect at all. Especially this one old boy. He kept makin' comments about Ernest's voice, and how he couldn't sing. That fired me up. Ernest Tubb was royalty in country music circles, and I wasn't gonna stand for no disrespect from some silly old boy from Hollywood. He didn't work on the movie much longer, I seen to that.

I had some other incidents during the film's planning

stages. Some was my fault, and some wasn't. One thing I done was mispronounce the director's name when I was on *The Tonight Show*. His name was Michael Apted, which I pronounced as Michael "Uptit." I was embarrassed, but Michael laughed about it.

After it was all said and done, if someone was to ask me for very many details about that night, like who was sitting with who or what somebody said to me at the reception after the movie, I'd come up short. I think my mind must have just gone numb. Either that, or it went to Butcher Holler and wouldn't leave.

The very first thing I thought when that film started rolling was how glad I was that I insisted they film these early scenes right there in Butcher Holler, Kentucky. They was about ready to try and build some kind of a set there in Hollywood, when I put my foot down and told 'em to make it real or not at all. So off they went to Kentucky, and they thanked me for makin' 'em go there after it was all over. It wasn't easy, though. Them big trucks carrying all the cameras and cables and microphones and stuff couldn't make it to Butcher Holler. So they drove as far in as they could and then hand-carried the equipment the rest of the way. Them Kentucky hills is steep.

The hills wasn't the worst of it. The film folks got eat up by ticks and chiggers, and they was awful nervous about the snakes they knew slithered around in the hills.

Bernard Schwartz, the producer, wanted to capture the weather just the way it is in Butcher Holler. He didn't allow no shooting breaks for snow or rain, for hundred-degree weather or twenty-degree weather.

Right off they showed Levon Helm, who played my daddy, talking to the actor who played our cousin Lee Dollarhide. Lee looked a mess, nothing like he did in real life. Of course, watching Levon Helm made me get tears in my eyes, just like when I went to Butcher Holler while they was filming the movie. He did a good job playing Daddy. Close to perfect, I'd say. The next thing I noticed was that Mommy looked real drab in the movie. Mommy was anything but drab. She wore blood-red lipstick. The woman who played her was a pretty woman, but they had her looking kind of drab and dowdy. My mommy was the only woman in Butcher Holler who'd wear blue jeans back then. Mommy was lively. She was feisty. They couldn't show the actress's feet in the movie because she couldn't dance like Mommy. I don't think they really showed her feistiness in the movie, and that's why I'll tell you some more about her and Lee Dollarhide in a while.

Since the movie started right when Doo came back from the army, when I was already thirteen, things I'd wrote in the book about early childhood was left out. They couldn't have told everything, or they might have had a movie that would have gone on for days. So I have some extra stories to tell from them days, too.

Tommy Lee Jones done a great job playing Doolittle, and even Doo admitted it. I say *even* Doo, because when Tommy Lee first signed on for the part, Doo wouldn't help him a bit. Right after Tommy Lee took the part, he come to a show I was playing in Las Vegas. I remember him knocking on the door to the hotel suite, and me lettin' him in. He was wearin' a green sweater just like he'd seen Doo wear in some picture. And he'd dyed his hair red like Doo's. Doo was sittin' on the couch watching a ballgame and he hardly even looked up. Tommy Lee kept tryin' to talk to him and get him to agree to help him with the role, but Doo just sat there 'a lookin' at that durned old television. It was jealousy, plain and simple. And maybe he thought Tommy Lee was 'a gonna make fun of the way he talked. Doo didn't like some famous actor 'a sittin' there trying to copy things about him. Finally Tommy Lee excused himself and left. I was embarrassed, but you couldn't talk to Doo when he was in one of them moods.

I'll tell you how Doo's attitude started changing. When they started filming in Butcher Holler, Tommy Lee rented a Jeep, bought a jug of moonshine, got drunk, and started driving around the back roads of Kentucky like a madman. He got arrested before he even made it to his first day on the set! Worse yet, he resisted arrest and ended up getting beat up the side of the head for it. Universal Studios had to go bail him out so he could get to work. So the next time Doo saw Tommy Lee Jones, he was hungover, fresh out of jail, and sportin' a big lump on his head. Well, I think Doo decided right then and there that Tommy Lee Jones was a man he could like. From then on Doo tried to help him any way he could.

That don't mean Doo always liked it. It didn't bother me a bit when Sissy tried to mimic my ways, but when Tommy Lee followed Doo around trying to walk like him it made Doo crazy. He just hated it. In fact, Doo said he never felt like he met the real Tommy Lee Jones until the movie finished filming. Only then was Tommy Lee Jones hisself, and not Doolittle-Junior! I guess actors is that way, always trying to get into the part and forgetting themselves for the time being. Doo finally tried to help him, though, even when it was making him half nuts.

Later, when the Academy Award nominations come out and Tommy Lee wasn't nominated, Doo was fit to be tied.

"You ain't got nobody to blame but yourself, Doo," I said. "He come to you for help, and you didn't do nothing until it was too late."

Doo knew it was true, so he didn't even argue with me about it.

The only thing that I had a problem with in the Patsy Cline part of the movie was the scene where Charlie Dick sneaks some beer into Patsy's hospital room when I met her that first time. That never happened. Not when I was there. The scene bothered Owen Bradley, too. I know why they done it; to help show her character as a strong woman and she didn't care much about what folks thought she should be doin'. She did it her way, just like Frank Sinatra.

But those things I noticed weren't all that important. Like I said, I was proud of the movie and proud of all the people who acted in it. The strangest thing was when the final scene come up and the credits started to roll. I told Doo it seemed like everything had gone by too fast. I'd seen my life in exactly two hours and four minutes!

After the premiere, Universal threw us a little party, but to save my life I couldn't tell you where it was or what happened there. I do remember me and Sissy and Doo and Tommy Lee being on a little stage talking to people, thanking people for coming. But that's about it. The worst thing that happened was that Doo had durn near a truck-load of whiskey delivered to the Spence Manor, where we had rented a suite and where all the Hollywood folks was stayin'. Me and Mommy ended up going home to Hurricane Mills the next day, 'cause I didn't want to see Doo sit there and drink until he'd gone through the whole load.

To tell you the truth, at both the premiere party and on the way home that next day, my mind was still back in Butcher Holler.

A lot of folks ask me if I really remember Butcher Holler. A few more are likely to wonder if I'm lyin' when I say that my very first memory is about a funeral that happened when I was only eleven months old. Well, folks, I ain't no liar. I not only remember Butcher Holler, I feel it, smell it, and taste it. I take a little bit of Butcher

Holler everywhere I go. I first sang to my little brother and sisters in Butcher Holler. Since then, I've sang in the world's finest concert halls. Sometimes, when I'm on a giant stage in front of thousands of people, I close my eyes and drift back to the swaying trees and bubbling streams of the only home I knew until I was fourteen. I can smell the freshness of the mountain air I breathed as a child. Yes, I *do* remember Butcher Holler.

But memories can be funny. Sometimes you remember things just like you were reading a story in a book, with all the little details and sights and sounds. Other memories are more like snapshots, pictures peeking in here and there. That's how my very first memory is, like a series of pictures that come and go.

It was when my Grandma Webb died. Even though I was only eleven months old, I can still see my daddy, Ted Webb, carrying me alongside the men taking his mama's body from the house and carrying it to a willow tree near her front gate. Daddy carried me in his arms while them pallbearers stepped on stones to cross a creek. They buried Grandma in the hills of Kentucky where time and weather have made her headstone a fading marker. Daddy was wearing a white shirt and he was crying. I'd never seen him in a white shirt, and I'd never seen my daddy cry. Both of 'em scared me to death. Maybe that's what made the memory stand out for so many years.

I guess it might be important that my first memory is one of loss. It was important to me to tell about it in this book. Like I said earlier, a lot of what has happened to me in the past twenty years has been about losing people.

Butcher Holler, Kentucky, is a coal mining and moonshining community about twelve miles from Paintsville in eastern Kentucky, about eighteen miles from the West Virginia border. You can ask anybody in Paintsville how to find Butcher Holler; they'll direct you to a gravel road that ain't really gravel. It's called "red dog," and it's made from slack that wasn't quite coal. It burnt for years and turned red. You'll only drive so far until you have to get out and walk along a path into Butcher Holler. During the Second World War, they thought about making a red dog road into the holler, but people got to thinking about it and said they didn't want one. They figgered that Hitler might fly over Kentucky and see that red line leading into the mountains, and think it was a target instead of a little old holler.

Of course the trick is sometimes finding your way out of Butcher Holler, as some unlucky revenuers on the track of moonshiners found out over the years. That's just another side to mountain life, the world Doo and I came from.

If mountain people was anything when I was growing up, they was resourceful. They wasted nothing and they was loyal. No stranger ever entered Butcher Holler without folks yelling from shack to shack, "Stranger coming up the holler, Stranger coming up the holler!"

They didn't know a lot about the world outside the

holler because they didn't need that world. They could make their own way. There's some people in that holler today, I'm satisfied, who don't know the name of the President, and don't care. It don't help the people in the holler to know the President's name. People have asked why there is no road to my old home place instead of just a dirt path. Why would there have been a hard road back in them days? Most folks traveled on a horse, a mule, or in a homemade sled pulled by a mule. I didn't even see a car until I was thirteen, and that was Doo's Jeep. There wasn't no development in rural eastern Kentucky then, or now. Nobody ever went to Butcher Holler except the folks who lived there, or their kinfolks when they came to visit. If you walk a mule on a hard road, you got to put steel shoes on the mule. We couldn't even afford shoes for ourselves. We each got one pair of brogan shoes a year, and each pair was two sizes too large so we could grow into them before we got another pair the following year. And mine were just like the boys'.

My daddy thought everybody in Butcher Holler was born to stay there, and most of the time that was true.

I was five years old and under the table when I remember Mommy saying: "Ted Webb, you're going to get me and these kids out of this holler! Nobody here is ever going to get ahead in life or get no education."

I was in Butcher Holler not all that long ago, and for the first time in my life, I looked around and thought, "How in the world did I ever get out of here?" The answer is easy, of course. Doolittle Lynn took me out.

The most modern thing that ever happened back in there was when Daddy bought a battery-operated Philco radio and **we** listened to newscasters Lowell Thomas and Gabriel Heater. On Saturday nights we listened to the Grand Ole Opry in Nashville. Daddy wouldn't let us play nothing else 'cause he didn't want to run down the batteries. He could probably buy a new one for a dime; I don't remember.

I remember hearing Ernest Tubb singing "Rainbow at Midnight" and "It's Been So Long Darlin' " on the Opry. Everytime he sung, I cried. Again, I was probably two years away from getting married. If anybody had told me in the 1940s that in 1967 I'd have a hit duet, "Sweet Thang," with Ernest, I wouldn't have believed them. But then, if anybody had told me in the 1940s that I'd ever get out of Butcher Holler, I wouldn't have believed them, either.

We had a one-room schoolhouse that my own great-grandpa, Bid Webb, built and my grandpa, my own daddy, and us had attended. The school had a row for every grade, and that made for a mixed bunch. Some kid who hadn't gone beyond the fourth grade might be almost six feet tall and sitting behind a little girl who was only eight or nine years old. Almost nobody wanted to go to school in Butcher Holler during my time there, and the county stopped the welfare payments to families whose kids didn't attend class. So a lot of parents made their kids go to school just so they could get more money for groceries and such. I mean, I've seen fifteen-year-old boys enroll in school for the first time so their mommies and daddies could get money. Them boys wore bib overalls and brogan shoes, those heavy shoes that come to the top of your ankles.

Those old farm boys were tough and mean, and they'd kick the fire out of the teachers. Our little country school had trouble keeping teachers 'cause the big ole boys ran them off. That's one reason learnin' came hard in the hills.

They might not have wanted to go to school, but people in Butcher Holler could come up with ways to make a living, even if it wasn't much of a living. They didn't throw nothing away. They could find a practical use for anything. Remember when everyone was worried about that Y2K thing that might come on New Year's Day, 2000? Some writers, in big newspapers like the *Los Angeles Times* and such, said there might not be any electricity or running water or gasoline or telephones. It didn't worry me a bit, thanks to my upbringing.

I love to watch the Arts and Entertainment channel, and there was a show on August 11, 1999, that said that the whole nation was predicted, by some experts, to go dark at midnight on New Year's Eve, 1999. And if there wasn't any electricity, a lot of folks wouldn't have had heat and wouldn't be able to cook. If there wasn't no running water, how would folks drink, and how would they flush the toilets? If there wasn't no gasoline, how would folks get to work? How would folks pay bills, since the mail trucks run on gasoline too?

I'm the last person that wanted to see that Y2K prediction come true. But I lived without electricity, indoor plumbing, or central heat every day of my life until I was a grown woman. I don't know if air conditioning had been invented, but I know we'd never heard of it. We'd never heard of a furnace or central heat, either.

But, by golly, we could survive. Take hunting, for example, my daddy loved 'possum and trapped them, but Mommy was the hunter. The woods around Johnson County is full of wild game. 'Possum is greasy meat, so Mommy would cook it as long as she could to cook the grease away without letting the meat turn dry. Then she'd put sweet potatoes and sage on top of the 'possum and put it all in a big bread pan and into a wood stove oven. I remember eating that meal until I left home at thirteen.

After I met Doo, I learned to fish and hunt just like Doo and my mommy. In them days, Doo would kill 'em, but I'd skin 'em, cut 'em up, and put 'em in a freezer locker. I learned to hunt and fish just like my brothers when I was still living in Butcher Holler. I was a good shot, too, and still am. The reason folks in the hills are such good shots is that it can mean the difference between eating and not eating. I don't know how it is that even though we couldn't always afford food, we always had shells or bullets.

Shortly after we was married, Doo and me moved to Washington state where he could find work. Doo had worked in the Kentucky coal mines and he didn't want to do it for the rest of his life. But when we got to Washington state, Doo often had to leave to find another job or run moonshine or Lord knows what. I remember he'd go off for days at a time after we got to Washington, leaving me and my babies alone.

Well, one of them times we got down to where we was eating mostly dandelion greens, like a lot of poor folks did and still do. One day when I was about at the end of my rope I saw a pheasant across the pond, probably a hundred yards away. I grabbed Doo's old .22 rifle. That gun was broke, because one day Doo'd got so mad at me he picked it up and broke the stock off. But I guessed I could still shoot us a meal with it.

I ran outside, took aim, and got that bird in the head with one shot. It could never have happened twice.

I waded out in that pond in water plumb up to my neck to get that pheasant I'd shot. I can remember sitting one foot slowly in front of the other to be sure the water didn't get too deep. When I was certain it was safe to take a step, I did. I cleaned that bird, and it was the first meat the kids and me had in three weeks.

I'm getting a little ahead of myself, but I'm just trying to make a point about how those of us that lived without *any* conveniences learned to survive. A person just did whatever he had to do in order to earn a living, or just to stay alive. I bet nobody in Butcher Holler, Kentucky, was worried about Y2K.

In the mountains, we worried about things like stayin' alive. Folks seemed to always find a way to scuffle a living, even if they had to make moonshine or steal. One of the most clever fellers I ever met was an ole boy who came to Butcher Holler when I was thirteen, wanting to take folks' pictures for twenty-five cents. But meetin' him ended up causing my feelings to get hurt about as bad as they ever have been. And it was a scar that I carried with me a long time. I still carry it. Here's the story of my picture and Grandpa Ramey.

Twenty-five cents was one-fourth of a day's wages for Daddy. So some people might think it was a waste of money for folks who often went without food to spend money on pictures. But those folks don't understand how mountain people take up with one another. We wanted pictures of each other, so we didn't think it was no waste of money when this camera feller showed up. We'd stand in front of his box and he'd put a sheet over his head. He'd go off with the film 'cause we'd give him our word we'd pay him when he came back with the pictures. It was worth it, too, when we was sitting around at home on a winter night. We'd pull out pictures of friends from across the holler, and look forward to spring, when visiting was easier.

Thinking about that camera feller coming back with pictures, knowing he'd get paid like we promised, reminds me of another good thing about the folks I was raised with. Their word was worth gold. I'd have rather had the word of most neighbors in Butcher Holler in the 1940s than to have any lawyer's contract today.

This here feller eventually came back with our pictures, and he gave all of us a bunch to pick from. We only had to pay the quarter for the one we wanted. I picked the one of me that I thought was best, but I didn't make up my mind alone.

I thought I'd ask my grandpa to help me. His grandkids called him "Grandpa," and his kids called him "Poppy." His real name was Nathaniel Ramey, the Ramey part being changed from the Indian name of Raney. Grandpa was a full-blood Cherokee Indian. Indians didn't talk much in those days. They just sat real quiet and stared into space like they was thinking a lot. Sometimes they read, although most nobody in Butcher Holler could read. I think the Indians was still bitter about the way the white man cheated them out of most of this country in the 1800s, and I don't blame them one bit.

About all my Indian grandpa did was sit in a rocker, smoke a pipe, and grunt. If you spoke to him he'd grunt some more.

When I was little, I'd sit right under his feet and talk ninety miles per hour, the way little girls do. He'd sit in silence until I finally shut up. Then he'd grunt, and I took that as a cue to talk some more. So I'd rattle on.

"Mommy, why won't Grandpa talk to me?" I used to ask.

"Poppy don't talk much," she said. "But he loves you and he likes to hear you talk."

I took mine and Mommy's pictures to Grandpa. I was

showing them to him and going on and on about which one I thought was best and why. By then it didn't bother me if I thought he was listening to me or not.

"Grandpa," I said, "look at these here pictures. Which is prettiest, Mommy or me?"

He quietly laid down his newspaper, pulled his pipe from his mouth, and spoke the first words I ever heard him say. Remember, I was close to being a teenager, and I was real sensitive.

"Young lady," he said, "you'll never be as pretty as your mother."

These were the only words he spoke to me about it, and it broke my heart. At least that's how it felt to the tender heart of a country girl who had an inferiority complex about her appearance.

Grandpa was an unpredictable spirit, and, like most mountain folks, he sort of figgered he was his own law. If somebody did something to somebody that was wrong, they faced the consequences from the person that had been wronged. No policeman hardly ever interfered. He might have been killed. And no fancy lawyers got guilty people off the way they do today on technicalities.

In my day and time, if a man trifled with another man's wife, the husband could kill him and nobody did a thing about it. A man didn't even flirt with another man's wife. In fact, he often didn't even speak to her, unless she was with her man.

I might have been about ten, I'm not sure, when

Grandpa was walking with the woman he was gonna marry—my grandma. They were just courting, but everybody in the holler knew they was boyfriend and girlfriend, and that they was probably going to get married. I'm sure Grandpa stole a kiss or two now and then, and we called that "sparkin'." But nobody did much else in the way of affection until after they was married. And nobody in his right mind would have been too friendly to a woman that was "spoken for" the way my grandma was.

This ole boy was following Grandma and Grandpa along a path and Grandpa thought he was following too close. So he told the feller to drop back a few paces. In fact, I think he told him to go plumb away.

The old boy didn't go.

Grandpa turned and pulled a pistol from his bib overalls and shot the heel off the man's boot. I told you that the men and women in Butcher Holler were good shots.

Folks said all you could see going down the trail that day was dust from that man running. Grandpa walked over and picked up the ole boy's boot heel. The guy never came back for it. If that feller hadn't run, Grandpa would have likely shot him dead. That's just how things was in the holler.

And that night of the movie premiere, after I sat there next to my husband and watched *Coal Miner's Daughter,* I couldn't help but think of a couple of the holler people who made a big difference in my early life, people

I hadn't talked about much in my first book. And when I got to thinkin', I realized that two of the most important people, next to my immediate family, was a cheatin' husband and a chicken thief.

Two

Swim Big Sandy
or Drown . . .

THE CHEATIN' HUSBAND belonged to Aunt Boyd. Aunt Boyd wasn't really an aunt, but we called her that. In Butcher Holler almost everybody was related to each other. Even when someone wasn't a relative, we often called them "Uncle" or "Aunt" anyhow. Come to think of it, this story would make a good country song, 'cause it's got a cheatin' man, a woman on the warpath, and a baby that ended up awful close to dead because of it.

Aunt Boyd thought her husband had been fooling around with another woman. My mommy said that one day when I was about a year old, I was leaning against the old nail keg when Aunt Boyd began to get all worked up about what she was going to do to the woman who she thought was slipping around with her man.

Daddy kept a big stick behind the cabin door for security in case somebody tried to break in, and Aunt Boyd saw it.

"If I ever catch my man with that woman," she said, picking up the stick, "I'm going to knock her head off." She explained all of that to Mommy. Trouble is, she also demonstrated. She drew that giant club over *her* head and accidentally hit me in *my* head!

Mommy said I cried for five days. A big knot came on my head. Within another week, knots as big as hens' eggs came up behind my ears. Then knots started coming up all over my head.

Mommy started "doctoring" me with her Indian medicine and talking to God every night. She was bound and determined not to let me die.

"God sent you down here for a purpose," Mommy told me later. "Loretty, it's not that I loved you any more than the rest of the children, but I knew you were different."

And she vowed she wouldn't let me die.

But all her Indian doctoring couldn't help my head, and about three weeks later that hole from the blow began to fester and rise, infected and filled with fluid.

Daddy and Mommy carried me to the Paintsville hospital, where a hole was drilled behind my ear and another hole was drilled close to it. They cleaned the pus and fluid from my head and inserted cotton into those two holes.

I should have been left in the hospital. Maybe I would have healed sooner with constant medical attention. But Mommy and Daddy didn't have no money to pay for a hospital stay. I don't know how they afforded any of the treatment. Maybe the county paid for it. Maybe the doctor did it for free.

My head was shaved for four years. Because of the stuff still inside my head, I had no balance. I didn't learn to walk until that sickness finally cleared up. I was four years old before I took a step.

Mommy carried me in a quilt she had made from cut-up overalls, and when she got tired Daddy would carry me. I can see that quilt today. Mommy got it in her head that one of the most important things she could do was to keep my feet warm, and that led her down a path she'd never have taken unless she was scared for one of her babies.

My people had the work ethic. They worked hard for the little they had. They didn't take handouts. I recorded a song called "They Don't Make 'Em Like My Daddy Anymore." It contains a line that says that Daddy never took a handout. The truth is, there was a time when my mommy did ask for a handout and I know it must have near killed her to do it.

I was around three when Mommy went into Murphy's Five and Ten Cent Store near the Big Sandy River. She told the clerk how her and her husband had to carry their daughter twenty-four miles a day to get medical attention, and how the doctors had suggested that she just let me die at home. Mommy told the clerk that she had determined that I was gonna live.

Then she told that man that my feet were going to freeze inside that homemade quilt. She asked the clerk to give a pair of shoes to the little girl that she refused to let die.

The clerk said he wasn't givin' no handouts, no matter whose feet were cold.

I'll never know what was going through Mommy's mind when she walked out of that store, not a penny in her pocket, her baby in her arms.

"Go on down the road, Ted," she said to Daddy. "You take Loretty and go on, and I'm going to stop at another store. I'm going to ask somebody else for a pair of shoes."

Daddy went ahead, carrying me in that little denim bundle on his long and weary walk home. I didn't have no appetite and was real underweight. But even a skinny child is a hard load to carry for twenty-four miles, especially for a small man and a little woman. Daddy was only five feet, eight inches tall and weighed 117 pounds. Mommy was only five feet tall.

Mommy acted like she was taking off for another store. But that's not what she done when Daddy was out of sight. She went back to the store where the clerk wouldn't give her the shoes and she stole the little red shoes that she loved. Mommy never told me she stole them shoes until I was a grown woman.

Mommy said she was practically running with the stolen red shoes until she caught up with us. We didn't stop until we got to the Old River Bridge across the Big Sandy River not far from our house. Then Mommy started to put those shoes on my feet. They were bright red and had buckles. I can see them to this day. I can picture Daddy's face when he saw 'em and knew what Mommy had done.

When Daddy started to run, I asked Mommy why he took off like that. "Loretty, he just wants to get home and put them new shoes away so they don't get dirty," she said. Truth was, he was runnin' home to hide what Mommy stole.

And when Mommy told me this story all those years later, she also explained to me that usually a storekeeper would have called the police over a pair of stolen shoes. Daddy had to be scared because neither he nor Mommy had ever stolen anything in their lives, I reckon. But for some reason, nobody ever came to the house looking for them shoes. I just couldn't wear 'em in public. They were my secret shoes.

I wrote a song about those shoes, "Put My Little Red Shoes Away," in 1999. I'd trade every pair of shoes I own to have them back, too. And I wrote about the Old River Bridge after it got tore down. That song is called "I'm Going to Swim Big Sandy River or Drown."

Sometimes that's how you got to look at life. You can either swim the river or drown. I think that was how Mommy was looking at things when she stole them shoes. I don't think there is much that a strong will and constant prayer can't accomplish. That's been one of the secrets of my strength as I've faced life's hard times. I'd recommend the formula to anybody.

Like I mentioned earlier, mountain people are protective of what little they have, and back when I was a kid, if what they were protecting was their moonshine, they could be deadly. That's how the Webb family lost our cousin, who was one of our best friends, Lee Dollarhide, the chicken thief I was telling you about earlier. The way Lee was showed in *Coal Miner's Daughter* has bothered me to this day. In the movie, Lee had long, greasy hair and looked like he needed a bath. Lee wasn't like that. He was clean and was a sharp dresser. It hurt me to see him look that way, but that's Hollywood for you. Even though I tried to get everything right when it came to that movie, there was parts that was wrong. I remember how the movie showed our house in Washington state with an electric washing machine on the front porch. Well, Doo and me sure didn't own no washing machine, and we didn't have no electricity. I washed our clothes by hand on a washboard, just like my mommy did in Kentucky.

But that movie sure had one thing right about Lee. Moonshine was the reason he died. Close to the beginning of the movie, Doo goes looking for Lee to get some moonshine. Lee ends up talking to Doo about helping him run shine, since, as he put it, in the holler a man's got three choices: coal mine, moonshine, or moving on down the line. Doo reminded Lee that when he was a kid, he'd help run liquor for a nickel a day, and if he was gonna do it now, he'd be more expensive than back then. Well, Lee was not just running his moonshine, because he'd had a still go dry. He was stealing shine from some boys over at Greasy Creek. Doo told him it was dangerous, but Lee just shrugged it off. Doo didn't go in with Lee, and he was lucky he didn't, because about the next time Lee run over to Greasy Creek, the owners of the still shot him.

Lee was one of my closest friends in Butcher Holler, and he was the kindest man I ever knew except for Daddy. We didn't have much to eat, and many nights we had nothing at all. Nothing. Other nights we had chicken because of Lee. He stole 'em, of course. Shoot, Lee even stole chickens from Doo's daddy one time.

I never told cousin Lee about Grandpa saying I wasn't pretty, but somehow Lee seemed to know that I thought I was as ugly as a stump. He always made it a point to tell me I was pretty. "Loretty," Lee would say. "I want to tell you something. You're pretty now, but one of these days you're going to be a beautiful woman."

I'd run to the mirror and look and look to see if I saw any sign of "pretty" showing up. After all, I never thought Lee would lie about something that important. In the end I decided he was honest—just blind. I wasn't pretty, not with freckles and plain features like I had. Plus, I had them buck teeth and bowed legs.

Lee lived right beside us, and he'd hear me singing as

my voice carried through the air. He told me how much he enjoyed it, and he asked me to sing more and to sing louder. He especially liked to hear me sing when he was running off his moonshine.

When Lee got shot, there wasn't no money for his funeral. I'd never heard of an undertaker, and I didn't know what it meant to be embalmed. So Lee Dollarhide lay inside a wooden coffin inside his mama's cabin for three days. Then he was carried to the graveyard and buried, box and all, under the Kentucky soil. Today, Lee and his coffin is dust, and have been for years. He's in a grave that's not far from Mommy's and Daddy's. I decorated them last Memorial Day.

Lee's laying in his mama's cabin for three days wasn't all that unusual. That's just how poor country folks honored their dead. Somebody would stay with the body day and night.

You may remember that Ray Stevens recorded a song about "Sitting Up with the Dead." Every time I hear it, I'm reminded of Lee Dollarhide's body layin' in his mama's cabin, as well as a story they tell in the holler about an uncle of Mommy's. This uncle was too cocky for his own good. And on top of being cocky, he wasn't quite right in the head. He was always saying that nothing and nobody could scare him. Well, a bunch of them old farm boys said, "We'll show that son of a bitch."

So the next time somebody died, they got the family to ask Mommy's uncle to sit up with the body all night so they could get some sleep. He said that would be fine.

Then those boys put wire on the dead man, put his coffin by the window, and hid outside. About two o'clock in the morning, they pulled on the wire, and that dead man sat bolt upright in his own coffin.

Mommy's uncle looked at him, said nothing, spit his tobacco, and fell back to sleep in his chair. So the next night the farm boys tried again. They again pulled the wire and let the dead man sit at a right angle. They just left him there, dead, sitting straight up in his coffin.

Mommy's uncle stirred and slowly rose from his chair. He walked to the coffin.

"You son of a bitch," he said. "You're dead, and I'm getting paid to sit up with you. Now you lay back down!"

I told you he wasn't quite right in the head. But it made for a good story around Butcher Holler.

Lee Dollarhide never had much use for the law. He was little, and could easily slip through handcuffs each time he was arrested. He'd come to our house, and Mommy and Daddy would hide him above the ceiling. I'd see them throw him up a rope so he could pull a three-pound lard bucket with some food in it up to his hiding place.

I'll never forget a Christmas Eve, when I was around five, when Mommy gathered all of us children around to say Santa Claus wasn't coming. There wasn't going to be anything for Christmas, she said. Not anything for anybody at our house. She claimed that the snow was too deep for Santa to make it to our house that year.

Then she got the idea to draw a checkerboard by hand. She used yellow and white corn for pretend checkers, like most folks used black and red as real checkers. That hand-drawn checkerboard, and them pretend checkers, was our family's Christmas present. Kids today get bored with fancy computers and electronic games. They have boats and airplanes that fly and sail by remote control. But I truly believe they almost never have as much fun as we did with the corn and homemade checkerboard.

That Christmas Eve we all got ready to go to sleep in the shuck bed—flour sacks Mommy stuffed with dried corn shucks. We never thought about getting anything for the holiday, but that night, before I went to sleep, I told Mommy I believed Santy Claus was gonna come to our house. Mommy just shook her head and looked real sad.

There was no consoling me that night. I was just havin' a fit, and I wouldn't quit squallin' and hollerin' that Santa Claus was coming. Mommy tried to get me to calm down, but I was having none of it. I just sat up cryin' hard as I could.

About the moment I was at my loudest and saddest, the door to our cabin flew open and a cold wind swept through the room. We had newspapers nailed to our walls for insulation, and them papers flew everywhere. Right in the middle of the flying newspapers stepped a man who said he was Santa Claus! I was too little and too excited to notice that this "Santa Claus" was Lee Dollarhide wearing a mask and with a pillow under his shirt. Not only that—even though I'd heard of Santa Claus, I'd never seen no pictures of him, so when Lee said he was Santa, I was ready to believe it.

Santa walked to the shuck bed and emptied a sack full of hard candy. When I got older Mommy told me that Lee had robbed a candy store on that Christmas night. He was our Santa Claus that Christmas, and Butcher Holler's Robin Hood for years.

They was lots of nights, especially at the end of a winter, when all of the canned goods Mommy put up was gone and we'd pile into that shuck bed still hungry. I know now how that must have hurt Mommy and Daddy. But on some special nights, we was awakened by a pounding at the door. It was always well after midnight, and a couple of hours before daylight. And it was always the same story. Lee would appear with a couple of squawking chickens that he carried by the feet, their wings flapping.

"I found these here chickens," he'd tell us children. Mommy and Daddy wouldn't say nothing. They'd just kill, clean, and fry the meat in no time so their kids could eat. And we devoured it. Mommy kept every part of every chicken, even the feet. She'd scald the feet and peel 'em, and put them in the pot to make chicken and dumplings. Everyone in my family has eaten boiled chicken feet and heads. Sometimes Mommy cooked the chickens with wild onions or poke. I like wild onions to this day, and picked some wild Tennessee poke in July 1999 to make a poke salad.

I remember asking Mommy why Lee always happened to be around when we had chickens. She just said he was the one who brought us the food. I was probably eight or nine by then, and I didn't ask any more questions. I didn't know that Lee was stealing them chickens, but I sensed Mommy didn't want to talk about it.

One time, before I left home, Lee stole three more chickens and some feed. I guess he thought he'd feed us for one night, and that we could keep another chicken or two alive to eat later. That's why he stole the feed. But the feed sack had a hole in it. The sack leaked chicken feed from where he stole it right to our front door. The law simply followed the trail. The police busted through the door and arrested Lee when he had a drumstick in his hand. I didn't know what was going on. They wouldn't come up there to arrest the moonshiners and such, but they got good ole Lee for feeding a poor family.

They took Lee to jail for that deal, but he escaped again.

Long after Lee died, people asked if I think he done wrong in his life. I said no, and that I think he went to Heaven on that very night the moonshiners shot him. And I'll wager that the Lord had a platter of fried chicken a-waitin' on him.

Three

On Becoming a Woman . . .

I LEARNED EARLY ON that becoming a woman could be scary business, especially if you don't know nothing about it. One day when I was almost thirteen, I started cramping in my stomach and didn't know why. I remember thinking that I'd had plenty to eat that day, so I couldn't be having hunger pangs. And believe me, poor people know what hungry feels like. Then I felt something wet, and for a minute I was afraid I'd gone to the bathroom in my pants. When I looked down, to my horror I saw blood between my legs! Lord, I didn't know what was happening! I thought I was sick, that I might even be bleeding to death. Still something kept me from running to my parents like I'd usually do when I was afraid. Something inside me said this was some shameful thing I couldn't even tell my own mommy or daddy. The blood leaking from me made me feel dirty. So I ran to the creek and sat down, hoping that water would wash whatever awful thing was happening to me right on down the stream.

Mommy had never told me about periods. It wasn't a topic of general conversation in the holler, even between a girl and her mother. None of my girlfriends had ever mentioned 'em. So for the next couple of months, every time my period came, I tried desperately to hide it, and I'd sit for hours in the creek, trying to keep clean.

I can't tell you how afraid I was. It was awful. I just knew I was dying, and from some horrible thing I didn't understand. Then one day I was washing fruit jars in a tub of hot water and Mommy was canning turnip greens. I'd been cramping something awful, holding my stomach, and finally fainted.

"Loretty," Mommy said, grabbing me. "Are you having your monthly?"

"Am I having what?" I asked.

"Are you bleeding down there?" she asked.

I hung my head and nodded.

"Oh. It's time," she said.

"Time for what?" I was sure she was gonna tell me it was my time to die.

"It's time you got your monthly," she said matter-of-factly.

Then she explained that I'd bleed once a month for the rest of my life, except when I was pregnant, or until I was too old to have babies. But she didn't explain how babies was made or what that bleeding had to do with it. The day I left home the only thing I knew about sex was that boys stood up to pee and girls sat down because they was made different "down there."

The one good thing that came with them "monthlies" was that Mommy let me off the hook when it came to working.

"You don't need to help when you're having cramps," Mommy said. She told me to stop helping with the canning. She put me to bed, tore strips of flour sacks to put into my panties, and gave me an aspirin.

My younger sister, Peggy Sue, once reminded me that I told her I wasn't going to be like my mommy, not explaining things. She said I told her when she was twelve that she would bleed once a month. But, she said, I didn't tell her where she'd be bleeding from, or what it meant. I made that same mistake with my oldest daughter, Betty. I left out the most important parts. Both girls laugh about that to this day. They was just kids, and probably wondered if they'd bleed from their gums or feet, or wherever. So when them girls began to flow "down there," they was as frightened as I had been when it first happened to me! The one way I was different from Mommy was that the minute I realized what was going on, I did try to explain the whole story.

I don't think being from Butcher Holler had much to do with Mommy's reluctance to talk about such things. I fear that back in them days, that conversation was one a lot of girls in New York City or San Francisco didn't have with their mommies, either. And knowing how *not knowing* feels made me want to explain as much as I could to my own children. That includes everything from sex education to the music business to raising goats, too. I'm sure that sometimes my children wished I didn't explain so much. But once I got the hang of explaining, I just couldn't stop myself.

Right after I started having my period, Mommy and Daddy decided I should start sleeping on a little bed in their room instead of with the rest of the kids. Daddy said I was too big to be sleeping with my brothers. It never occurred to me that he and Mommy were thinking about the fact that I was becoming a woman.

Later on, after I found out that married people have sex, I wondered how Mommy and Daddy ever had any once I moved in. I don't know when they was "personal." Must have been after I went to sleep. They had a feather bed, and it didn't make much noise, so maybe I just didn't wake up.

If somebody had told me that I'd soon go from sleeping in my parents' room, from being a grade school student and classroom janitor, to being a married woman, I'd 'a told 'em they was as crazy as Mommy's not-right-in-the-head uncle. I don't see no point in talking too much about me courting Doo. I put all of that in my first book, and it was in the movie too. But I'll fill you in a little in case you missed that story the first time.

I think some people have some wrong ideas about hill

people. Some think hillbillies all get married young, others believe everybody's marrying their cousin. Well, people in Butcher Holler, and that includes my parents, didn't think no thirteen-year-old should be getting married. A lot of my cousins were in their twenties before they got married. When Doo come home from the army in 1948, he didn't seem twenty-two years old to me. He looked like some little toy soldier in his uniform.

Being raised in such an isolated place, I didn't have much of an idea of what you might call "expectations." Expectations of going to school beyond that little one-room classroom, getting a job outside of the coal mines, having a life anything different from what I'd seen around me. I thought you lived at home until you got married, and then you lived with your husband. That was about all I thought of marriage. Age never seemed to come into it. Thirteen? Fifteen? Twenty? Twenty-two? If you "fell in love" with someone, you married 'em. What was love? Well, I guess they been asking that question forever.

At thirteen, I never had dated no boy, and I never had sparked either. I believed I was ugly, too ugly to ever get a husband, and maybe even too ugly to ever get a boyfriend. Lots of folks know that our school had a social one night and pies was auctioned off to raise some money. Doolittle Lynn bought mine, and that's how we first got together. The pie contest was a kind of beauty contest. I never dreamed anyone would pay more than a nickel for my face, even if it came with a pie. So when Doo pulled out a five dollar bill and made me a "beauty contest winner," he became my hero.

His Jeep was the very first car I'd ever seen. But I didn't like the idea of riding in it; never wanted to get into no vehicle that wasn't pulled by an animal. I was already a little crazy about Doo, but I still made him walk me home that night, all of us carryin' pine torches. When we got to my house, he gave me my first kiss. After that I was more than a little bit crazy about him. I went in the house singing.

"Who was that out there?" Mommy asked.

"Doolittle Lynn," I answered, feeling like my heart was still in my throat. I was already thinking I might be in love with him.

She and Daddy had a fit. They didn't like the notion of me seeing Doo one bit, but that didn't stop me. I'd have sneaked around to be with him, and did a time or two. There wasn't anything they could say or do. Once Daddy even whipped me, and that was one of the few times he ever raised a hand. They knew a lot about Doo's family. They knew there was a lot of hard drinkers among the Lynns, and they seen Doo's daddy, Red Lynn, leave his wife and children over and over. They divorced and remarried four times. Red would just go off and get drunk, then drop out of sight for a couple of years. At one point the law even told Doo's folks they couldn't get married no more. I guess they'd used up their times at bat. It wasn't the kind of family life my parents wanted for me.

Doo and I had three or four dates the next month. Doo went to work in the mines and once he had a paycheck in his hand, he asked me to marry him. I don't know if I wanted to get married, but I didn't want Doo to get away, either. Looking back on it, I wonder if I didn't fall in love so hard because no other boy had ever paid any attention to me. Doo made me feel beautiful for the first time in my life. Even Lee Dollarhide's compliments hadn't been able to make me feel so pretty.

Sometimes I think people forget just how intense a young girl's emotions is. Girls can fall hard during the early teens, when love is still something mysterious, and not judged by real-life experiences. I believe I loved Doolittle more at that time than at any other. As our married life went on, my feelings changed. I loved Doo until the day he died, but while I ended up turning a blind eye to a lot of his ways over the years, that early kiss was a distant memory.

I told Doo that he'd have to ask Mommy and Daddy for their permission to marry me. In them days, a man was supposed to ask a girl's daddy for her hand. Doo couldn't get a straight answer from Mommy or Daddy when he approached them separately, so he walked right into their bedroom when they was almost asleep to ask for my hand. The reason he did was because I'd told him he should try to talk to 'em together and when they was bone-tired. They didn't even get out of the bed. Daddy knew Doo wouldn't have come into their bedroom unless I had told him to do it. That meant Daddy knew I *really* wanted to marry this man. Daddy knew I had enough Webb in me to get what I wanted once I set my mind on it. If he had told Doo "no," I might have waited a whole week before I made Doo ask again, or I might have run off. I don't know.

Here's something else I didn't know. I wasn't Doo's first choice. When Doo went off to the army, he had a girl waitin' on him. When he come back, she was married to somebody else. So he went to that pie supper and found me on the rebound.

From the beginning, Doo was always calling me a stupid hillbilly, and in many ways, I was just that. Of course, there's a big difference in being stupid and being ignorant, when you just ain't been around enough to know what's what. Here's what I mean by ignorant:

On the way to the courthouse where we got married, I had to go to the bathroom. Doolittle took me to the bus station, which had the only indoor toilet in Butcher Holler. I had never been to the bus station, so I'd never used or even seen an indoor toilet. I sat down and it started flushing by itself! Water began to swirl and flush. I thought the toilet was a machine that was going to swallow me. I jumped up off the seat, pulled up my panties, and ran back to Doo like a scared rabbit. When I told him what had happened, he like to had a fit.

"God damn it, woman, you are the most stupid thing

I ever seen," he said. Then he told me about indoor toilets and flushing.

Me and Doo waited at the courthouse from eight o'clock until eleven-thirty in the morning for Daddy to come to the wedding. Mommy couldn't come 'cause she had to stay with the other kids. Hours seem like days when you're waiting. I got afraid that Daddy had backed out, and that he wouldn't give me away. Directly he came along, but he stood just on the inside of the door to the courthouse and never stepped inside. He could hear what was going on. When I saw that scene in *Coal Miner's Daughter*, I choked up. Like I said, Levon Helm was so much like Daddy, he brought a lump to my throat.

I got married but didn't have no ring. That was bought fourteen years later on the installment plan. It cost thirty-seven dollars.

The second the justice of the peace said "I now pronounce you man and wife," Daddy turned his back and walked right out the door. He never spoke a word after saying in a low voice "I do" when he gave me away, and I didn't see him for days. His heart was broken.

I saw my daddy walking away in the hard rain that fell all that day. And I remembered my mommy's words that morning, when she saw it raining so hard. She said, "Loretty, if you get married in this rain, you'll shed every tear that it rains." And I have.

I didn't know whether to be happy because I had me a husband, or hurt because I knew my daddy was so disappointed. That was such painful confusion. But when you are a thirteen-year-old bride, there are many confusing times. For me, they were just beginning.

Doo signed the marriage license O. V. Lynn, Jr.

"Who's that?" I said.

"That's my name," he said. I thought his name was Doolittle but, as I said earlier, most folks called him Doo. It turned out to be Oliver Venetta Lynn, Jr. I actually married a man whose real name I didn't even know until ten minutes after we was man and wife.

When I saw *Coal Miner's Daughter*, it embarrassed the tar out of me when it showed Doo trying to make love to me on our wedding night. It's still embarrassing for me to talk about such things. I was a guest on a radio show not long after my autobiography came out. The interviewer had advertised that I'd be there, and he'd had some letters about the visit. He said most of the mail he received asked him to ask me about my wedding night. I don't know why folks has so much interest in other people's wedding nights.

"Loretta," the radio interviewer said. "Let's talk about your wedding night."

"Let's don't!" I said. "Let's talk about yours!"

"I don't understand," the man said, "you wrote about it in your book."

"Well writin' about it in a book and talkin' about it out loud is two different things," I said. The show's host told me later he was taken off-guard, and he started spinning records and never asked me another question.

Well, I'll tell the story again here, and correct something about it.

Before we went to bed, Doo told me to put on a flannel nightgown that his mother had bought for me that day. I did—over my clothes. Doo sent me back to the bathroom to take off my clothes and I came back wearing the nightgown, a slip, and my panties. He sent me back to remove the slip, got annoyed, and tore off the panties.

I hated it even though Doo told me that this was what all married folks done. All I knew was that this man who I thought loved me was on top of me, doing things I didn't like. I especially didn't like the part about having to spread my legs.

The movie showed me hollering while we had sex, but we didn't have no sex that night. I just couldn't do it, and Doo didn't force me. In fact, it took a week before we actually did it. Doo finally went to sleep that first night, and I laid there and cried. It was three weeks before I could face anyone. I wasn't going to go around people who knew what we'd done, or tried to do, inside that there motel.

Doo said everybody knew anyhow.

By the way, the courthouse burned to the ground five days after we got married. That should have told me something. So our marriage got off to a bad start from the first. It got worse the next morning when Doo whipped me. I know that people got the idea from *Coal*

Miner's Daughter that Doo hit me that next day because he was frustrated about me not doing my part sexually the night before. That ain't exactly the case.

Long before I ever wrote songs, I wrote lines with rhymes. The trouble was, I didn't know what a lot of words meant. I still don't always know, and it has got me into trouble many times in my life. The story about baloney making people horny is just the tip of the iceberg. In fact, years after I got into the country music business, I was part of a show that Perry Como put on here in Nashville. When he left town, he told somebody I was a phony. He didn't think anybody could be that ignorant. I ain't a phony, but I'll admit to being ignorant.

I think Doo really did want to cheer me up and make me feel better about the previous night on our first day as man and wife. He got up and said he'd go get breakfast for me and him. It was still raining hard, a cold and miserable day, but when Doo looked out the window he started singing.

"Oh what a beautiful morning, oh what a beautiful day," Doo sang.

He was wearing shorts and a top that were sewn together. It was the ugliest thing I've ever saw. I think he wore them clothes in the army.

He kept singing while he got dressed. I was sitting there in bed rocking backwards and forwards with my arms wrapped around my knees.

Finally I decided to try and get myself together. If

Doo could try to put the wedding night behind us, maybe I could, too. So when he opened the motel door and a gust of cold wind blew in, I thought I'd make a funny rhyme with a word I'd heard them big boys at school sneak around and use.

"Shut the door you little whore," I said.

What a thing to say, and that sure did it! Now I promise you, I didn't have any idea what a "whore" was. I'd only heard the word, and it sure rhymed with "door."

I don't think being called a "whore" after sexual frustration was what Doo needed to hear. Especially since he didn't know me well enough yet to understand that I didn't understand what I was saying. He turned in his tracks and bent me over his knee. He beat my bottom and I bawled. If my daddy or Grandpa Ramey would have walked in that room, they'd 'a shot Doo on the spot, but nobody got shot and I finally was able to have sex. In fact, through all our married life I never withheld sex from Doo. I thought wives was supposed to do it for their husbands and even though being a wife didn't come natural to me, I tried to be a good one.

I don't think I had any idea how much it bothered Doo that I didn't like sex in those days, or even for a long time after. Years later, if someone really made him open up about it, he'd say that my reaction bothered him a lot. I guess it made him feel like he was doing something wrong, and from the beginning I convinced myself that it was my fault he went looking for other women.

Four

The Damned Old Dog
Won't Even Eat It . . .

BACK THEN I DIDN'T UNDERSTAND that sex was our biggest problem. I thought it was my cooking. I wasn't no cook and never claimed to be. I never had to do much of it because Mommy was so good in the kitchen. So I'd usually just try to cook up some beans and fried potatoes and cornbread. Simple food. For one thing, Doo liked steaks, and I never even ate beef until we was married. The Webbs couldn't afford steaks. Doo said he hated everything I made. I really tried to cook the way Doo liked. I'd get up at five in the morning so I'd have a half hour to get breakfast ready for him. He'd take one bite and throw the food off the back porch to our dog, Drive, a name we just happened to pick. Then he'd stomp off to work in the coal mines.

I'd cry most of the day and finally start fixing supper

in the afternoon. We called it supper back then; "dinner" was something you had on Sunday. But the scene was always the same. Doo would come home, dirty and tired from the mines. He'd clean up and then sit down to eat. He'd take one bite, or sometimes he'd just look at the food. Then he'd heave it over the porch. Sometimes he throwed the plate along with the food.

Drive sometimes ran when the food was thrown.

"See there," Doo yelled, "the damned old dog won't even eat it!"

"Why 'course not," I said. "He's so fat he cain't eat no more."

Knowing what I know now, about how Red Lynn treated his family, it don't surprise me that Doo threw food out in the yard at the drop of a hat. Shoot, Red once threw out a whole Thanksgiving dinner just because one of his kids started eating before he did.

Try as I did, every morning Doo stomped out to the mines. Every night he stomped out, too. I couldn't figure out why Doo hated my cooking so much. Me and Drive liked it fine. I tried every trick I could think of, including having some of my friends who was good cooks and Doo's own mama cook up his supper. Doo wasn't home much, and when he was home, he didn't have much to say to me.

I had one menstrual period less than a month after I married. I didn't have another until after my first child, Betty Sue, was born. I didn't even know that what Doo and me was doing in bed caused babies, so when I started feeling sick, I went to see Doc Turner just like always. It never crossed my mind I was getting ready to have a baby.

"Well, Loretta," he said. "You're not sick. You're pregnant."

Mothers who don't tell their daughters about sex and how babies are made aren't doing their daughters any favors. 'Course today, kids know everything from television and the sex education they get in school.

I was four months pregnant when Doo run me off. I wasn't sure why at the time. He seemed to have lost interest in me, and everything I did made him mad. The best explanation I could come up with was my bad cooking. It happened late one night, about ten o'clock. Doo up and told his brother Johnny to take me home in his Jeep. He was sick of being married to me.

When you look back over your life and see how much you've had to face, and how you've dealt with it, it's interesting to try and pinpoint the first time you faced something that might tear you apart. The first time you had to reach inside yourself and pull out strength you didn't know you had, strength that hadn't even been needed up until then. Strength that was 'a hidin' somewhere waiting for the time it was needed. That was probably the first opportunity I'd had in life to be strong: when Johnny Lynn dumped me out in the dark, and I had to hunt that lonely path to Mommy and Daddy's doorstep.

I'm not saying that I did anything brave during the

time I was living back at home, but something inside me was changing just a little. I saw that life wasn't no teen-age girl's idea of a fairy tale. I've decided that strength is a building process; it ain't something you just all of a sudden get. It ain't some miracle that drops in on you. It's one hard time after another, toughening you up for whatever might be hiding around the bend. Like they say—if it don't kill you, it'll just make you stronger.

Mommy and Daddy welcomed me home, of course. They just couldn't understand why Doo had been so aw-ful. After all, he was the one who'd marched into their bedroom and asked to marry me. He'd done the right thing instead of trying to get me to be having sex with him without being married.

I didn't bring no clothes home with me the night Doo's brother dropped me a half-mile from home, so Mommy took me over to pick up what little I had the next day. Me and Doo had been living in a coal miner's cabin at the Van Lear Coal camp, where Doo was work-ing. It was a pretty good house, with a kitchen, bed-room, and front room. It had no electricity or running water, but I liked it fine. When Mommy and me got there we had a surprise. Doo's mother had already been there and cleaned out all the furniture. The place looked like nobody had ever lived there. My sorry wardrobe was still hangin' in the closet. A couple of worn-out shirts and things. A bottle of talcum powder that Mommy had got me for Christmas had been knocked over on the floor.

* * * * *

Meanwhile, I kept wondering how everything had turned into such a mess. Why would my bad cooking cause Doo to throw me out? Well, as it turned out, it was not about my not being a good cook; it was about me not knowing anything about how to please a man. He'd found someone who did know. He'd gone back to the woman who'd gotten married on him when he was away in the army. (And people keep wondering where country songs come from!) He probably *didn't* like my meals, but them suppers he throwed to the dog was just a cover-up so he could stomp out and head over to his girlfriend's house.

Nowadays men say they're working late.

When Doo got home from the army, I was working at the school helping the teacher, Miss Bessie. Me and Miss Bessie were still good friends, and one day she stopped by to see me. Sometimes people tell you things that are gonna hurt you because they set out to hurt you. Sometimes they are just gossips, and sometimes just too dumb to know any better. But Miss Bessie was none of those things. She came to tell me something I needed to know because she was my friend. She wasn't gonna let me sit over at Mommy's all day long, crying over the idea that cooking had washed me out as a wife. As far as Miss Bessie could see, it was Doo who had washed out as a husband by being unfaithful.

After Miss Bessie told us about Doo's girlfriend, all I could think about was how mean he was! I'd have never married Doo if I'd knowed he really wanted someone else. I never suspected a man could be that awful. The only man I'd ever been around was Daddy, and he was never mean to nobody. I grew up thinking all men was as kind as Daddy. Daddy never looked at another woman, and everybody in Butcher Holler knew he was a good and faithful husband. If people was slippin' around in the holler, Mommy and Daddy never spoke about it to us kids. And Daddy was home every night. I never even heard them say a cross word to each other. It made me mad at Doo, and even madder at the other woman.

Even back then I wrote my way outta hurt. Miss Bessie suggested that I ought to write this woman a letter, so I sat right down and done it. I told her that Doolittle Lynn was a married man with a baby on the way. It didn't matter whether she'd knowed him first, either. Of course, the first thing she done when she got the letter was show it to Doo. The first thing he done when he read it was find me and jump all over me for messin' in his business.

In fact, the words he said to me that day burned into my heart. He said, "If I ever had any love for you, I lost it today." That broke my heart once again.

I think the seeds were sown that very day that would grow into songs like "Fist City" and "You Ain't Woman Enough."

The baby was beginning to show in my stomach and I had nothing to wear, so Mommy made some maternity dresses out of feed sacks. Then, a couple of days after I turned 14 on April 14, she somehow got a pair of shoes for me. You remember how Mommy felt about shoes. And she believed sick kids and pregnant women *really* needed to wear shoes. She always worried during any woman's pregnancies because she'd lost so many babies herself. Usually, though, we went barefooted in the spring and summer, and would wait for shoes until just before winter came. Mommy wasn't gonna allow her pregnant daughter to go barefooted, but there was one small problem with her good intentions. She bought them shoes a couple of sizes too big because she thought my feet was still growing.

Now here is another one of them things where one incident leads to another and still another, like dominoes falling. It was as a result of Mommy's belief that pregnant women needed shoes that I got some inside information of Doolittle Lynn's doings. Because them shoes was so big, I developed a blister that gave me blood poisoning, and I wound up in the Paintsville hospital with Doc Turner taking care of me.

"Loretta," he said, "you're not sleeping with Doo, are you?"

"No," I said, "me and Doo's not married now."

See, I'd somehow come up with the idea that if you weren't living with a man you weren't married no more. I thought me and Doo was no longer husband and wife just because he had throwed me out.

"You're wrong," the doctor said. "You and Doo may

be separated, but unless you've gone and got a divorce, you're still married."

I didn't have no divorce, so I said I guessed he was right, I was still married.

"I think you'd be doing the right thing by not sleeping with Doo until he comes back to get you," the doctor said. "Now don't sneak around and sleep with him!"

Doc Turner, bless his heart, knew I had enough problems without coming down with something you had to take penicillin for. Mommy explained to me what Doc Turner meant when I told her what he said.

You'd think I wouldn't have ever wanted to see my husband again. But the truth is, I still loved him with all the unrealistic emotion of a teenager, and cried over our situation all the time.

I also knew I was putting Mommy and Daddy through a hard time. I was living back at home—broke, fourteen, uneducated, unemployed, and expecting a baby. And I knew as well as anyone that Daddy could hardly afford to feed the children he had at home.

Maybe it was the Indian in her, but my mommy had "the sight." She could read coffee grounds and tell you what was 'a gonna happen, maybe not the exact thing, but enough clues that you knew if good or evil was waitin' around the next corner. And she always seemed to know about some day-to-day things. Like when we had mail. We lived a long way from the post office, and there was a creek that sometimes flooded to make your way harder than usual. In the winter it was a terrible walk. So Mommy would get out her coffee cup and swirl the grounds around to see if it was worth the trip. I trusted Mommy's "sight," or instinct or whatever you want to call it, because I never knew her to be wrong.

One day Mommy told me to find a four-leaf clover.

"Put the clover in the Bible where it says . . . 'And this shall come to pass.' The old saying is true," she said.

I found a clover, put it inside an old King James Bible, and I wished that me and Doo would get back together. Looking back, I'm surprised that Mommy gave me that advice. Mommy liked Doo better than Daddy did, but according to both my parents, he wasn't good enough for their little girl. They was against the marriage, and they had to resent Doo for getting me pregnant and kicking me out while everybody in Butcher Holler knew about his girlfriend.

On the other hand, Mommy wanted me to be happy. And she knew I'd never be happy until I was back with my husband. A man and his wife was supposed to be together. And that's why it happened like this: one day me and some girlfriends walked the twelve miles to see a movie in Paintsville. Because I was pregnant, I had to sit down and rest a lot. I figgered I had time to do it. I wasn't in no hurry, since my life was going nowhere.

We saw a film called *I Wonder Who's Kissing Her Now*.

I was walking back to Butcher Holler when somebody hollered at me.

"Hey," said a voice, "wait a minute!"

It was Doo.

"What for?" I said to him. I wanted to see him, but then on the other hand I didn't, if that makes sense. I secretly wanted him back, but I wasn't in no hurry to get hurt again.

"I want to talk to you about the baby," Doo said.

Well, I thought to myself, *if he wants to talk about the baby, maybe I should talk to him.* I told the girls to go on ahead.

The closer Doo came toward me, the more I was afraid to hear what he might say, or what he might not say.

"I want to buy the baby some clothes," he said. And he said he was gonna do this and he was gonna do that, and on and on. In some ways, he was talking to himself, convincing himself that the marriage hadn't been so bad, that he did want the baby I was carrying. I just stood there trying not to cry.

I told him I knew about his disease and wouldn't have nothing to do with him sexually. Well, he told me he was cured and if I wanted to ask Doc Turner, I could. I knew he wouldn't lie if he was willing to bring Doc into it.

We walked along the path to where it split. Doo was supposed to go his way and I was supposed to go mine, back to my folks' house. That's where he talked to me about giving our marriage another try. After all, he said, we was about to be parents. And he said he still loved me. I was a sucker for that kind of talk.

My daddy wasn't a sucker for it. My girlfriends reached our house real soon. Mommy run outside when she saw 'em.

"Where's Loretty?" she asked.

"Doo's talking to her," one of the girls said.

That's all my daddy needed to hear.

I looked up and saw him hurrying down the path toward me and Doo. But by the time he reached the spot where we'd been, we'd already started up the other side of the holler.

I went home with Doo that night.

It had broke my daddy's heart when I left home in the first place, only to get dropped off pregnant, unhappy, and crying. Just about the time he got to thinking he and Mommy could somehow make things all right for me, I left home again with the same man I'd left with before. Daddy wouldn't speak to me for three or four weeks. You cain't imagine how that broke my heart.

But hearts was fixing to get broken worse. Doo was about to talk me into movin' as far away from Butcher Holler and the only ones I knew truly loved me—my family—as he could get: Washington state.

Now I'm gonna tell you about the days in Washington state. I lived there almost thirteen years, so it was a big part of my life. It was a part that didn't get much attention in the movie *Coal Miner's Daughter*, except to show

Doo helping me get my music career started. In that first book I talked about how sad I was to leave home, about learning to be a good cook, and about friends we met in our new life. I talked about my sadness over my daddy's death. Those thirteen years was probably the hardest I ever spent. I learned firsthand what my mommy and daddy went through when they had nothing to feed their kids. Now it was my turn. And whether you are in the woods of Washington or the woods of Butcher Holler, poverty is poverty, and hungry is hungry.

With lots of young girls, their biggest hopes are when they are teenagers, and in their early twenties. But mine didn't come until later. These were the years when I struggled to become a woman, and wasn't even sure what all it meant to become one. For a long time, my biggest hope was that we had enough food to eat, that my husband was going to come home at night, and that he wasn't gonna get mad at me and the kids.

A lot of the stories my kids was worried about me telling happened during the time we spent in Washington. I guess they was afraid me and Doo would look like we was candidates for *Jerry Springer*. Well, sometimes the truth is hard. We had some terrible times during them years. I wouldn't have made it through if it hadn't been for two things: I've always been a hard worker, and I believe in God.

Five

I Felt Like I'd Never See
Any of My Family Again . . .

DOOLITTLE WAS ALWAYS ambitious, wanting to better himself. He'd also been in the army, and understood that there was a world outside Butcher Holler. So it should have been no surprise that when Doo heard of work in Washington state, where his dad was panning for gold, he decided to go, come hell or high water. Doo had been to Washington state when he was younger, and the way he talked, it was God's country. And he wasn't the only one who decided to go west. My brother Junior went with him to look for jobs and also pan for gold. They promised to send for their wives, although I'm sure some folks figgered that was the last that me and Junior's wife Bonnie would ever see of them two.

I was seven months pregnant, and even though this

was my second separation, I didn't feel abandoned, just lonesome. I really believed Doo was off to build a better life for us, especially since he was taking along my brother. Part of the way Doo convinced me to go was to tell me that Washington state would cure my migraine headaches. Like my daddy, I've had bad headaches all my life. Well, Doo told me that the air was so pure up there that folks didn't have no migraines, and of course, I believed him. The air is pure, but it didn't stop my head from hurting.

Doo and Junior didn't have no money, so they hitch-hiked all the way to the Northwest. There was no inter-state highways in that day and time, so they faced a lot of danger hitchhiking on dark two-lane roads. One time a driver let them off a long time after dark, when the only light came from the moon, the stars, and car head-lights. Doo and Junior waited awhile, but no car lights come down the road. They took off walking and came on a place with lots of grass. Doo said he couldn't see much because that night was as black as a coal pit. But he insisted that Junior and him sleep right there. No mo-tel was around, and they didn't have no money anyway. They rolled out their bedroll, just an old blanket. Junior woke up around daylight when he could barely see. His eyes focused on lots of straight and standing rocks. They was tombstones. Junior and Doo had fell asleep inside a graveyard.

Mountain people, and a lot of other folks, are superstitious about graveyards. Some think they're disturbing the dead if they go there for anything but a burial. Others are just flat-out afraid of graveyards at night.

Well, Junior jumped from the grass and commenced to running—back toward Kentucky! He was yelling and running right down the highway. Doo said he saw Junior waving his arms up and down as he ran into the dawn.

"Junior!" Doo shouted, "where are you going?"

"I'm bound for Butcher Holler!" Junior yelled. He didn't look back.

Doo took out after Junior and pulled him to the pavement. If Doo hadn't caught Junior, I guarantee he'd of showed up in Butcher Holler in a few days. Junior didn't give up easy. He hit Doo and told him to let him go home. They had a fistfight right there in the middle of the highway.

Now wouldn't that have been a sight? What if a driver had come along and seen two grown men rollin' around? That's one car that wouldn't have stopped.

Finally Doo settled Junior down and made him start walking and hitchhiking again toward Washington. Doo said him and Junior had two or three fights like that during their trip.

After they got to Custer, Washington, Doo and Junior soon found work baling hay, milking cows, and doing all kinds of jobs for two bachelor farmers, Bob and Clyde Green. So Doo sent for me and Junior sent for Bonnie.

As usual, Mommy had to stay home with the other kids, so it was Daddy who took me to the train station. Me and Daddy didn't say a lot that day. I was his second of eight children. I was the first to marry, and the first to leave home. For me to go off and be with my husband was the natural order of things. But natural or not, it hurt, and tears run down his cheeks all the way to the station. As that train pulled out, I saw my daddy still standing there wiping his eyes.

I'd never been on a train, and I haven't been on one since. I rode that thing for four days and three nights without a penny in my pocket. Mommy made me a giant sack lunch before I left for the Van Lear train station and handed a letter to me. She told me to give the letter to the train conductor, and said he'd be the man who wore a uniform and yelled "all aboard." I never opened that letter, but I suspect Mommy asked him to look after me. And he did just that.

Every night, the conductor would swivel my chair in such a way so I could lay down. Nobody else got that kind of personal attention. Then he'd give me a pillow. He was supposed to charge me twenty-five cents, but he told me not to say nothing to nobody about it. So I didn't. Mommy's sack lunch was chicken gizzards and Moon pies. I still love fried chicken gizzards, but cold gizzards for eighty-four hours of travel can get old. Well, this same conductor walked into the dining car and took sandwiches and milk and brought them to me. He told me not to mention that either, so I didn't.

I still remember looking up at the ceiling of that train in that recliner seat. I remember the clacking of the rails and the ringing of the bells. I'd just about fall asleep, and we'd pass one of those contraptions along railroad tracks that rang. Clang, clang clang! I was used to the silence of the country, so the ringing always woke me up. The train rocked and the baby was beginning to kick. Daylight hours was even worse. I swear, watching the country pass by from that train window was like traveling to outer space. It couldn't have been any stranger to see the land change from hills to flatlands to mountains and back again than seeing planets and stars and moons flying by. I had no idea that the world was that big. And with every mile, I felt like I'd never see any of my family again.

The closest town to where we lived in Washington was Custer, with a population of 325 people. But me and Doo's home was actually a farmhouse owned by the Green brothers. Our house was close to theirs, so Doo was handy when they wanted him to work, and I ran over there and cleaned their house while they were in the fields. Eventually the bachelors' mother died and Aunt Blanche Smith came to live with them. She taught me how to cook so that Doo never again threw out my food. Aunt Blanche was a great cook who was careful about everything. She reminded me of the old blind Butcher Holler midwife who had delivered seven of Mommy's kids. She'd cook beans only after counting them one at a time to make sure she didn't get no rocks in the pot.

Besides the bachelors, I also cooked for the thirty-six ranch hands who worked for them. My cooking might not have pleased Doo back in Butcher Holler, but it pleased them hungry men who did fieldwork and common labor. They'd be hollering for "more helpings" while I was hurrying to finish the first. The bachelors worked me seven days a week, and I was glad to give them that much time. They paid me by letting us live rent-free.

There was a big problem with me working for rent. I've thought about it in the years since, and I can see where homemakers can get into this same mess. You may be working as hard or harder than your husband, but if you don't have any cash coming in, he sometimes don't think of you as pulling your weight. And in Doo's case, he figgered any money he earned was his, not ours. That wouldn't have been so bad if I'd been earning cash, but my work went straight toward the rent. So when Doo got paid, he bought whatever he wanted. During our years in Washington state, he ended up buying a boat, some camera equipment, guns, and a lot of whiskey. Doo shot a lot of wild game for our meat, but to tell you the truth, we could'a had more meat from the store for the money he spent on shells. When he'd go off fishing or hunting with his buddies, me and the kids usually had to count on making what food we had last, or hoping the Green family would help us out some.

When I think back on them years in Washington, I always think about the kindness of the Green brothers. They fed us when we didn't have food, and made us feel like family. In them years we always spent Thanksgiving and Christmas with the Greens, and I did the cooking, along with their Aunt Blanche. The very first Thanksgiving was something else. I ate and ate and ate until I thought I'd pop. One of the bachelors finally said, "Loretta, you're gonna have that baby this very night if you don't stop eatin'!"

"No, I ain't," I said.

Then Doo and me went back to the house and went to bed. We slept on this old army bed, a twin size that we could barely squeeze into with me pregnant. I had been scared to death thinking that I'd have the baby in my sleep and we'd smother her in that little bed. Well, sometime in the night I come up outta that bed with the first pain. Never again would I think anyone could sleep through childbirth unless they had a doctor there drugging 'em! I was screaming and hollering, and Doo was running around like a chicken with its head cut off. He got me into the car and we set off for the hospital in Bellingham. Doo was driving so fast he was sure we were gonna get stopped by the police.

"Loretta, if a cop flags us down, you keep right on screaming," he said. I remember thinking that the comment didn't make sense. Well, of course I'd keep on screamin'—it was me having the baby, not the cop.

I had Betty Sue after thirty-seven hours of labor. She

weighed less than five pounds and was sixteen inches long. The nurses said Betty Sue was the smallest full-term baby ever born in St. Joseph's Hospital in Bellingham. Her little head was so beat up by the forceps that she was just pitiful.

Doo almost wouldn't claim her.

"This isn't my baby," he told the nurses.

He had always told me that I was going to have a boy, and as I explained, I believed *everything* the man told me in them days, except for his yarns about being faithful. When Doo told the nurses they was wrong about the sex of my baby, I just assumed he was right. I didn't want to take the wrong baby home, obviously.

When the nurses first brought Betty Sue into my room, I told them to take her away.

"I had a boy," I said. "Don't bring no girl in here. I had a boy. Where is my little boy?"

Doo was so determined to get the right baby that he went to the hospital nursery. He picked out a nine-pound baby boy and told the nurses it was his, and he ordered them to take that baby to my room. They wouldn't do it, of course, and finally convinced Doo that tiny little girl baby was his. The minute I held her in my arms, I loved her more than anything.

Once we had children, the differences in mine and Doo's upbringing was even more obvious to me. I had grown up with a soft-spoken, gentle father. And Doo grew up in a household where no holds was barred. In his mind, if a child didn't finish his meal, or if he started eating before Doo said he could, that was grounds for a whipping. Doo's little brother Jimmy lived with us in them days, and he pointed out to me that the times was very different then. You could get put in jail these days for whipping kids as hard as some folks did back then. Doo believed in the old idea of spare the rod and spoil the child. I never thought that way, but since he considered me still a kid too, he never paid a lick of attention to my child-raising ideas.

And some of the worst times had to do with Betty Sue. Doo was harder on her than he was on any of the kids, and part of the reason was that Betty Sue was a lot like her daddy. Some of our kids would back off from a fight with Doo. Not Betty Sue. They was knockin' heads from the time she could talk. She'd refuse to eat her peas, and he'd yell and scream for an hour. She'd sass him, and he'd tie her to the clothesline outside, even though she couldn't stand to be out in the sun very long at a time. I'd spend my time running around trying to undo what he done, afraid every minute he'd turn on me because of it.

Betty Sue is still with me to this day. She and Cissie run my theater and other operations at my ranch in Hurricane Mills, Tennessee. She used to run her own restaurant. She runs my heart all year round. But that day when I first held my first baby, I wasn't much more than a baby myself, and I had a whole lot to learn about the world. I was a baby with a baby.

Six

Like Nothing Had Happened . . .

ABOUT A YEAR AFTER I LEFT Kentucky, Daddy got real sick and Mommy sent money for us to come home, with a short letter that like to scared me to death: "If you want to see him alive, you better come quick."

I was pregnant with our second child when we got that letter, but nothing could have stopped me from making that trip. I figgered I'd made the trip to Washington while I was pregnant; I could durn well make it back to Kentucky pregnant. So we went back home to Butcher Holler. By the time we got there, Daddy had got better. The big news in Butcher Holler was about jobs opening up in Wabash, Indiana. Doo decided to stick around awhile and look into it.

And so Butcher Holler is where our son, Jack Benny, was born. When I went into labor, Doo and Mommy took me in a truck to the hospital and Doc Turner in Paintsville, Kentucky. By the time we finally got inside the old contraption, I just wanted to lay down.

The truck bounced all over the road, the ride was rough, and in some places the mud was so deep we got stuck. Doo and Mommy was both smoking up a storm. I thought I'd die from all of the smoke before I ever delivered, or else the baby would bounce outta me right there in the truck. But somehow we made it to Paintsville and Jack just barely got born in a hospital, praise the Lord.

A lot of people think I named him after the comedian Jack Benny, but I didn't. I had never even heard of the famous Jack Benny. I liked the names "Jack" and "Benny," and that's the long and short of it. Jack was a lot like Daddy. For some reason, as he grew up, Doo made fun of him because of it, too. I always felt Doo carried a little resentment toward Daddy because he thought nobody would ever replace him in my heart. The truth is, once my kids was born, I just had more people to love.

It was during that visit back to Butcher Holler that Doo's cheating got throwed right in my face again. It got throwed in the face of the whole family, because he got caught running around with the wife of one of my brothers. The whole thing got found out when Doo and my brother decided to go up to Wabash to see about them jobs people was talking about. I stayed in Butcher Holler with Betty Sue and the new baby.

Well, my brother came back to the holler one night crying and carrying on. I woke up and asked Daddy what was going on, but he just told me to go on back to bed. Mommy was more realistic about what I needed to know. She marched right in where I was sleeping and told me that my brother had caught his wife and Doo in bed together.

The next morning, Doo's mama got in charge. She told me to come with her to Wabash and get Doo, and I followed right along. I think that because I'd just had a baby, I was too tired and confused to argue. But I didn't know no better, anyway. So Doo's mama dragged me back to Doo, and like a good wife, I stayed. The way I looked at it, even at fifteen, when you get knocked down, you get back up, dust yourself off, and get on with it. My brother left his wife for quite a while after that happened. By the time they got back together, me and Doo was on our way back to Washington state in an old junk car Doo bought.

The Green brothers welcomed us back like we was family. I think they felt sorry for me and the kids, and as much as they liked Doo, they wasn't always sure he was taking good care of us. In fact, when Jack Benny was about five, one of the brothers even offered to adopt him. Jack was always helping the brothers, handing them nails when they was working or running little errands for them. Like me, they thought the sun rose and set on that boy. I know the Green brothers thought they could give Jack a better life. And here's the truth: if it hadn't been for my music, they could have from a money point of view. But they could have never given Jack as much love, and besides, nothing could make me permanently part with one of my children, then or now. Only God could.

Even after getting caught cheating with my own sister-in-law, Doo didn't change when we got back to Washington. He'd tell me he was going to go off working, or hunting, and he'd be gone for as long as two weeks. I knew he was with women. I knew he was cheating, and I was already beginning to learn to live with it. I'd stay home working in the bachelors' garden, and in my own garden, with my babies sitting on a blanket beside me. Times we ran out of food, the bachelors helped, we went without, or I boiled dandelion greens. It was in Washington state that I killed that pheasant with a rifle with no stock.

Ernest Ray, my third child, was born in Washington. Hank Williams died during the time I was pregnant with Ernest Ray. I heard it on the radio, and when Doo come home that night, I was still crying. He thought I was sick from the pregnancy. "No," I said. "Hank Williams died."

"Well, what in the world has that got to do with all this carrying on?" he asked.

"I love Hank Williams," I said. "Ain't nobody ever gonna sing like him again."

And they ain't.

The events around Ernest Ray's birth are painful for me to think back on. Doo was off working construction, and I had to get a girlfriend to drive me to the hospital. I struggled with Ernest's delivery for three days and nights. (And I'm still struggling with him.) Doctors urged me to have a cesarean, but I was too young to sign the consent form, and they couldn't find Doo. I had a bed by the window, and I'd watch for Doo every day. I was in there that whole week watching women's husbands walk up the drive carrying flowers and candy. I remember how the doctor who delivered Ernest Ray was real mad at Doo for not being with me, and for being so hard to find.

One night I heard him tell the nurse: "If that son of a bitch comes around here at three in the morning, you make him go see that little girl."

Doo didn't come to the hospital in Washington until six days after Ernest Ray was born. I went ahead and named Ernest Ray after a boss of mine who was always nice to Doo and me, a fellow named Ernest Crandall.

A lot later, Doo confessed he'd spent the money he'd saved to come back in time for the baby's birth on a new camera.

Like I said, Doo's money was Doo's. We might not have bread in the house, but he had a fishing boat in the yard and camera equipment in the closet. I never liked that boat in the first place because I'm terrified of water. When Doo would take us to the ocean, I sat inside and clung to the sides as the high waves of the Pacific tossed our little boat here and yonder. I wore a life jacket, but never found out if it would keep me afloat, thank God. Usually, I ran up and down the bank hollering at my family out in the waves.

This one time I was sure I was gonna lose one of my babies to the water. Doo kept insisting that I let Ernest Ray try to learn to ski. I was dead set against it. Ernest was five, and couldn't have held his own in the rough ocean, especially while wearing a pair of skis. Each ski was two feet taller than he was. So Doo concentrated on teaching Jack Benny and Betty. Jack was out in the water, and Doo was hollerin' at him to stay up on the skis.

Ernest Ray was hollerin' too. "Me could 'ki but me mommy won't 'wet' me!" Ernie always called me "me mommy." I still smile thinking about it.

All of a sudden, Doo pulled the boat to shore, grabbed Ernest by the collar on his life jacket, and hurled him into the Pacific. I was positive he was gonna drown or get eaten by a shark. Ernest's little hands and arms were beating on the water. He was fighting to stay on top. Of course, the life jacket held him up. But he was a little boy who didn't understand that. Neither did his mother.

"Help! Help!" I began to scream, running faster now up and down the shore. "My baby's drowning! Help!"

"Help me, me mommy, I'm drowning on down," Ernest screamed.

A crowd gathered in no time.

Doo saw all the people my screaming brought 'round,

and he waded out in the water, snatched Ernest by his life jacket, and brought him in. But even now Ernest remembers the horrible fear he felt that day.

From the look on Doo's face, I knew I was in trouble for causing such a commotion. I sort of slunk back into the crowd.

"Damn, woman!" he yelled. "I'll throw you in the water if you don't shut up!" You can imagine what them other campers lined up on the beach thought of us— h-i-l-l-b-i-l-l-i-e-s! And I didn't care.

I was afraid, however, he was going to whip my butt right there on the beach. But since he had an audience, he just fussed and fumed and packed up to leave.

Looking back on it now, I'm surprised Ernest Ray didn't go a little crazy from the way Doo tried to toughen him up. And since Ernest Ray would be the first to admit he drinks way too much now, he might even say he did get a little crazy from it.

I remember when Ernest Ray was around seven years old and we went to Yellowstone National Park. We were walking across this bridge over a great big waterfall. Doo wanted everyone to look down over the side of the bridge, but Ernest was scared to go over to the edge. That irritated Doo, since it didn't seem manly. Ernest kept inching toward the wall, and Doo kept getting madder 'cause Ernest didn't run up and lean out over the edge. Finally, Doo ran up behind Ernest, picked him up by his ankles, and dangled him upside down above that roaring waterfall and river.

It scared Ernest so bad I thought he'd wet his pants. I know I like to have died.

A lot of folks, men and maybe women too, have throwed a kid into water to make 'em learn to swim, or scared them in some mean way. But it's not right. I knew it wasn't right back then, and I still know it. But for Doo, it was simply him "making men" out of his boys.

One thing about Ernest that has always stayed the same: he is always in a good mood. He was that way from the start. People tell me they've never met anybody else who is always happy. When he was a baby, I'd get up at daylight to fix Doo's breakfast and look over at Ernest Ray in his bed. He'd look back at me and smile. I could put him on the blanket in the field next to the other babies and he'd kick and giggle and smile, right in the heat of the day.

I don't want to leave the impression that all of the trips our family took in Washington was terrible. Sometimes these trips were fine. We'd get white bread for our baloney or fried egg sandwiches—and we'd eat the leftover bread slices just like cake. Sometimes we even had pop to drink—one Coke apiece. That was something we never had except for special occasions. Doo would bring that camera he bought and take pictures. He would get in a good mood and he'd sing and tell jokes. He could be a charmer, Doo could. Those times were wonderful, and I'd forget all about the women and the drinking and the temper.

In the years since Doo died, I have found myself thinking back more about the good times and not much about the bad times. I'm not sure why.

Another scene out of my life that never made it into my first book and movie was Doo's green bean rampage. I always canned food during the garden season. I had two cookers that were used for canning beans. I put beans inside Mason jars and put the jars inside the pots. I put towels over the bottom of the pots so the jars wouldn't bust.

This one time I got up at 4 A.M. and canned green beans that I had picked from my garden. I worked all day to put up a hundred quarts. Doo came in tired, hungry, and drunk. Supper wasn't ready because I'd spent all of my time canning, and Doo was furious about it.

He began to throw them quarts of green beans. They probably weighed two pounds each, and if a person threw them hard enough and hit somebody in the head, they might kill them. Doo threw them hard enough to dent my new refrigerator. It was one of the first new things I ever owned for my house. Each time he threw a quart it exploded all over the kitchen. I was screaming because I was afraid the breaking glass was going to cut me or one of the kids. The kids was scared half to death, and I run 'em into the front room to get 'em out of the firing line. Doo just kept getting madder and throwing harder until he broke all hundred quart jars. Then he stomped out of the house.

Green beans was stacked on the kitchen floor up past

the refrigerator door. They was on the walls. They was in the windowsill. They was stuck to the ceiling.

I cried and shoveled beans for hours. I put the beans in a wheelbarrow and pushed them to a place behind our outdoor toilet. The birds ate the beans, and a lot of beans rotted. If the birds ate them, they probably flew off to die. When the beans was all gone, I hand-picked the broken glass and threw it away in a big oil barrel so none of the children would get cut.

During this same tantrum he ran his fist through a glass cabinet, too. It was a real pretty cabinet, and I wish I still had it because I bet it would be worth some money. But Doo got so mad at my screaming that he was ready to punch me out. Instead, he turned around and put his fist through the glass. Six months later, his hand was still hurting and a doctor ended up digging a piece of glass out of him.

I don't know where Doo went after his outburst; probably somewhere to get some supper and more whiskey.

My old neighbors, Harlan and Edna Brown, and the Green brothers put the word out that I needed food to put up and Mason jars to put it up in. People from all over the area started stopping by until I had fresh vegetables and jars coming out of my ears.

I turned right around and started canning again. That's the way we usually handled Doo's drunken temper tantrums: we just went on like nothing had happened. Communication has always been a problem in our family, and even all these years later, I fear it still is. There's times I know my kids and me should have more heart-to-heart talks than we do.

Seven

I Often Threw
the First Punch...

AFTER ERNEST RAY WAS BORN, I took a notion to have another baby, and I wanted another girl.

Ten months later, I had Cissie. She came two weeks early. Cissie was one of them kids that was a pure joy to be around. She was always happy and positive—and she knew how to work her daddy, too. Times when Betty Sue would dig her heels in and end up in trouble with Doo, Cissie would start to cry a little, and he'd soften up. Of course, she was the baby of the family for nine years, and she liked that position just fine. She still likes it. Her and Patsy, the youngest twin, fight all the time over who's the real baby of this family.

I took to being a mother a lot more natural than being a wife, probably because I'd helped with all my brothers and sisters. I'd even wanted to bring my sister

Peggy Sue with me to Washington state back before I left on that train. Of course, my mommy and daddy wouldn't even listen to that kind of talk.

After Cissie came, there was one time I got so mad at Doo for staying out that I was ready to pack up the kids and try to get back to Kentucky on my own. Two of Doo's friends played roles in this story.

As much as them Green brothers liked me and cared about me, they'd run off with Doo when he was in a woman-chasing mood as easy as not. And my boss, Ernest Crandall, looked out for my husband as well. Men will usually stick up for each other. Especially if they are protecting a friend's right to run around on his wife. I liked Mr. Crandall so much, but when push came to shove, it was Doo he backed.

I had started picking strawberries early on during our years in Washington state, mainly because it put actual cash in my pocket. It was a seasonal job, but for a few weeks a year, I had cash money. The strawberry pickers got paid by the carrier, which is a wood box that holds eight quarts of berries. Each time I picked a carrier, the man punched a ticket that I took down a road and traded for cash. The man who had the cash for us was Mr. Crandall.

With money in my pocket, I started to get a little more backbone. One year during strawberry season, I caught Bob Green and Doo snuggling up with with two local Indian girls. I pitched such a fit that for once, Doo believed I might actually walk out on him. Doo was so afraid I'd leave him and take the kids with me that he took 'em to bed with him.

This news soon got around and by week's end, when I went to trade in my tickets, Ernest Crandall wouldn't give me the money. Like everybody else, he had suspicions that I'd use the money to leave Doo. Would I have gone if I had got the money? Yes. But without cash, there was nothing I could do. When I finally cooled off, Mr. Crandall started giving me cash again. But I started understanding something then. Women who have some money of their own got choices. And having choices is mighty important.

I think women try a lot of tricks to try and get their men to stop drinking and cheating. I remember one time that I did nothing but make a fool outta myself tryin' to make a point. Strawberry picking season was under way, and Doo invited a bunch of the pickers to our house to drink beer. One of the pickers was a woman I knew he'd been sleeping with and I thought I'd give Doo a taste of his own medicine. Maybe I'd have myself a beer and smile at a man or two.

The trouble is, I can't drink. I only had about four swallows of beer. (Some people can gargle that much.) It wasn't long before I headed to the door and threw up all over. I didn't even have a chance to flirt with nobody. I did nothing but cause Doo to break up the party.

He dragged me into the kitchen, run the sink full of water, grabbed me by the hair and shoved my face in the sink. He knew how scared I was of water, and held my head under until I began to choke, then he yanked me out by the hair until I caught my breath. As soon as I did, he pushed my head back under the water.

He said he was sobering me up.

He got the kids out of bed at about ten o'clock that night. They were all still little.

"Look at your old drunk mother," he said, and of course, he was dog-drunk himself. "Ain't she a sight? Ain't you kids proud to have a drunk for a mother?"

It's a sorry story, but true.

Still, I worry that people who read *Coal Miner's Daughter* or saw the movie think I am some helpless woman who couldn't, and wouldn't, take up for myself. My foot!

Doo was not the only one in the family who could turn mean as a snake. His brother Jimmy, who has been one of my best friends throughout life, recently reminded me that I was often the one who threw the first punch. Remember, I was the only girl amongst a bunch of brothers. I was always a scrapper, and I fought with more folks than Doo, which brings me to another scene you never saw in *Coal Miner's Daughter*.

One time a woman and her husband moved from Missouri to Washington to be close to her parents. The Missouri woman was picking strawberries with me and mentioned that they didn't have no place to live. Since there was empty rooms on the second floor of the house

Doo and me was living in, I said they could stay awhile for free. Until they got on their feet. That was a dumb move.

Anyhow, this old gal got mad 'cause she thought I had my record player cranked up too loud. Doo had bought me a Hank Williams record for our anniversary, I was playing it over and over for some of my friends from the strawberry patch. I thought the gal had her nerve in complaining about me in my own house. I don't mind being asked to do something, but I hate being told to do something, and won't take being ordered to do something from anybody, not to this day.

That's another reason me and Doo fought. If he demanded that I do something, I'd say no, just to be contrary. He might eventually get his way, but it was after the fight.

Anyway, this woman told me to turn off my loud music. I told her to go on off and pick some fruit.

I sure wasn't expecting her to jump me, but that's what she did. I was sitting down and she was standing up. Durned if she didn't haul off and hit me, then start pullin' me around the room by my hair. Here's one big truth about a fight: you can't hit anyone when you've got long hair and they're pulling you by it. They're out of reach. Sitting down didn't help me much, either.

She kept pulling my hair, and I kept trying to pull away, which just hurt worse. Then I saw a butcher knife on the cabinet, and was able to struggle to within arm's reach of it. I grabbed it in one sweep and put the blade against her. Lordy! It must have been Grandpa Ramey comin' out in me!

"Turn me loose or I'll put this right through you," I told her. I ain't sure I would have done it, but she didn't know that. You can sure get somebody's attention quick when you got the butcher knife.

She turned me loose and I stood up straight. I'll bet the old gal thought I was mean enough to shave her head. I threw her out of my house and told her to go mooch off somebody else. She packed up and left, taking a beautiful rose-patterned crochet doily my mommy had made. I never could prove she stole it, but I sure thought at the time she did.

I got off with just a bruise or two, but I had to admit she bested me until I got that knife in my hand. She did that because she got in the first lick—the first punch. If you get that first punch, you're likely to win. I know; I've gotten plenty of first punches, and plenty of wins.

I ain't proud of that story or this next one, but this one has such a good ending I got to tell it anyway. I was sitting at home rocking Ernest Ray one night. Cissie wasn't no more than two months old. I remember my hair was up in pin curls because Doo promised to take me out for the first time in a long time. Doo come in drunk, singing and raising the dickens. He was carrying a bottle of whiskey. The first thing he says is that he's going to turn right around and go somewhere.

"You promised I could go with you tonight," I said, and put Ernest Ray down.

Doo shook his head, and yanked out one of my pin curls.

That fired me up because I knew durn well he was on his way to see some woman. I hauled off and hit him squarely on his mouth, knocking out his two front teeth. I was actually aiming at his shoulder and missed. Them teeth shot outta his mouth and blood went everywhere.

I can still hear them teeth hitting the floor and bouncing. Pop, pop, pop.

For a second I thought he'd kill me. Fortunately, he was hurting too bad and went to yelling and jumping around the room. The babies was crying, the blood was spurting, and I kept getting ready to duck. Truth is, Doo was lucky to be drunk that night since it probably eased some of the pain. Finally he yelled that we needed to find him a dentist.

The closest telephone was at a nearby farmer's house so we all traipsed over there. What is that line from "A Boy Named Sue" about the mud, the blood, and the beer? In our case it was "the booze, the blood, and the babies," all invading some farmer's house at 3:00 A.M. to call a dentist.

"I neeth my teeff pulled," he told the dentist, who was probably still half-asleep. 'Course, Doo was talkin' about the roots, which was still in there with the nerves all exposed and hurtin'.

The dentist couldn't understand Doo, but Doo could understand the dentist, who told him that he wasn't coming out of his house at that hour to do no dentisting.

Doo started yelling into the phone, threatening to kill him, and I guess the dentist believed he'd do it, because he finally said to come on over. The dentist got the last word, though, because we had to pay him on the installment plan.

For a long time, Doo went without two front teeth. He looked like an eight-year-old boy who's lost his baby teeth. His smile was real ugly. He looked so bad that he didn't take up with any other women until we had enough money to pay for his false teeth. And that was several months later. It tickled me half to death.

It seemed like we got worse off as the years went by in Washington. We lived in three different houses while we lived there, and the last two was nothing compared to the Greens' place. But when Doo decided he needed to live someplace else, he just packed us up and we was gone. One of the houses was a two-room weighing station for the coal mine way back in a place where there had been mines, and there was still sinkholes as big as whales. I had to walk about half a mile down into this one old mine where there was water dripping for our drinking water. The kids had to walk a mile or so just to catch the school bus. It was one thing when Doo left us for a week at a time when we lived down the road from the Greens. When we lived close to the bachelors, I knew I wouldn't starve to death. It was another thing when we was out there in that old shack of a coal station.

The fellow who owned that place used to come around when Doo wasn't there. One time he come up there drunk and run me around the house about a dozen times. I must have been around seventeen. The rent was late so he told me he was gonna "take it out in trade." I outrun him, though.

I remember that I didn't have money to buy Betty Sue no underpants, and I ended up making panties from old dresses. There wasn't no elastic, so I'd pin 'em together with safety pins. I'd say: "Now, honey, don't get on them bars and hang upside down today. The kids will see you don't have real panties on." Betty Sue never listened to me no more than she listened to Doo. She'd be hanging on the bars right off. I swear she'd just as soon show you her hind end as her face. She ain't afraid of nothing; never was.

One time, my old friend Blanche come all the way out to see us. She brought milk and beef and white bread. I thought it was heaven. She just couldn't stand to see us living like that. Who knows, maybe the fact that we seemed to be going downhill is what got Doo thinking about me singing for money.

In 1959, not long before I started singing, something happened that opened my eyes about me and Doo and about the way other people live. It was a little old black-and-white television. Doo bought it on time, and we was still paying on it when we finally left Washington. People sometimes laugh about how unrealistic *Leave It to Beaver, Ozzie and Harriet,* and *Father Knows Best* was. But

I wasn't laughing when I first saw them. They seemed like they were living in Heaven.

I'd always thought that it must have been Mommy and Daddy's marriage that was the weird one. So many of Doo's friends run around on their wives and drank that I slid right into the belief that our life was just like everyone else's. I started studying the families on those shows, especially during the times when Doo was off for weeks at a time hauling logs or hauling hay. I saw the families on these programs and started getting a feeling deep down inside of me, a feeling that we were the ones who were weird. It was the way Doo and me was living that was different. Oh sure, I now know those shows glossed over everyday problems. But back then, what I saw was a clean, safe place where men didn't bust a hundred jars of green beans. A place where wives like me didn't knock their husband's teeth out and hope he didn't kill them over it.

I wanted to live like the people on that television screen.

Eight

"Whispering Sea"

WHATEVER ELSE OUR MARRIAGE was back in them days, and whatever you think about Doo's hardheaded ways, I know this: without Doo and his drive to get a better life, there would have been no Loretta Lynn, country singer. He pushed and shoved me every step of the way, starting with the time he bought me that Harmony guitar at Sears, Roebuck and told me to learn to play the guitar and sing. I could never have done it on my own. "Shy" isn't the word for what I felt onstage. Terrified is more like it. I mean, it took courage just to sing for Doo, who thought I could sing better than Kitty Wells. I'm not saying I could; I'm just saying that Doo thought so.

Doo came home one day and said he'd got me a job. I thought he meant another job cleaning house or cooking or something like that. But he didn't. He'd gone and got me a job singing inside a tavern in Blaine, Washington, right on the Canadian border. I'd never been inside a tavern and I'd never sang in public. And he'd done gone and got me a job. I was gonna be singing with the Penn Brothers, John and Marshall, and their group, the Westerneers.

I always sang to the kids, but singing in public had never entered my mind. That was for people like Kitty Wells and Ernest Tubb. And I didn't even know one song all the way through. I told him I didn't want no job singing in front of people, and he told me he'd let me know what I wanted. I argued and cried and carried on, but Doo got his way, just like he always did.

I went off with Doo to sing at the tavern, and begged him all the way to change his mind. But he wouldn't hear of it. He was determined that other folks was going to hear me sing. Maybe he wanted their opinion, but I doubt it. Whenever Doolittle made up his mind, he didn't seek nobody else's opinion.

Me and three or four musicians all sang, and our sound was picked up by one microphone. In other words, each instrument didn't have its own microphone. The people were dancing and yelling, and most of 'em was drunk so they wasn't really listening. I was glad about that. I sang into the microphone and looked at my feet. I wouldn't raise my head to face the crowd. But I knew they were there, just a few feet away. I could hear them.

Then, after every song, I turned my back to the crowd. I just couldn't face the people. I was so scared, I didn't even want to walk through the crowd to use the bathroom. Also, I was embarrassed to think people would know what I was doing.

"Doo," I whispered into his ear. "I'm dying to pee. Walk me out to the weeds out back. Nobody won't see me there, and I won't have to talk to nobody."

"Woman," he said with disgust. "You're ignorant. Get your ass to the ladies' room and use it."

"I cain't go to the ladies' room, Doo," I said. "Everybody will think I'm peeing."

He walked away from the stage and came back with a glass of tomato juice. He made me drink it all up so I'd *really* need to pee. I finally gave in, and Doo led me to the ladies' room.

What happened next is something I ain't talked much about. But I'll tell it now. The first person to "hit on" me at a show was another woman!

After I went to the bathroom and stepped out of the stall, a woman approached me and said she liked my singing. That embarrassed me and I couldn't think what to say. But then she told me how much she liked my outfit. It was much easier for me to talk about sewing than singing.

"I made it myself," I said.

"Let me see how it's made," she said. She started looking over the dress, feeling around at the seams and touching me. I guess I mistook that glint in her eyes for interest in my sewing talents.

"Oh sure," I said. I didn't realize the woman was undressing me. I thought she was trying to figure out the pattern. I was dumb as a post.

My jumper was off and I was halfway undressed when Doo kicked the door down. He saw me, half-stripped, grabbed the woman, and slung her out the door into the crowd.

"Why'd you do that, Doo?" I asked. "I was showing that woman how I made this here jumper."

Doo told me to get myself together and to get myself back onstage. I had no idea why he was mad. He would never tell me, either. It wasn't until I got to Nashville and the Grand Ole Opry that I learned what had been going on that night. When I was playing the Opry, I started writing songs with a woman who was a lesbian. Shoot, I didn't even know what that word meant. You'd have never guessed she liked women by the way she acted, and she never come on to me at all. Finally a close friend from the Opry told me to stop bringing the woman to the show.

"People are going to start talking about you and that *friend* of yours," he said.

"What do you mean?" I asked.

"She's a regular down at the Jungle Club," he said, his eyes kind of squinted.

"So?" The Jungle Club didn't mean nothing to me.

"It's a homosexual hangout."

That word didn't mean nothing to me either. But he wouldn't say nothing else that night. Then I showed up with the woman again and he explained it all to me. I nearly fainted.

I run right back and told my friend what this Opry star had said about her and the Jungle Club.

She laughed. "You just go ask him what he was doing in the Jungle Club."

Now, in reality, I don't give a flip about who somebody wants to fall in love with, and I stayed friends with the woman to this day.

Here's something else I didn't explain at all in *Coal Miner's Daughter*. I started my own band a couple of months after I started working with the Penn Brothers, and here's why. They was tired of paying me my five dollars a show, and was fixing to fire me. The steel player, Roland Smiley, who we called "Smiley O'Steel," warned me, and said that if I left, we could start our own group. So I left and we put together a little combo. My brother Jack was living in Washington by then, so he played lead guitar while I was on rhythm. Roland came with us on steel. We billed ourselves as Loretta's Trail Blazers, and got us a paying job at Bill's Tavern. I had to make some money; after all, me and Doo was paying babysitters.

I kept singing in those old dives in Washington because Doo kept making me. I would have been a whole lot happier if he'd got steady work that let me stay home with my kids without having to work myself. But Doo had decided that I was a professional singer.

Doo heard that Buck Owens, who sang at one of the rowdiest bars in Tacoma, Washington, was running a talent contest. So we went to see Buck about getting a chance to perform. Buck told Doo it was impossible because he was already overbooked. Doo kicked up a storm about how far we'd drove, and finally Buck let me sing. I was scared to death, but I'll be doggone if I didn't win that night. I got a watch for Doo as the prize. Then I went a block down the street and entered another talent contest, where I won myself a watch. But, like a lot of things in the music business, they didn't last long. I think it broke down in about three days. The funny thing about that talent contest was something that happened years later. I was on a 1997 Ralph Emery TNN special, and they got Buck to do a live appearance through a satellite feed. Buck got on and told me he had had a crush on me for all them years.

"Buck, I didn't know that," I said.

"Yep," he said, "but we had two problems—my wife and your husband!"

We just laughed.

I'm afraid Buck would have had his hands full with Doo, because he was awful jealous. Maybe he knew how easy it was to cheat, or maybe he wondered when I'd start thinking that what is good for the gander is good for the goose.

I've got lots of stories to tell you about times Doo got

jealous of the artists I worked with. All it took was for some old boy to look at me twice or say something about me. Except for Faron Young. Faron was a different story. We was sitting home watching Ralph Emery's *Nashville Now* show one night in the early eighties, and Faron Young was his guest. Ralph asked Faron what he'd want to take with him if he was stranded on a desert island. Faron never missed a beat. "A case of beer, a bottle of whiskey, and Loretta Lynn," he cracked. Doo laughed till his face turned red. He loved Faron, and knew there wasn't any danger of him trying anything with me.

Here's a story that will explain why Doo could laugh at Faron's wisecrack. I went on a lot of package shows with Faron, and once in the mid-sixties at a show he was headlining, a bunch of us had gathered in his room after our shows. There was a crowd of both men and women—musicians, artists, backup singers. A little bit before it was time for him to go on, Faron jumped up and announced:

"Ladies," he said, "I'm fixin' to drop my laundry, so those of you who don't want to see that had better hit the door." Of course, he meant he was going to be in his underwear while changing britches. He turned to me and didn't even ask.

"Loretta," he said. "Hit the door."

My feelings was hurt until Doo explained that it was Faron's way of showing me respect. Doo got a big kick out of his ordering me out like that. Faron was another who used to drink and raise cain. But he was always a gentleman around me.

The watch I won on Buck Owens's show might not have run long, but that show was a real important part in getting my career going. The show was broadcast in Canada, where Norm Burley of Zero Records heard me sing. He contacted us and asked if I wanted to make a record. I didn't even want to sing in public, but I got really excited that somebody thought I was good enough to make a record. He had heard me sing "Whispering Sea" on the Buck Owens show, and it had a special meaning for him.

His wife had died, and he went to a rock in front of his home every night on the Pacific Ocean to talk to her spirit.

In my song "Whispering Sea," I wrote about sitting down by the sea and it whispering to me about an old love affair that used to be.

I think Norm must have cried when he heard that line. People were moved to emotion real easy in them days. I still am that way. I'll tear up at a sad song in a minute. In fact, I think most people would be better off if they were more emotional. But you can't let yourself drown in them tears. So I told Norm that whenever I cried a little too long, I thought about what God said to Aaron about his continued grief over the deaths of his own two sons. You might remember that in the Bible, they burned to death for going into a tabernacle while wearing shoes. God told Aaron he cried long enough, and to stop moping. That's what He said in so many words, anyway.

I have thought about those words a lot over the years. And sometimes I have to give myself a little reminder: You've cried long enough. Quit moping.

Maybe it was because I wrote that song that he treated me and Doo like family and helped us every way he could. He paid for the gas for us to go to Los Angeles to record "Whispering Sea" and another song I wrote, "Honky Tonk Girl." I got the idea for it from watching a woman I used to pick strawberries with cry in her beer over the father of her nine kids. He'd left her for another woman. She sat in the same booth every night in this bar I played, and drank her beer and cried.

I always loved playing Canada. I feel like it is where I really got my start, with Zero Records and the audiences along the border. There was only one time when I worried about the audience up there. I'd been playing some little clubs that was usually packed, and all of a sudden the crowds dried up. I was sure they didn't like me or my music no more. But I had one last date to play, and when I got there, all them folks that had been missing showed up. I run right over to this one girl I'd got to know.

"What happened?" I asked. "You ain't been here for over a month!"

"It was Lent," she said.

Well, I hadn't heard of no "Lent" except for the lint that gets on your clothes. I asked her what she was talking about, and she explained that Catholics give up what they love the most during this time called Lent. I must have still looked puzzled.

"Don't you get it?" she said. "We gave you up for Lent."

It was after we got the record pressed that Doo decided the only way to get the record on the radio was to visit the stations ourselves. We went with Norm Burley's blessing and a little of his cash to help on expenses. He told us right up front that if we got something going and a big label offered me a deal, he would let me out of our contract. We packed up our car, an old Mercury, and went back home. We left Ernest Ray and Cissie with my mommy, and Betty and Jack Benny with Doo's parents. Then we took off.

It still saddens me that Daddy didn't live to see it all happen. We started out promoting in 1960, just a year after he died. One thing the book and movie didn't tell was why I was so mad at Doo when we went home to bury Daddy.

The night my daddy died, I dreamed that he was dead. I woke up crying, and Doo said, "Loretta, when you dream someone died, it means somebody got married. Peggy Sue probably got married. Just go back to sleep."

I went back to sleep and in my dream I was walking around my daddy's coffin, wringing my hands and crying.

Doo said, "You know what probably happened to your old man? If he's dead, I bet it's because he was running around with some eighteen-year-old girl in Wabash. His old heart just couldn't take it." I knew it was just a dream, but when the Green brothers came and told me I had a call from Wabash, Indiana, I hoped Doo was right and maybe Peggy Sue had got married. I used a phone for the first time in my life and got the worst news of my life. My daddy was dead. Doo drove three days and nights and we got to the funeral forty-five minutes before it started.

The months that we spent driving around this country promoting my record was some of the best times Doo and me ever had together. Maybe it was because we had a common goal, or maybe Doo believed he'd found a way to finally fight his way out of poverty. Maybe it was because for the first time he saw me as a partner; probably not equal, but very necessary. But he treated me better on the trip than he ever did all them years in Washington. We laughed and talked and planned. There was so many times when Doo would want me to visit the station alone, and he'd sit out in the car waiting. It would get so hot he'd nearly faint, but he waited until I'd got 'em to play the record and maybe even do some little interview. You couldn't get by with visiting stations like that now, but I have to say that back then, we run into more nice folks than mean ones.

One person who was real encouraging back then was a guy named Bill Mack, a disc jockey on WBAP in the Dallas–Fort Worth area. He's now on a 50,000 watt station, and he's also syndicated on 2,000 other stations. He is also the man who wrote LeAnn Rimes's hit song, "Blue," that she recorded a couple of years ago.

Me and Doo walked into his show with "Honky Tonk Girl" and asked him to play the record. He was one of the nice disc jockeys that gave me some time on the air. He's another one who soon saw that our promotion tour wasn't exactly a big-dollar deal.

I was on the air with Bill and he said, "Loretta, that sure is a pretty dress you're wearing."

"Thank you," I said. "I just washed it."

"Oh really," he said, "where did you find a laundry around here?"

"I didn't find no laundry," I said, "I washed it in the back of the car."

And I had. I had a basin of water that I had put in the floor and had put my cotton dress inside. We didn't even have enough money for food, so we sure didn't have none to wash clothes.

"Oh," Bill said, grinning and shaking his head. "Well, how did you get it dry?"

"I blowed it dry out the window," I said.

Doo had paid four dollars for that dress, and I wore it whenever I wasn't wearing my cowgirl suit. I held it out the car window like a flag in the breeze to dry. We must have been a sight.

On that record tour we ate a lot of canned goods and other foods that didn't spoil quickly. We almost never ate in restaurants, because we didn't have the money. Actually, I still like to take my own food on the bus. Back in the mid-seventies, when I was writing *Coal Miner's Daughter*, I said I thought that promo trip had soured me on sandwiches for good. Well, as it turned out, I was wrong. I've always got baloney on the bus, and if you visit me there, you could probably count on me fixing you one.

But on that first tour there sometimes wasn't even money for baloney, so I started stealing fruits and vegetables from people's gardens. It started one time down in the rural South when we was broke and real hungry. I thought it over and, like cousin Lee Dollarhide, I figgered out stealing food was about the easiest way for a poor person to get a bite to eat. I remember sneaking under the bottom of three strands of a barbed wire fence. It was broad daylight and I didn't want to be seen. So I crawled close to the earth, like an animal sneaking up on prey.

I got under the fence, and then sneaked down the plowed row of a watermelon patch. I rolled the biggest melon I could find back to the car.

I have to admit that this whole scheme was my doing. It scared Doo to death. That first time I sneaked into a watermelon patch, Doo drove at least seventy-five miles before he'd stop the car. He always thought the law would catch us, and we'd wind up in jail with nothing to offer as bail except copies of "Honky Tonk Girl."

"Doo," I said, "it would be better to go to jail. We'd get fed three times a day."

I was serious. Watermelon is tasty, but not very filling even when you eat it right down to the rind. You just pee a lot and get hungry again in thirty minutes.

But one day Doo pulled up to a radio station and I learned that my watermelon-stealing days might be drawing to a close. When I introduced myself, the deejay smiled a great big old smile and said, "Well, Loretta Lynn, congratulations on your hit!"

"Hit?" I said.

"Your hit record!" he said.

He told me that "Honky Tonk Girl" was on the *Cash Box* charts. I asked where I could get a copy of this here *Cash Box* that listed hit songs. He handed us a copy, and me and Doo was so excited, it just tickled us to death. There was my song, listed right along with songs by Ernest Tubb, Johnny Cash, the Wilburn Brothers, Patsy Cline, Hawkshaw Hawkins, Stonewall Jackson, and forty others, many of them members of the world-famous Grand Ole Opry.

Since I had that hit on Zero Records listed next to Grand Ole Opry stars, we figured the next step was to get on the Grand Ole Opry. I never gave a thought to getting a manager, to auditioning, or all of the other junk artists go through today. Why would I need anybody but Doo standing behind me? We drove straight to Nashville.

Nine

Mention the Grand Ole Opry, and They'll Smile Every Time...

THERE WASN'T NO SIGN hanging at the Nashville city limits that said, "Welcome Loretta Lynn and Zero Records." We got inside the Grand Ole Opry that first night only because we counted out our pennies and sat in the audience. People sometimes talk about the Ryman, which is where the Opry was back then, as a rustic, old-fashioned building filled with down-home Americans—folks in bib overalls, inexpensive housedresses, boots with farm dirt still clinging to 'em. It didn't seem that way to me. Considering where I came from, the Ryman and the people inside was uptown. I remember that on that first night, a cold drink fell from the balcony onto my head. But it sure didn't douse my dreams.

We slept in the car and put what little money we had into Opry tickets and more baloney. We talked to anybody who would listen to us. People couldn't believe we thought I could get on the Opry without having any real connections. But Doo said it could be done, and I believed him. I know I was naïve. *Very* naïve. And sometimes I think it was a blessing. We kept hammering away at it, and before long they gave me a chance. Of course, I had an advantage that most artists don't have when they come to Nashville, then or now. I already had a hit record.

One thing that surprised me when we got to Nashville is that so many people who live here don't like the idea of the Opry! From the time we arrived, town people we met started telling us it was just a hick show with hillbilly music. But I thought it then and I think it now: the Opry put Nashville on the map. You can go anywhere in the world and mention the Opry, and people know what you're talking about. Maybe they've never been to America, and so they ain't never heard the Opry. But they still know what it is. You can take the number one show on American radio or television today and go to Europe, mention the title, and the people will have no idea what you mean. But mention the Grand Ole Opry and they'll smile every time.

Actually, before I ever played the Opry, I got to appear on Ernest Tubb's *Midnight Jamboree*, which comes on after the Opry goes off the air at midnight. Doo was a good talker when it came to my music, and Ernest Tubb believed in giving people a chance. A lot was made in the movie about Patsy Cline hearing me sing on the *Midnight Jamboree* and inviting me to come see her in the hospital.

But something else that first night made a pretty big impression on me. This is something I wouldn't have dared write in my first book. Not unless I'd wanted Doo to whip my butt. I was up on the stage fumbling around, trying to tune my guitar, when a man's voice said, "Let me help you with that, Loretta." I looked up into the face of one of the most handsome men I'd ever seen. The man who tuned my guitar that first night was an Oklahoma boy named Cal Smith. At that time he hadn't had no real big hits yet, but he was Ernest Tubb's front man and rhythm guitarist. Of course, some years later, Cal would record one of the biggest hits in the history of country music—"Country Bumpkin." I got a little crush on Cal that night because he was so good looking. I'll tell you more about that later.

I got on the Opry the way I've got a lot of things in my time—just because I didn't know I couldn't do it. I've heard all of these people talking about having to pay bribes, sleep with Opry big shots, and stuff like that. Not me. Doo talked to the Opry people first, including former Opry manager Ott Devine. He told Ott that the Opry would be a whole lot better show with me on it. Doo had the courage of a bullfighter. And of a bull, too. Because when anyone said "no" to Doo, they was just waving a red flag in front of his face. Finally Ott agreed that I could perform, and one of my heroes, Ernest Tubb, introduced me on the Opry. I sung the only hit I had, "Honky Tonk Girl."

I was invited back to sing the same song for the next seventeen weekends in a row at the Opry. A lot of people wondered how in the world I was getting so much time on the show when I didn't have no connections. I think my shyness hurt me a lot. I didn't talk much to anyone, so they thought I was stuck on myself. Some speculated that I was sleeping with some Opry official. I wasn't, of course. It was all Doolittle's doing that got me on. And luckily, "Honky Tonk Girl" kept me there.

Back in the early sixties, there was a lot of prestige for a country singer to be on the Opry, but not much money. I believe it paid seventeen or eighteen dollars a night, and three additional dollars if you sang a second song. The Opry musicians was paid more than the singers.

I shopped in the Salvation Army store and bought material to make my own stage clothes. One afternoon, an Opry official saw me coming out of that store and told me it cast a bad light on the Opry when local folks saw the show's singers acting like poor people. That hurt my feelings a lot. I was doing the best I could, growing my own vegetables, raising chickens for meat and eggs. Doo had a job by then, but it didn't pay much. The kids was with us by that time, and it was hard to support a six-member family on a working man's wage. It still ain't an easy thing to do. I bought shirts for the boys, and dresses for the girls, for ten cents each.

It's funny looking back on it, but it wasn't just the town people who made fun of what they considered hill-billies. I loved Roy Acuff. I think everybody did. Roy was the Opry. Him and Ernest Tubb, Minnie Pearl, Bill Monroe. But Roy used to make fun of my country ways when he was the emcee on the Opry. He was one to talk! Behind his back, them town people was makin' fun of him!

Before introducing me to the crowd, he'd say something like, "Loretta, how many eggs did you gather to-day? Loretta, how much butter did you churn?"

I'd tell him and everybody would laugh. Come Sunday, many of the Opry stars, including Acuff, would come to my home to eat the food they teased me about. Patsy Cline would come, too, especially if she learned Doo had shot a rabbit. She loved rabbit more than anything.

As much as I respect the Opry, I have to say it has some curious ways. For example, Conway Twitty recorded fifty-five number one songs. That's more number ones than any other artist in any form of music has ever recorded. Yet he was never invited to join the Opry. Conway once had a hit called "Grandest Lady of Them All." It was about the Grand Ole Opry, and how it's the Mother Church of country music. I was one of dozens of guests on a tribute to the Opry. I think it was a CMA

Show. The entire cast sang "Grandest Lady of Them All."

Guess who was not on the show? Why would they not have Conway, who made the song a hit, sing his own song? By then I had the nerve to say pretty much anything I wanted. So I told Roy Acuff I thought it was wrong for Conway not to be there. Acuff said he agreed but didn't have no say in what the CMA done.

One of the biggest thrills at the Grand Ole Opry was meeting Kitty Wells. I believe Kitty is one of the greatest ladies to ever hit Nashville. It was Kitty that I patterned myself after, and I've told her that many times. Kitty can be tougher than some think, too. I've seen her get outright smart with people when they deserved it. One time right in the beginning of my career, Kitty and me was on a radio show together. This deejay looks at me and says: "Well, sounds to me like *somebody* is trying to sing like somebody else." Kitty knew I was too bashful to take up for myself, so she narrowed her eyes and said, "Well, at least she picks the best."

Another thrill was meeting Minnie Pearl. There was another great lady. When I first met her, she was out pushing a record she made with Archie Campbell. That was when I was pushing "Success." Minnie come up to me one night, winked, and said, "I can't sing and neither can Archie. But we got a record out!"

Minnie was always saying, "Loretta, come on over to my house. Let's take a walk together and talk." One of my great regrets is that I didn't do it because I knew that there was something Minnie wanted to talk to me about, to tell me. Or maybe she just wanted for us to spend some time together. She was after me for ten years to come over to the house. You always think you'll get around to things you want to do. Time can run right out on you.

Her husband, Henry Cannon, took care of her at home after she had a stroke in 1991. Finally, a couple of years before her death, he decided he couldn't do it no more and put her in a nursing home. I was real upset about it at the time. I thought she should have stayed home and had more nursing help if she needed it. Maybe it had to be. It ain't for me to say.

I will say this: I regret not going to the nursing home to visit her. I couldn't do it. My memories of her were so beautiful, I couldn't face seeing her after them strokes. Not only that, but it was right after Doo and my two brothers died.

One of the best breaks we got right off in Nashville was meeting up with a woman named Faye Morgan, who was backstage one night. Faye was a real friend to struggling musicians. We was so broke when we got to town that, as I mentioned, we lived hand-to-mouth and slept in our car. When Faye realized how desperate we were, she offered to put us up at her house for nothing. One bit of advice I will give anybody writing a book. Double-check that all your friends got their name in it. When my autobiography come out, Faye said she was upset that I didn't mention her. Well, dang it, I did mention her in the book. She just missed it. But, Faye, for what you done for Doo and me, I'm gonna thank you again.

Having those three months to save up and look for a place made all the difference. It wasn't just a money problem, either. A lot of landlords wouldn't take people who had kids, and certainly not four of 'em. But we finally found a place for a hundred dollars a month on Barber Drive in Madison, a little town east of Nashville. That was a lot of money for us to put together every thirty days. I was starting to earn a little bit from the Opry and Doo was working for $1.10 an hour at a gasoline station. He was grossing $44.00 a week, and after taxes, was bringing home about $37.00. After whiskey, it was about $30.00. That meant he was clearing $120.00 a month, and spending $100.00 for rent. Depending on my Opry appearances, we had twenty to forty dollars for food, electricity, and clothes for us and the four kids. Of course, as I mentioned, I shopped the Salvation Army store, so I saved a pretty good amount.

I have never been afraid to make do.

Ten

Still Thinking of Patsy . . .

TALKING ABOUT THE OPRY and my first years in Nashville always makes me think of Patsy Cline. She was my first friend in Nashville, and one of the best women I ever knew. When I met her, I had nothing going but a song out on a little Canadian label. She was a superstar who never once acted like she thought she was any better than me or anybody else.

Patsy's recordings are not "country" to my way of thinking. They are great records, just not country. She wanted to make records that were more country, and she could have done it, too. Owen Bradley, her producer, used to laugh and say that Patsy wanted to yodel on every song she heard, even the love ballads. He'd say, "No, Patsy. I'm not gonna let you ruin this ballad!" I'll tell you what, though, she could yodel with the best of 'em. Patsy Montana couldn't hold Patsy Cline's guitar when it come to a yodel.

Me and Patsy was so close when she got killed that I didn't know what I was gonna do. I walked around in a daze for weeks. And to this day, when I walk onstage, I think: "This is the way Patsy told me to come on the stage. This is the kind of song she said to start with." She taught me a lot about being onstage. I didn't have years of playing clubs under my belt like lots of artists do when they start touring. It was only about six months from the time I started until I had that hit. Patsy always told me to hit 'em hard coming and going. I might come out onstage and start with a ballad, or I might end with one. She'd say, "Don't you do it, Loretta! Start upbeat and leave upbeat. Don't ever leave an audience on a down note."

Patsy and me stuck up for each other. If Doo done something to me that Patsy didn't like, she spoke right up. I did the same with Charlie Dick, Patsy's husband. Doo liked Patsy and knew she and Charlie were our best friends in town. But he also knew I was learning from Patsy. Patsy would say to me, "You're crazy to stay with that man." I'd say, "You're living with one just like him." And we'd laugh. Them two men run around together *and* they run around on me and Patsy together.

But looking back, I have Doo and Charlie's friendship to thank for me having my twins. I thought I was pregnant in late 1962. It turned out to be just a scare, but it made me and Patsy nervous about getting pregnant since we both thought we had all the kids we needed. We told Doo and Charlie it was time they got "fixed" so we couldn't have any more kids. They went down to a clinic to get fixed, and Charlie said he'd go in first. While he was in there, Doo got cold feet and made a run for it. Two weeks later I got pregnant. Boy, did I get pregnant!

Patsy was always leaving Charlie. One day she called me up and said, "Loretta, get over here quick! I'm gettin' outta here. I'm leaving Charlie and this time it's for good."

"How am I gonna do that, Patsy?" I said. "I ain't got a car." Of course, even if I'd had a car, it wouldn't have done me no good. I was twenty-seven years old and couldn't even drive yet.

"Don't worry about that," she said. "I already called you a taxi. It'll be pulling up in your yard any time now."

Sure enough, within a few minutes, here comes this taxicab. I went over to Patsy's and helped her and the kids pack up. We drove in Patsy's car to a motel on Dickerson Road, and I stayed with her the rest of the day while she talked on and on about how she wasn't ever going back to him. The next day she drove right back to her house and unpacked. I have to laugh at them days because that's just how she was. I guarantee you if she'd really wanted gone, nothing could have made her stay. She did and said exactly what she wanted.

Well, that ain't exactly true now that I think about it. Career-wise, Patsy run up against some walls. One

thing Patsy told me she wanted to do was record a whole
album of gospel songs. She especially loved "Amazing
Grace" and "Just a Closer Walk with Thee." Even with
her popularity, Decca wouldn't let her do it, because
they believed gospel wouldn't sell big enough. Patsy did
record some religious songs from time to time, but it was
mainly because of her contract with Four Star Records,
which had struck a deal with Decca. That company insisted she cut only songs they published, unless they was
public domain songs that didn't require royalties. Sometimes when Owen couldn't come up with enough good
songs from Four Star, he'd slip a gospel song on an album.

One of the last things Patsy talked about to me was
the gospel album she wanted to make. By that time I
was on Decca Records and being produced by Owen
Bradley, the same as Patsy. It bothered me a lot that
Patsy never got to make that gospel album. So a week
after her death, I told Owen I wanted to record an album
of hymns in her memory. Things had changed just
enough and I was on such solid footing with Decca by
then, that they okayed it. I called the album *Hymns*, and
included six gospel standards and six new ones I wrote
myself.

I'll tell you a quick story here about something that
happened when I made *Hymns*. I had just finished with
a song I wrote called "The Third Man," which, by the
way, I didn't put my name on at the time because I knew
a songwriter who needed the money worse than me. She

had nine kids and her husband had run out on her—the hound dog. The song is mostly a recitation, a spoken song. It is a song about the men who died on crosses the day Jesus, the third man, died.

We finished the cut and Owen thought it was inspired. Then we played it back. There was a strange noise in the background, something that couldn't be accounted for no matter how the engineers checked and double-checked. I was both uneasy and disappointed because I didn't know if I could get the same emotion again. All of a sudden, there was that same noise coming from right there in the studio, from somewhere in the couch, it seemed! It was enough to raise the hair on the back of your neck!

I was being managed by the Wilburn brothers at the time. Teddy and Doyle went in search of the noise. In a dark corner, they found Doolittle Lynn, passed out drunk and snoring on two planks next to the wall. After the Wilburns finished yelling and chasing Doo around the studio, I went back and cut the song over. It turned out good, but I'm surprised after that mess.

I wish more country stars recorded gospel albums these days, because most of us "go back"—as they say—to religion. That's where a lot of people started singing, in church. And Patsy's heart always went back to religion. Mine does, too.

Another thing I wish is that singers recorded more with musicians right there in the studio, rather than just singing to tracks that the pickers already had recorded.

I think the music is usually better when it's not pieced together. It's got more "spark" to it when it's all done at the same time.

Patsy and me started out with one thing in common. We both had husbands with tempers, but we gave as good as we got. I've said before that if Doo hit me, I'd fly right back at him. If he smacked me once, I smacked him twice. Well, Patsy was like that, too. And she'd talk back to Doolittle Lynn when she didn't like how he talked to me, too. Doo never had no woman who'd talk to him that way. The women we'd known in Butcher Holler and Custer, Washington, might tell me I ought to talk back, but they kept their thoughts to themselves when they was around Doo. Not Patsy. She never kept a thought to herself in her life.

I think Doo secretly admired Patsy, even though he thought she mouthed off too much and drank a little with the boys. Here's how I know that. When she died, it hit him almost as hard as it hit me. It liked to have killed him. He'd gone to work that morning and had the car radio on. That's when they announced her death and started playing nonstop Patsy Cline songs. He wheeled around and come back to the house. I hadn't put the radio on yet that morning, but I knew what had happened because her booking agent called and told me. "You better turn on the radio, Loretta," the agent said. "Patsy is gone."

"No," I said. "Me and her is going shopping."

About that time Doo walked in looking like death warmed over.

"You heard," he said, taking one look at me.

"I don't believe it for a minute."

"It's true, Loretta. It's all over the radio."

And it was true, no matter how much I tried to wish it away. Over the years, I've thought so much about her and how she gave me some of her strength when she left this world. Lord knows, Patsy had enough of it to spread around.

There have been times when I felt her spirit, but none as strong as in 1976, when I told Owen Bradley I wanted to do an album called *I Remember Patsy*, featuring all her songs. We started out recording "I Fall to Pieces." Owen decided to do it as a waltz instead of a shuffle, and it came out terrible. I didn't like it and he didn't like it. But we went ahead and put down the tracks to the rest of her songs before I started to sing. Well, I couldn't sing a lick. Nothing sounded good. I was either above the pitch or below the pitch every time I opened my mouth. This went on for the whole recording session.

"Honey, let's just pack it up for today," Owen said, after about three hours of trying. "We'll come back another day and try again."

What I think happened is that I didn't feel I was good enough to be singing Patsy's songs. Hardly anyone is, you know. She was one of the greatest vocalists I ever heard in my life, no matter if you are talking country or pop or anything else. I've never heard one who could match her. The closest I can name is Trisha Yearwood. She could do a great job on a Patsy Cline album. But in my mind, Loretta Lynn wasn't good enough.

Owen started locking up the doors, but just as we was starting to leave, something stopped me. "I'm ashamed of you! You can do this," I heard Patsy say, as clear as if she was standing right behind me.

"Let's go back," I said to Owen. "You just run the tape and I'll sing."

I walked back to the vocal booth and Owen rolled the tape. I went through every one of 'em without taking a break. I will say that I went flat on the very last note on "She's Got You," but Patsy didn't say nothing about it and Owen liked it, so we kept it. The song hit number one in the charts, even with the bad note.

After that I decided to put a Patsy medley in my show, and that was hard. Patsy's songs have a lot of emotion. And you ain't ever gonna sing the slow songs like her. But sometimes when I'd start to sing, I'd look out above the crowd, where the cigarette smoke was drifting, and there she'd be. Patsy would sit there in her red pants, with them little gold shoes on her feet. She'd smile and I'd sing.

Now, the deejays never treated Patsy right after she passed away. They just quit playing her records much. I like to think me singing Patsy's songs helped some—kind of renewed interest in her music. That helped her kids, too. I'll tell you something else. Some people think if it hadn't been for my movie, there wouldn't have been a movie made of Patsy's life. If that's true, it makes me proud.

Eleven

This Is Gonna Be a Helluva Show! Bobby's Pants Is Unzipped, and Loretta's Drunk!

DOO HAD SINGLE-HANDEDLY promoted my first record. He had brought me to Nashville, got me on Ernest Tubb's *Midnight Jamboree* and on the Opry. Now I needed veteran management, and we both knew it. That was a great thing about Doo. There are some singers' husbands who think they know everything about the music business and end up making some bad decisions on behalf of their wives. But Doo understood there was too much that he didn't know. Plus, the last thing in the world Doolittle Lynn wanted to do was to have to put on a tie and show up at business meetings.

We signed with the Wilburn Brothers, who managed their own careers, published songs, and booked a few other acts for personal appearances. There was four of the brothers, Teddy, Doyle, Leslie, and Lester. They had built quite a management company, as well as Sure-Fire Music and Wil-Helm Talent (with Don Helms, who had played steel for Hank Williams).

It wasn't easy to get them to sign me because when I first played a tape recording for them, Teddy thought I sounded too much like Kitty Wells. But Doyle, Teddy's brother, said he thought he could hear something special in me. Now here's where it got sticky, and where Doo and me should have checked with other managers about contracts. I signed a lifetime song publishing, management, and booking contract with the Wilburns. That came back around to bite me later.

Doyle played my songs for Owen Bradley, who was in charge of Decca Records, and he said: "I already got Kitty Wells." But when he heard "Fool Number One," he wanted to cut it on Brenda Lee. Doyle agreed to let him have the song for Brenda if he'd sign me, too. Owen later said it was the best trade he ever made. Still, Owen waited until I got enough songs that he believed set me apart from Kitty before we started making our records together. I stayed on Decca, which later folded into MCA, for the better part of the next thirty years.

When I look back on my early sessions, one of the things that sticks out is that Owen would flat leave the building when I'd decide to put a pop song on an album. I did on most of them, too. I always loved country music, but in Washington state, you didn't hear much of it. You heard pop singers like Perry Como or Rosemary Clooney. Or you heard rock singers like Elvis Presley or

Conway Twitty. I loved both of those boys. I even had a big old Conway Twitty poster hanging in our bedroom. Why Doo didn't jerk it off the wall is more than I'll ever know. But even though I was raised on Jimmie Rogers and Ernest Tubb, I started loving pop songs in Washington, even though most of them wasn't right for me. When I started recording, I always wanted to try at least one on each album. The funny part of it is that Owen Bradley is sometimes criticized for the "Nashville Sound," the smoothing out of country. But I think he just tried to make records that was right for the individual, because in my case and in Kitty Wells's case, he sure wasn't trying to make no pop-sounding records.

Above and beyond that, people have to understand that country music is always changing and going in one direction or the other. And we ain't never going to go back to the farm for good.

At first Doo was jealous of Teddy and later of Doyle. Part of his jealousy had to do with my career. Doo had been the one who had launched me in the business, and now it was Teddy and Doyle in charge. Doo didn't want to be my manager, but he sure hated giving up the control. Mainly though, Doo was worried about me being on the road with men. He'd start drinking and get worked up, imagining me running around with the other singers, the musicians, the roadies, the bus driver. But I wasn't cheating on him, and it made me mad when he accused me of it. There'd come a time when I thought it was almost funny, but not back in the beginning. I missed Doo a lot on them tours. That was the man that I was thinking about, not some guitar picker.

I remember once when the Wilburns and I had been on a month-long tour. We had probably done about twenty-eight shows in thirty days, while driving up to five hundred miles a day between shows. All I wanted to do was get home to my husband and my kids. The last show on the tour was in Knoxville, Tennessee. I called Doo and asked him to come to the show.

He told me he didn't have no interest in coming. It hurt my feelings, but that was nothing new.

What I didn't know was that Doo saw the Knoxville show as a chance to catch me cheating on him. But as I said, I didn't cheat. He didn't think our old car would make it through them mountains, so he drove to Nashville from our house in Goodlettsville and wouldn't you know he rented a Jaguar. Then he drove to Knoxville and called the hotel where me, the Wilburns, and others in the show was staying.

"I'm Doolittle Lynn," he told the hotel operator. "Loretta Lynn is my wife and I'm coming to your hotel so I can surprise her. Have her room key ready for me when I get there."

"I'm sorry, Mr. Lynn," the fellow said. "The rooms are under the Wilburn Brothers' names and they said that Loretta's room number is to be given to no one."

"I'm almost there," Doo told the operator. "When I

get there, you'd better have the key ready for me or I'll jerk the whole damn switchboard off the wall." And he would have.

After the show that night, I went to Teddy and Doyle's room along with my brother, Jay Lee Webb, who played lead guitar during my part of the program, and with Don Helms. We spent the time inside the room trying to write a song for Webb Pierce.

We never did get it completed, and we finished trying at about one o'clock in the morning. The men thought they should walk me to my room and make sure I was safe.

I opened the door, looked around, and saw that nobody had broke in during the show. Thank God they didn't come inside my room.

"It's fine boys," I said. "I'll be all right. You all go on to your rooms and I'll see you tomorrow."

"Okay Loretta," my brother yelled back.

I walked into the bathroom and sat on the toilet. It was only then that I noticed a slight movement of the shower curtain and thought there must be a crazy killer hiding in there. I was almost right. Suddenly Doo jumped out from the shower with a bottle of whiskey in one hand and a loaded pistol in the other. He was so convinced that he'd catch me with another man that he was shaking with anger. And he was ready to kill me and whoever I was with. It took me some talking, but I calmed him down by reminding him that it was my brother's voice that he'd heard calling back in the room. Finally he stumbled off to bed, where he passed out. But I believe with all of my heart that if Teddy, Doyle, or Don Helms had stepped inside my room that night to make sure the room was empty, Doo would have jumped out and opened fire.

I never understood Doo's jealousy over the Wilburns because they was the ones who taught me to handle men. He must have known they were looking out for me, not trying to romance me. Doyle and Teddy were always telling me I was too friendly, that men was misunderstanding my attitude, and was going to try to date me.

"Ain't nobody going to try to date me," I told the Wilburns. "I'm married with four kids and everybody knows it."

The Wilburns finally went to Doo and told him to tell me to stop being so friendly. He told me they were right, that men were going to try to date me if I didn't tone down my personality. And so I did because Doo had told me to. He never mentioned it again, and neither did I. But I soon learned that some men can be pretty pushy when it comes to chasing skirts.

Not long after that, in the early to middle 1960s, I played the Longhorn Ballroom in Dallas, Texas. It was a private party for a bunch of doctors. The owner came to me privately and said that he'd appreciate it if I was nice to the doctors. I thought it was dumb of him to think he had to ask. What did he think? That I was gonna be rude? I thought he wanted me to walk among them while I was singing, or visit with them between shows.

They sat near the stage, so I would walk down and sing to first one and then another. It wasn't long until one pinched me right on the butt. I didn't even stop to think. I just knocked the dickens out of him. He ran to the promoter and said I wasn't doing my job, and the promoter started yelling at me.

"You're breaking your contract," he yelled. "I'm not going to pay you!"

"No man is gonna pinch me on the butt," I said. "That ain't in my contract."

And I got my money, too.

I don't think the Wilburn Brothers was ever any more protective of me than they were one night when we played a show with a world-famous gospel group. It was a quartet who performed in church houses as well as the nation's biggest concert halls. During the 1940s through the 1970s, southern gospel quartet music was featured at what were called "All Night Sings." Perhaps a dozen quartets would sing from dark until daylight, and the fans came by the thousands.

This particular group was a headline attraction at many of them all-night affairs.

I had no idea that some gospel quartets sang about their love for Jesus and Christian ways, but actually lived an entirely different lifestyle.

The leader of the gospel group told me he wanted to show me his new bus. So I got on board with him—just me and him. We walked all the way back to the stateroom, the bedroom where he slept. On the floor, I noticed cases of whiskey.

"Why have you got this?" I asked. "You gospel singers don't drink, do you?"

"Oh, I don't," he said, with a shrug. "But some of the other boys do."

He had just closed the bedroom door when all of a sudden I heard the thundering voice of Doyle Wilburn.

"Loretta!" he yelled. "Where in hell are you?"

"Oh, Doyle," I said. "We're in the bedroom. Come see this!"

"You get your damned ass off of this bus right now," Doyle said.

"Why?" I wanted to know. I was embarrassed because Doyle was being so rude. But he wouldn't shut up.

So I got off, and him and the gospel singer had words. And then Doyle explained to me that the singer was not only a big drinker, he was always hitting on the women singers. Or any other woman he could find, as a matter of fact.

The Wilburns did so much for me. Teddy helped me to learn how to put on makeup. The brothers helped me with my stage show. And they were the ones who first taught me to walk in high heels. I had never worn anything but work shoes or cowboy boots in my life.

One of the funniest things that ever happened during my stage show had to do with the first time I wore them high heels.

We were doing a show in Salt Lake City, and the emcee was a fellow named Bashful Bobby. He started walking up the stairs to the stage, and I noticed that his fly was open.

"Bobby," I whispered. "Your pants is unzipped." I didn't realize that the mike in his hand was on and that the whole audience could hear me.

"Damn it, Loretta," Doyle Wilburn said, when Bobby finally got out to the stage. "Why didn't you just walk out and announce it?"

"Well, I think I done him a favor," I shot back. "His shirt was sticking right out through his fly. What do you think folks would have thought *that* was?" We squabbled a bit like brothers and sisters, until it was my turn to go onstage. I soon learned I should have practiced a few days by myself before trying to do a show in them high heels.

Bashful Bobby introduced me: "Ladies and Gentlemen—Decca Recording Artist Miss Loretta Lynn."

The spotlight hit my face and, like Bashful Bobby had before me, I started up the stairs to the stage. Only one of my heels got caught and I couldn't free myself. I was stuck right there. I tried and tried, and Bobby announced me again.

Then from the audience you could hear this loud voice: "This is gonna be a helluva show! Bobby's pants is unzipped and he's comin' outta the fly. And Loretta's too drunk to get onstage!"

I jerked that heel free and run on out. I did two or three songs wobbling around on that ol' heel, and finally stopped the music.

"Friends," I said. "I ain't drunk. But Teddy Wilburn wanted me to wear these here high heels and I ain't never had a pair of 'em on in my life. I'd go get my boots but he's got 'em locked up in the trunk of his car."

So I kicked off the shoes and performed for all the Mormons in Salt Lake City barefooted. They seemed to like it, so I started doing it at a lot of shows!

Back when I first started out, if I wasn't touring by myself on Greyhound buses, I rode with other artists in cars as a part of package shows. I've worked many a show with four singers and a driver inside the car, pulling a trailer filled with musical instruments and an upright bass fiddle on the roof. Many times I rode in a car with my brother Jay Lee, who came along to play guitar.

We'd bounce along two-lane highways and try to sleep while sitting up. Sometimes if I worked a show with an artist who had a bus, and he was going to play in the same town where I was going to play next, he'd let me ride on his bus. I slept in a bunk, one of three stacked from the floor to the ceiling.

When I traveled with Ernest Tubb, Cal Smith always gave up his bunk for me. Cal would ride in the car with Jay Lee and help with the driving. Even though he had his own room at the back of the bus, Ernest would sleep in the bunk across from me. He was so protective of me that he would raise cain if anyone cussed around me. Cal could let fly with a word once in a while, and Ernest would say, "Shofner"—that was Cal's real last name—"Lighten up with your language around this little girl."

Doo didn't much like going on the road once I got started, but I remember this one trip in 1963 when he drove me on a short Texas tour for a man who later became one of our good friends in Nashville.

Billy Deaton later moved to Nashville and managed Faron Young, but when I first knew him, he was working out of Texas. A talent broker is a person who buys an artist from a booking agent, then sells the artist to a promoter for a profit. In this case, Billy paid the Wilburn Brothers $300 for me to sing three sets. He sold my services to a promoter for $350. He booked a five-day tour on me and made $50 a day.

It's funny that I remember those amounts, but not how much the Wilburns paid me.

This one wasn't a package show, and in 1963 females were still considered "girl singers" who couldn't headline. But Billy was a singer as well as a talent broker, so he had a regional reputation and could get me the jobs. So you see, even with three national hits, "Honky Tonk Girl," "Success," and "The Other Woman," I was to open the show for Billy. This five-day tour was one of them few early tours where Doo went with me. Billy said we arrived in an old car, but he can't remember what kind. Neither can I.

One of Billy's shows was at a dance hall in Fredericksburg, Texas. I'd never heard of Fredericksburg, but then I hadn't heard of none of the towns that Billy put me in.

People was asked to pay three dollars to see me, and all of them was working folks. Many had earned their money doing backbreaking cotton picking. Three dollars was a lot of money for them folks, and the hall wasn't close to being sold out. But it soon would be. There were enormous cracks in the walls of this dance hall. I started singing with Billy's band, and my voice leaked through the cracks in the walls and into the street. Soon, folks was peeping through the cracks, and through the windows. The sidewalk got crowded real soon with onlookers. There wasn't no more room for nobody to stand. Directly, they began to come through the door, and they paid their three dollars. The place sold out. It held about three hundred people.

Doo sold eight-by-ten glossy pictures of me for $1. I think it was just a shot of me with my face leaning on top of a guitar. Billy said him and Doo laughed after the show because me and Doo made more money off the pictures than I was paid to sing. But that didn't matter. Billy and Doo drank up all of the profit.

Today, when I look across a crowd, I sometimes think of those Texans who made me "prove myself" and looked through the cracks before they bought a ticket. Today promoters charge too much for shows. I did a show recently and later found out they was charging $90 a ticket! If I'd known that, I'd have told folks to line up and I'd give some money back. Ain't no show worth $90. But that one show where folks listened through cracks in the wall for free and finally paid their three dollars will always be a memory. It's just one of thousands that I wouldn't take a million dollars for.

And part of the memory is of Billy Deaton, who is now in such bad health that it just about breaks my heart. After Billy moved to Nashville to work with Faron, he started booking a lot of the Opry acts. And long after some of the big talent agencies wasn't talking to some of the older artists, Billy was still trying to find them work. I still love Billy to death, and I hope Nashville doesn't forget folks like him.

Twelve

The Balancing Act...

IN 1963, OWEN BRADLEY asked Ernest Tubb who he wanted to sing some duets with, and Ernest answered, "Well, I think I'd like to sing with that little girl that's come to town—Loretta Lynn." I about came unglued when Owen told me. I run all over the second floor offices of Decca Records whooping and hollering. Finally Owen said, "There's people below you! You're gonna fall right through the floor!" I said I didn't care. It was the greatest thing that had happened to me in this music business. I came to town as an outsider who was resented by some. Patsy Cline's friendship made a difference in them first two years. But when Ernest Tubb picked me to sing with him, it pulled me clean inside.

When I was a little girl, I remember laying in bed listening to "Rainbow at Midnight" on the radio. That song was so pretty it made me cry. Mommy would say, "Loretty, if the music's gonna make you cry, I'm gonna turn off the radio." So I'd turn over and put my head under the covers so she couldn't see me. That's how much of an effect Ernest Tubb had on me.

Singing with Ernest was the same as when I later recorded Patsy's songs. I wasn't sure I was up to it. I knew that no matter what I did in my whole career, I'd never measure up to that man. And the last time I ever sang with him I felt just the same as I had the first. Don't get me wrong. I'm usually a pretty confident singer and writer, so I ain't putting myself down. But standing beside Ernest was like standing next to a monument. And you know what? Ernest Tubb is a monument in this business. I hope new fans don't overlook his music, because if you are looking at all-time country greats, he's right up there.

Doo always appreciated the fact that Ernest treated me like a fine lady. And I appreciated the fact that Ernest never drank around me. Oh yes, Ernest was a drinker, just like a lot of 'em. One night on the bus, Ernest said, "Honey, I hope you never see me drunk."

"Well, Ernest, a lot of people has said you drink quite a bit," I said.

Ernest nodded. "And they tell me I'm an awful drunk. So I don't want you to see it."

Doo was never once jealous of Ernest and the time we spent together, both in Nashville and on the road. They was great friends. Not drinking buddies, just great friends. Ernest Tubb liked Doolittle Lynn, too. I guess he understood something about him.

Doo's drinking would eventually kill him, but it was Ernest's smoking that took his life. He developed emphysema, which is a disease that limits a person's ability to breathe. I could identify with that, since I'd seen so many coal miners with black lung disease when I was a kid.

But Ernest kept working even though it got harder and harder for him to breathe. Sometimes, he was so winded after a song that he let the band play an instrumental until he could catch his breath. Ernest was never really the same after the emphysema got bad. He just couldn't sing with as much power, and he was tired all of the time. But even when he was told that his condition was incurable, he kept on going.

"I'll never give up," he once said. "As long as the people will buy a ticket to come through the door to see me, I'll work."

The heartbreaker of the music business is that people forget legends like Ernest. By the eighties, when he was sick, he didn't get invited to play the big concert halls very often or to do the package shows with the big stars. Instead, he played the honky-tonks where he started out. Ernest Tubb never thought he was too good to play a honky-tonk, but I know the smoke in those places didn't help his emphysema.

Every time I saw Ernest after 1980, he looked worse. And every time, I loved him more. He was behind so many "firsts" in my life. He was the one who first introduced me on his famous *Midnight Jamboree* at the Ernest Tubb Record Shop in 1960. He was the first to introduce me on the Grand Ole Opry. And he was the first to ask to record with me, even though I'd only had three hits at the time.

Years later, I was playing Las Vegas and I asked Ernest to be on the show with me. I surprised him and had the stage remodeled to resemble the Opry stage. That really touched him, and he told somebody that I was the only person he ever saw who never changed after she became famous. *That* really touched me.

Finally, Ernest got to where he couldn't talk, much less sing. The last year he worked, he cut his personal appearance schedule a lot. They put him in a Nashville hospital and then on a respirator. He died on September 6, 1984.

I didn't go to his funeral. Mommy had died not much before that and, of course, my son Jack Benny had died that same year. That was too much death, too often. I was grieved out.

Ernest Tubb died broke and in debt. An awful lot of folks, including me, would have had it different. But the man who had helped make so many careers just wouldn't take no financial help from nobody.

Ernest asking me to sing with him in 1963 was a big surprise, but it wasn't the biggest one I got that year. The biggest was when I found out I was pregnant again.

There I was, my career on the verge of getting white-hot, duet partner to Ernest Tubb, concert offers coming in right and left, and I turn up expecting a baby. I thought I was done with all that. Betty Sue, my oldest, was already in junior high, and suddenly I was fixing to have a baby in my life again. Oops, the doctor informed me—not one baby, but two.

I worked until right before the delivery. Me and Ernest recorded our best duets when I was eight months pregnant, "Mr. and Mrs. Used to Be," "Our Hearts Are Holding Hands," "Sweet Thang." Being that far along, I was real short of breath when we recorded and I remember how hard it was to get the high harmonies. Ernest wasn't no harmony singer, so I did all the parts myself. I stayed on the road until almost the last minute, too. Then on the day they was born I canned thirty-eight quarts of green beans. Sometimes it seems like I've spent half of my life on the road, and the other half having babies and putting up beans. It's always been a balancing act.

I named the babies Patsy, after Patsy Cline, and Peggy, after my sister Peggy Sue. Nine days later I was onstage in Germany. The package show lasted six weeks, and I bawled my head off every day. I was ready to quit the music business and take care of them babies. Even though I'd been on the road for the past four years, I'd always been home when my older four children was babies. Leaving grade school–age children is hard, but climbing on a bus or airplane when you've got babies that is less than two weeks old is so much worse that I can't describe it. Until the twins was borned, we had first one babysitter and then another, watching the four older kids. Doo's parents babysat with Patsy and Peggy for the first couple of years, until I hired Gloria Land as a housekeeper/nanny. She moved in and took charge of the house, the six kids, and when she could, she got in charge of Doolittle Lynn. Gloria still lives in a house on my property, and the kids love her like a second mama.

I often wish I'd had a stable babysitting situation with the older kids, because even if they couldn't have their mama home, they should have had more stability. All of that moving around we done in the early days bothered Betty Sue, maybe more than the rest of the kids. Still, she had her some fun as a kid. She loves to remind me how loyal her daddy was to country music. Every time she'd start playing a Beatles record, Doolittle would say, "You remember that it's country music that puts food on this table, little girl."

The older girls remember back when we was living in Goodlettsville, Doo was always after 'em to get outside and play, not to mope around the house watching television. Of course, what he didn't know was that, according to them, they wasn't out there just riding horses, or playing hide-and-seek, or playing softball. A lot of the time they was sneaking cigarettes and chewing bubble gum to cover up the tobacco breath.

The worst thing them girls could do, in Doo's opinion, was color their hair and paint their faces or their nails. One time, when Betty Sue put streaks in her hair, Doo like to had a fit. She come walking in with streaked hair and sunglasses, and Doo wouldn't speak to her for three days.

When Betty Sue was a young teenager she decided she was in love and told us she was getting married. I tried every way I could to talk her out of it, but like I've said, when Betty Sue dug her heels in, she couldn't be budged. And she had one thing to hold over my head—I'd done the same thing. I told myself that everything would work out good for her, but although she ended up having two beautiful children with her first husband, the marriage didn't last. I worried myself sick over Betty Sue, and times when she needed money I'd call Gloria and try to get some slipped through to her. Doolittle wasn't much help when any of his kids was having marriage troubles. He was one of them "you made your bed, now lay in it" parents.

Jack Benny, Ernest Ray, and Cissie were enough younger that around the time Betty Sue got married, their lives was still about being kids. It wasn't until later that they started having their own troubles.

Unlike the older kids, the twins was raised in show business from the very start. Whenever I played the Opry, Doo brought them along. He'd take 'em over to Tootsie's Orchid Lounge, across the alley from the Ryman. They'd wait for me to sing and Doo to finish his beers, surrounded by Tootsie's regulars like Roger Miller, Willie Nelson, Faron Young, and Little Jimmy Dickens. Years later, they'd go back to Tootsie's Lounge to play their own shows and get a career going as The Lynns. They are good entertainers, too. In fact, as I like to tell 'em, if they'd just let me run their careers, they'd be as big as any star out there right now!

Them girls became Doo's babies. Maybe it's like when a man gets married a second time and thinks he's got a second chance at being a good father. Sometimes the first wife will grit her teeth because he seems to treat the "second family" so much better. Sometimes I gritted my teeth, and I know my older four did too. Doolittle never even came close to being as hard on them twins as he was on the older four.

In some ways, Doo spoiled them girls rotten, yet in other ways, he was thoughtful about their raising. He was determined that they wasn't going to ever think they got special treatment because their mother was a recording star. Come to think of it, he made sure they didn't. They went to public school in Waverly, Tennessee. They dressed in inexpensive clothes. They didn't get to buy every durned thing they saw.

Peggy says their lives was pretty normal until 1980, when *Coal Miner's Daughter* was being made. One of the first things that happened was when kids at school started 'a buzzing about who was staying out at our house. Carrie! Well, of course, they was referring to the Stephen King horror movie, *Carrie*, starring Sissy Spacek. My girls never even heard of that movie. After *Coal*

Miner's Daughter, life became more like a zoo out at the ranch. But I'll tell you about that later.

Meanwhile, my world could get a little zoolike on the concert trail.

One of the worst times I ever had on the road in the early days was at a 1965 package show with George Jones, Buck Owens, Roger Miller, Faron Young, and Sonny James. Jones was the headliner, and he'd been on a binge the whole tour. One day he was sitting out by the motel pool and Faron Young brought some old girl in a bikini up to him. Faron said, "George, what do you think of this gal?" Jones could barely see through the bloodshot eyes, but he said, "Faron, that's the ugliest damn woman I ever saw." Well, Faron was drunk too, so he says he's gonna whip George's butt. There was a fight and Little Jimmy Dickens got in the middle of it. Somebody stopped 'em, but you can see what kind of a tour it was. I was glad Doo came along that time. And George should have really been *thankful* for Doo.

One night Jones was drunk and couldn't go onstage. He couldn't even get dressed. I did my show, and it was Jones's turn to go on. He didn't come out, so all the artists did three sets. And two times I said, "George is getting dressed." Finally I walked offstage and found Jones drunk in his dressing room wearing nothing but his underwear. Doo was trying to sober him up and get his pants on him. You ever tried to get pants on a drunken man? It served Doo right.

"It's no use," Doo said. "Jones can't even walk, much less stand up, much less sing. You go back out, Loretta, and do a third set." (I wouldn't be telling this story on Jones if he hadn't told it on himself.) I went out to do a third set. I'd sung all of the hits I'd had in my four years on Decca, and had to start doing cover tunes. It didn't work. The people began to boo louder than I could sing.

"We want George Jones! We want George Jones!" they chanted. Then they got even madder, and it was a real mad mob at its worst. Somebody hollered for the drunk "son of a bitch" to come onstage or they was a-gonna come backstage and get him.

"That's right!" hollered somebody else. "And I don't care how big a star he is. I paid good money and drove a far piece to get here. I'll kill the bastard."

I don't know if the guy would have killed George Jones, but he yelled at me that he would. He scared me to death. And when he did, thousands of people applauded and rose from their seats. I was afraid they was going to storm the backstage. Why, if that mob had got hold of poor old drunk Jones, one of them might have killed him, and nobody would have knowed who done it. The fans was about half drunk themselves 'cause the place we was playing served booze.

I went backstage where Doo was in Jones's dressing room trying to sober him up enough to go on.

"Doo," I said. "Somebody hollered that they knew it wasn't taking Jones this long to get dressed. Then somebody else said for him to come onstage right now or they was gonna come back here and kill him."

Doo told me to run back to the stage and sing a couple more songs before the fans stampeded Jones's dressing room. Some of them had already got to the backstage area. Doo knew he couldn't take Jones out of his dressing room and through any crowd. So he broke the window and shoved Jones out, still in his underwear. Then Doo climbed through the window, picked up Jones, and headed for our car.

I waited as long as I could and finally announced that Jones was gonna be a no-show.

The fans crashed through Jones's dressing room door about the same time Doo and Jones peeled out of the parking lot. They broke the guitar and tore the room to pieces. Nobody bothered me because they knew I didn't have nothin' to do with Jones's carryin' on. But they smashed my guitar. Doo dumped Jones at our motel room just in case anyone knew what George's room number was. Then he came back to the venue for me.

I believe that Doolittle Lynn saved George Jones's life that night, and I'll believe it till the day I die. When a mess like the one with Jones happened, there wasn't nobody in this world I'd rather have there to fix things than Doo. Not the Wilburns, not even Ernest Tubb. Doo had a way of figgerin' out things and taking care of 'em. He could read a situation and take action in a second. But the times he wanted to go on the road with me got less and less. Apart from the fact that Doo was bored on the road, he got real sick of people making comments about his being married to a meal ticket. And no matter how many times I came back and said there wouldn't have been no Loretta meal ticket without Doo, it ate away at him.

By the 1960s and early seventies, I had a string of hit songs and a pile of awards. In 1967, I won Country Music Association's Female Vocalist of the Year for the first of three times, and in 1972, I became the first woman to win the CMA Entertainer of the Year. Things was going so good that promoters starting advertising me as America's most popular female country singer.

I was making more money than Doo and me ever dreamed about. And Doo had figured out so many ways to spend it that it was a nightmare. Back then, I never spent a dime I didn't have to. I didn't even know how to use a credit card until the late 1970s when Conway Twitty taught me. Not that I needed to use one anyway. I signed for food and rooms on the road, and I didn't have time to run around and shop in any of them towns I played. Doo was the one who had his hand in the money pile, not me.

I know he felt it was a man's job to bring in the biggest part of a family's income, but the sad fact is, an entertainer—if they work hard—can pull in more money than you can imagine. Certainly more than Doo could make as a farmer. In fact, I've always said that this is one thing that bothers me. Teachers, nurses, coal miners—where is their fair share? But until we can figure out a way to even things out, successful entertainers can count on a very good income. The problem turns out to be, in so many cases, how to hang on to it.

When we lived in Madison, just as my career was getting started, Doo took mechanic jobs to help pay our expenses. But between the time we moved to the 45-acre place in Goodlettsville, Tennessee, and the time we bought Hurricane Mills, Doo run through a pile of so-called business opportunities. I played a part in this too, because I understood how he felt about being a wage earner and didn't try to stop him. I never wanted to make him feel less a man, not once. And I don't think I ever did. But that didn't help when the bills was due.

Part of my never questioning him had to do with my guilt over his drinking. Just like when he run off to other women and I figgered it was my fault, I blamed myself for the drinking. I thought he drank so much because of either loneliness or feeling like he wasn't pulling his share of the load. I still had a long way to go before I'd come to grips with alcoholism. So I never tried to slow down Doo's spending.

The first one that sucked our bank account dry was his rodeo. He had the idea that combining country music and rodeo was a potential gold mine. It may be for some big corporation, but it wasn't for us. He built an arena in Goodlettsville, bought bucking broncs, bulls, steers, calves for roping contests, and two Mack trucks.

It was during this time that Jack Benny and Ernest

Ray really started loving horses, especially Jack. He loved to rodeo, and did it most of his life. Actually, Jack started out trying to be a jockey, and did race in Tennessee. But he got too big, and moved on to rodeo riding. He rode broncs, bulls, you name it. It like to scared me to death every time he got in the ring. Maybe I had a forewarning about Jack and horses, because in the end, my fears about Jack and horses was right. But back when Doo was running rodeos, it was all just great fun for Jack.

It wasn't so much fun for me. I kept on playing the rodeo shows for Doolittle, trying to make the same money I'd be making through another promoter. The Loretta Lynn Longhorn Rodeo ended up not only keeping us strapped for cash, but interfering in my ability to put on the kind of road show I needed. Doo was forking over rodeo prize money right and left, and I couldn't even afford my own band! And Doo didn't see that I needed one.

I used so many house bands and pickup bands that I didn't know if my bands was coming or going. And most of the time they didn't either.

Then, in 1969, I was playing a show at Sunset Park in Pennsylvania, and the pickup band was awful. The steel player was in one key, the bass player in another, and the lead guitarist—well, I don't even know what he thought he was doing. I was more than embarrassed; I was mad as an old wet hen. Thank goodness I'd learned to play rhythm guitar good enough to accompany myself. When I finished that show I told the audience that the next time I appeared on that stage, they could count on me having my own band. I didn't say nothing bad about the band onstage with me. I didn't have to; they knew they'd messed up the show. All the way back to Nashville, I thought about what to tell Doo, how to convince him I had to have a band. Ain't that something? I was the one having to do the convincing. I finally come up with a plan.

Doo used to like to ride in them rodeos, and he rode the best horses he could buy. He usually rode in the Grand Entry, which is not a competitive event, just a parade of riders carrying flags. Meanwhile, the woman billed as America's most popular female country singer was working with terrible house bands at venues in the United States and overseas. It was embarrassing to be singing the nation's number one song with a band that didn't even know the melody.

So I come home and asked Doo a question.

"When you enter the rodeo arena, don't you like to ride the finest horse you can?" I asked.

"I do, and I will," he said.

"Well, when I get onstage I liked to be backed by the best band I can find. The next time I go on tour, I'm taking my own band."

"The hell you are," he said. "We can't afford no damn band."

"No," I said, "*we* can't, but *I* can, and I'm going to have one."

"You just want everything to go your way, Loretta," he said. "Is that the way this is gonna be?"

I toughened up and said, "Yes, Doo. This is my career. And that's the way it is gonna be."

Well, Doo cussed and stomped around. It was odd, because his judgment was usually pretty good when it come to my career. But he just didn't see no reason I needed to be paying a band.

That was one of the few times I stood up to Doo without no compromise. And I got my band.

They was a band that I had once worked with in Ohio at an outdoor show. That band knew each of my songs perfectly. They were the best band, except for studio musicians, that I'd ever worked with. I eventually hired the whole bunch. We named our group "Loretta Lynn and the Coal Miners." We stayed together for twenty-seven years.

Doo finally closed down the rodeo, but he jumped right into an even bigger mess. Like the rodeo, his hunting lodge seemed like it might be a good idea. But it wasn't.

The Chilcotin region of British Columbia, Canada—called Cariboo Country—is a beautiful place, and today there's all kinds of lodges, resorts, and vacation spots up there. Doo saw the potential back in the late sixties, and decided what he needed to do was build a lodge where men could get away from city life, head for the wilderness, and hunt and fish to their hearts' delight. Him and a Canadian partner got busy and put everything we had into a huge hunting lodge with cabins surrounding it. They added a big log building strictly for hanging out meat to cure. Doo took a boat up to Chilcotin Lake and truly he thought he was gonna run an empire.

He had a direct mailing and advertising plan. He had projections. Doo wasn't a bad businessman. So smart about many things that I never made a move in my career that I didn't ask his advice. And it was usually right on target. He really did see the big picture on both the rodeo and the lodge. Maybe it was just the details that fell through.

When I finally got off the road long enough to make the trip, my heart sank. Cariboo Country is already isolated, but it seemed to me that the place they built was harder to get to than almost any other place they could have picked. Not to mention that the water on the lake was so choppy I didn't know who'd want to get out there. Of course, I'm scared of water so I might have been a little prejudiced on that one thing. Well, hardly anybody came. That broke my heart for Doolittle because I knew how much these businesses meant to him. Still, whenever they went belly-up, he didn't seem to mind. He just moved on to something else.

The scariest time was after Conway Twitty and I started United Talent, an agency formed to book shows for ourselves and other artists. Doo started going down to the office after hours. He'd invite a bunch of boys over and they'd drink all night. Well, before that night was over, Doolittle Lynn had written a check on the

business. I don't mean that the biggest problem was that
he was going over to the liquor store and cashing a five-
dollar check for whiskey, although he'd do that, too. He
was writing checks to people sitting there with him.
Some fellow would have a hard luck story, and Doo
would whip out the checkbook. We never kept 'em
locked up when we got started. The worst that ever happened was one night when he wrote a $10,000 check to
a skid row bum. The money he spent was subtracted
from my share of the agency's profits.

I didn't know what I was going to do. One afternoon
when I come in off the road, I finally went to our ac-
countant.

"What am I gonna do?" I asked. "This is Doo's
money, too. We don't keep our money separate. If I shut
down his checks, he'll throw a fit."

The CPA, Joe Kraft, said he'd think it over and come
up with an answer. He phoned me that night.

"Loretta Lynn Enterprises isn't protected and it could
be broke into at any time," he said. "You've got to lock
up the checkbooks immediately."

So that's what we done. The CPA told Doo that because of some other break-ins, that's what had to happen. Doo didn't squabble a bit over it. He never had no
idea it was all because of him.

As I saw my tour money going down a never-ending rat
hole, I decided I needed to get a different plan, too. I
started buying up land. I'd sneak some cash out of my

earnings before Doo could get his hands on it, and when I saved up enough, I'd buy property. Lorene Allen, who worked in the office, helped cover my tracks. But I knew he'd kill me if I kept it from him completely, so I got a plan about that, too. I started giving Doo property for everything you can imagine: Christmases, our anniversaries, his birthday—you name it, I handed him a deed.

Doo wasn't real sure he liked me doing that. He'd say, "Well, where did you get the money for that?"

"I made payments like everybody else," I'd say.

"How much do you owe on it?"

"Nothing."

He'd look at me funny and shrug his shoulders. "I don't know if that's a good idea."

"It's just like money in the bank, Doo," I'd say. "If we need money, you'll have this land to sell."

Then I stayed right out on the road earning, so he didn't have no excuse to sell. That went on for the last ten years of Doo's life. Even after we moved to Hurricane Mills and he decided to give up rodeos and hunting lodges and other schemes to become a farmer, I kept right on putting money into land. I guess that's the "poor folks" in me. Poor folks know that when you own property, you've got something. Hit records can come and go, but the land stays put.

Thirteen

Holes in My Heart—
Friends of My Heart . . .

COAL MINER'S DAUGHTER, the movie, has a big hole in it. The Wilburn Brothers ain't mentioned. I hated that because I know some might have thought it was because I was mad over the lawsuit they eventually brought against me. I didn't want people thinking I was petty enough to write them out on account of that. They were supposed to be in the film, but there was a dispute between the Wilburns and the producers over how much footage should be devoted to them. The producer finally said "to hell with them," and their part was deleted.

We were going to use the Wilburns' tour bus in some early scenes, but when they left, the movie people painted Patsy Cline's name on the side of a bus and we used that. The fact is, Patsy didn't own a tour bus. So that left two factual errors regarding Patsy—the beer in the hospital and the tour bus.

The Wilburn Brothers played an important part in my early career. I grew to love Teddy and Doyle as if they were brothers. But things began to slowly go bad.

They stopped touring. I was needing to work, and they didn't need no work. Teddy moved to California and Doyle didn't want to work on his own. When they stopped working as a duo, Doyle often wanted to go with me to my shows, which I was now having to work by myself or with other artists. Then, Doyle's drinking got a lot worse and some of the boys couldn't get along with him. I didn't even pay attention to Doyle's drinking. I lived with one that drank, so it wasn't nothing new. But I finally told the Wilburns that even though I loved them, I wanted out of my management contract.

They said no. I left anyhow, and they sued me for $5 million. That lawsuit was in trial for eleven years. Lawyers kept postponing it. 'Course, they was paid a fee each time they went to court to move for a continuance. Lordy, I told 'em I'd outlive the thing! I had to testify against the Wilburns, and it broke my heart. I told friends I didn't think I could do it, and they advised me to see a doctor. He took my pulse and blood pressure, then gave me a nerve pill. It was the first one I ever had. The doctor told me to take the pill thirty minutes before I was scheduled to testify at the Davidson County, Tennessee, courthouse.

I'll never forget sitting on that witness stand with tears streaming down my face, looking at the faces of the men I loved so much. But because they had helped to make my career didn't give them the right to ruin it.

In the end I won, and was given my freedom from the Wilburns. I had to get on with my career.

I wrote many a hit while I was with them. The 1960s was a time I wrote more than ever before or after. I did it out of loneliness and love and there ain't no better songwriting inspiration. There wasn't nothing else to do after a show. If Doo wasn't with me, I missed him. If he was, all he done was get drunk at the show and pass out on the bus or in the motel room. On the bus, I'd write to the whir of the wheels. In a motel I'd write with the "background music" of people partying and raising cain out in the halls. Loneliness turned into a pile of hit songs, and the Wilburns retain the publishing rights to this day. "Fist City," "I Want to Be Free," "To Make a Man," "You Ain't Woman Enough," "You're Looking at Country"—they are all BMI award winners for radio airplay and all in Sure-Fire Music. Shoot, even "Honky Tonk Girl" is in Sure-Fire.

Here's another gripe I got against alcohol, or at least what it can do to people. Doyle Wilburn died in 1982. Officially, I believe the cause of death was diabetes, just like Doo's would later be called. But, like with Doo, I think the real cause might have been alcoholism. Neither one of them would probably have had the diabetes if not for the amount they drank. At least it wouldn't have got

Loretta's mommy and daddy.

Mooney Lynn.

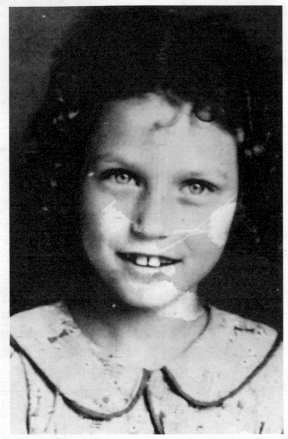

Loretta as a child.

Loretta with kids in Washington state.

Loretta's first recording session.

Loretta with brother Jay Lee and Smiley O'Steele.

Loretta on an early live show.

Loretta on an early Grand Ole Opry appearance.

Loretta and Conway Twitty.

Loretta with her mommy at the premiere for *Coal Miner's Daughter*.

Loretta and Mooney.

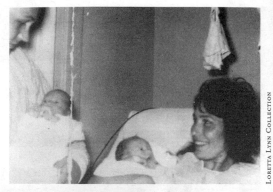

Loretta, Doo, and the twins at the hospital where they were born.

Loretta on *The Tonight Show*; John Davidson filling in.

Loretta at the Hollywood Walk of Fame.

Loretta with Tammy Wynette.

Loretta on the Ralph Emery show with her family.

Loretta at a family reunion, mid-80s.

Loretta in *Coal Miner's Daughter* dress.

Loretta and Doo on a tractor.

Loretta on the Opry.

Ernest Ray and
Jack Benny in their
military uniforms.

the twins.

Loretta with
Crystal Gayle
and the
Boston Pops.

Loretta with her family.

so bad. Near the end, Doyle was too drunk and later, too sick, to say much. I talked to him one night and thanked him for all him and Teddy had done for me. I told him I was heading out to a show and would come to the hospital the day I got back. Before I hung up, I told him I loved him. By the time I got back to Nashville, Doyle was dead.

I got to thinking about friends who fight. Me and the Wilburns fought like kinfolk, but we would never tolerate anyone else saying a bad word about the other. In fact, there ain't much we haven't said to each other's faces, in offices, studios, on buses, and in court. But I never said an evil-spirited word about either one of 'em behind their backs.

Like there was a "Wilburn" hole in my movie, there is also a "Johnson" hole in this book. In *Coal Miner's Daughter*, I wrote a chapter about my friends the Johnson Sisters: Loudilla, Loretta, and Kay. Them girls was my first official fans, the ones who started my fan club and stuck with me for years. Shoot, we started the whole week's long event called Fan Fair together, even though none of us got the credit for it. A few years back, the girls and me disagreed on a big issue. They got rid of the Loretta Lynn Fan Club reps we had in each state. I didn't think it should have been done, because in my mind, you can't run a fan club without representatives in every state. The rift grew and changed and turned out to be so big that I shut down the fan club, and we parted company. Trouble that size usually only happens in families, and in many ways, the girls and me was a family. I ain't seen or spoke to them in a long, long time. I'd hoped that they'd come to Doolittle's funeral, but they didn't. I looked for 'em that day. Doo had moved heaven and hell to go to their daddy's funeral. I don't hold it against them, though. They might have thought they wasn't welcome.

Loretta Johnson has been sick the past couple of years, and folks will bring stories about her health to me. I worried and worried about her, but never had the courage to pick up the telephone until while I was working on this book. When I finally phoned, they didn't want to talk. So I will just say this: Girls, I still love you no matter what all was said and done. I pray for you, Loretta. I pray mighty hard, and I know if I was sick, you would do the same for me.

Losing the Johnsons leaves not only a hole in this book, but one in my heart.

It's hard enough to find tried and true friends in any walk of life, but in the entertainment business, it's double hard. People ain't around all the time, and some entertainers get paranoid about somebody they think is taking up a top spot they ought to have. Jealousy is truly a troublemaking little devil, and for that reason I love the singers who don't even know the meaning of the word.

Every so often, an interviewer will ask me what female singers I considered my competition in the music business. I have to honestly say, nobody. It's not that I think I'm better than anybody else or they are better than me; I'm just different. That's what sets an artist apart. Owen Bradley knew it when he made me wait until I had songs that defined me and set me apart from Kitty Wells. If you turn on a radio and ain't got a clue as to who is singing because they sound like every other voice on the radio, in my opinion, that singer is in trouble. And that is the story of today. Not that I don't believe in competition. It makes you work harder, and that never hurt nobody. Still, since nobody was doing exactly what I was, I didn't think much about it. But if I was asked who made me sit up and take notice the first time I heard 'em, I'd start with a voice I heard on a car radio in 1967.

I was driving to a show with my brother, Jay Lee, when a song and a singer come on the air that took my breath away. I reached out and turned up the radio. The song was "Apartment Number Nine" and the deejay said the singer was an Alabama girl named Tammy Wynette.

"Dag gone!" I said to Jay Lee. "Did you hear that?" He was shaking his head, 'cause he'd heard the same piece of magic as me.

If I was the kind of singer who worried about competition, Tammy would have scared me half to death.

When I got back to town and learned more about Tammy, I knew I was gonna love her. She come to town with three little girls and not a penny to her name. I like people who will chase a dream, no matter how tough it is. I especially like women who aren't afraid to get out on their own. Tammy didn't know nobody in this town when she packed up her car and drove to Nashville. She traipsed around looking for somebody to help her until she run into Billy Sherrill. She couldn't have found nobody better. Along with Owen Bradley and Chet Atkins, Billy was not just a powerful man, he was a good man. And he could spot a star in Tammy.

One thing I did as fast as I could. I welcomed Tammy Wynette to town just like Patsy Cline had welcomed me. And like Patsy, Tammy became my best friend. Best friends are like husbands, you only need one at a time. Tammy wasn't outspoken like Patsy, but you could never count her out if words was flying. I remember one time around 1980, Tammy was on some show with several other women artists. While they was backstage, this one girl who'd had a couple of hits said, "I think you older women ought to move over and give us younger ones a chance." Tammy didn't miss a trick. She just smiled sweetly and said, "Move me."

That tickled the tar out of me.

I don't think Tammy ever got over her fear of being poor. Most poor folks don't. I never did; Patsy Cline never did. But here's the difference. I ain't scared of being poor. The day they tell me I ain't got a cent, I'll just put up some green beans and drag out one of Doo's old rifles to shoot my dinner. I ain't gonna go hungry.

Tammy worried about it. She kept her beauty operator's license up to date because she was afraid the bottom would drop out of her singing career. Then on the other hand, she'd spend more money than she had, because, like a lot of people raised up poor, she loved nice things. As a matter of fact, she loved 'em too much, and sometimes that put her in money trouble.

I'm not that way. All I ever cared about was having a comfortable home, a soft bed, and enough to eat. Cars don't mean nothing to me, and neither does fancy houses. But to Tammy, that meant she was making it, and I don't fault her for it.

Tammy's health was a problem for years. Her body would form scar tissue every time she had an operation, and she'd have to have it removed. Then she'd get more scar tissue from that operation. It just went on and on, and she was in pain all the time. I honestly don't know how she stood it, especially working as much as she did.

Tammy and I used to get together and stay up talking like teenage girls. Once in the mid-eighties, Tammy was hospitalized in Atlanta. I was playing a show in Macon, Georgia. I was about to go to bed that night when there's this knock on the hotel room door. I thought, "What the fire? Who could that be?" I opened the door a little and there stood Tammy Wynette in a housecoat and slippers.

"What are you doing?" I asked. "You are supposed to be in the hospital!"

"Well I'm not there," she said with a big grin. "But I'll sneak back in before they know I'm gone."

She'd had somebody fly her from Atlanta to Macon, drive her to my room, and they was coming back to pick her up the next morning! You can't tell me that at least one of them nurses didn't know she'd snuck outta there. We stayed up the whole night and told all the George Jones stories we knew. Then her pilot knocked on the door and they made their run back to Atlanta. That night, when it come time for me to sing, I had almost lost my voice. So I apologized and said, "Folks, I spent the whole night sitting up with Tammy Wynette gossiping about George Jones. Now I know she is supposed to be in the hospital, but believe it, for at least a few hours she was in my hotel room right here in Macon."

Tammy was always pulling little jokes. Most people who didn't know her well found that odd, because she never came across as a funny person, but more of a serious one. She could be funny, though; believe that, too.

Tammy and me used to laugh about the fact that we had these images we never lived up—or down—to. Tammy was right in the middle of dumping a husband when she recorded "Stand By Your Man." Then for the rest of her life people used her as the poster child for long-suffering wives. Shoot, Tammy would drop 'em right and left if they wasn't treating her right. I've heard Tammy say, "Oh, yeah. I stood by 'em all right." Then I was out there singing my songs, which made me sound like the one who'd whup up on a man in a minute. And

I was the one staying married and standing by Doo through God knows what.

One of the funniest sights I ever saw was in the mid-eighties when Tammy and George Richey come to Hawaii to visit Doo and me at the place we'd bought over there. We got to the airport to pick 'em up and there they stood holding full-length mink coats. It was hot as it could be, and there they stand in mink and sunglasses. I had to laugh because they sure looked like a couple of country stars right then. All I could think of was Cal Smith singing "Hello, country bumpkin."

They stayed for two weeks, and while Doo and Richey were out fishing or roaming around, Tammy and me did nothing but lay around the house and girl talk. We didn't move unless we wanted something to eat. I'd haul myself up off the couch and head to the kitchen. Tammy would ask me if I'd bring her a sandwich. Baloney one time. Peanut butter the next. Next time, she'd be the one that would get up and head to the icebox to make something for us. We had a ball doing absolutely nothing.

The only time we ever even come close to having words was at the 1977 Academy of Country Music Awards in Los Angeles. Tammy came to my dressing room and asked me if she could dress in there with me. I said she sure could. Just as she was walking out to rehearse her song, she asked me to keep a watch out for Dinah Shore and let her know if she come backstage. So I did, and about the time Tammy was finished, I noticed

Dinah standing in one of the halls talking to somebody. I went over and told Tammy, and she rushed out so fast she forgot her hat. I still have it somewhere.

I didn't see Tammy again until several days after the show, and I asked her if she'd got to talk with Dinah. "Oh, no," Tammy said. "I was ducking her." Well, Tammy was going out with Burt Reynolds and he was gonna meet up with her there. They didn't want to run into Dinah. That came close to making me mad.

"Tammy," I said. "Why'd you drag me into that? Dinah is a friend of mine! If I'd known you two were trying to pull something on her I'd have whupped you both!"

She just laughed. Later Tammy told some folks that she couldn't have married Burt 'cause they'd fight over the mirrors too much.

Tammy worked too hard. Her health was too bad for her to be playing the dates she did during the last few years of her life. She was gone way before she should have been. And for me, the saddest part of it is that I truly do not believe she ever found real love. I think she was searching for it right up to the end. And that includes both George Jones and George Richey. Neither one of 'em was the right man for Tammy. And even though she never said so, in so many words, I think she knew it.

After Tammy died in 1998, I was surprised to hear George Richey was gonna sell that beautiful house they owned on Franklin Road in Nashville. Tammy loved that house. It was one of the things that was always a reminder that she wasn't still picking cotton. I own two houses in Nashville, over in an area called Elliston Place. They are big, but they ain't fancy—nothing you are gonna see on *Lifestyles of the Rich and Famous*. One of 'em is rented out as office space. And after Doo died, I didn't like staying out at Hurricane Mills as much, so I thought maybe I'd put in a bid on Tammy's house. It would be a little like keeping it in the family. I was told the asking price was $7 million. Since I didn't want to mortgage the farm to buy it, I backed off. Later I heard it had stayed on the market for quite a while and George finally sold it for a whole lot less. If he'd called me back, I'd be over there moving my stuff into one room and building a shrine to Tammy in the next.

Another voice I heard that caused me chills was a great big one coming from a little girl. That little girl was Tanya Tucker belting out "Delta Dawn." You ain't ever gonna mistake Tanya for nobody else on the radio, or in person. Now, Tanya is a lot like Patsy Cline when it comes to her saying what she means. Folks, you don't ever have to wonder what Tanya is thinkin' 'cause Tanya is gonna tell you. I love that girl. Tammy loved her, too, and for the same reason I do. She don't try to be anything she ain't. She's always just herself. Tanya is one of them people who, if she is your friend, she is really your friend. You don't have all that many friends in show business. Not real friends. You got people who want to run around with you or get something from you.

But the true-blue friends is hard to come by. Tanya is one that will do anything for you. If you're sick, she'll fill in for you in a minute. If you don't need filling in for, she might bring you some potato soup to cheer you up.

We started out being friends, with me acting like a mother hen over her at awards shows. I still remember the 1973 Country Music Awards show, when we was both up for Female Vocalist. Tanya was only fourteen years old, same as me when I was a newlywed. That was an exciting year for me. I won Female Vocalist, and Conway and me won Duo of the Year. Tanya said later she would have felt funny winning against the adults, but I, for one, wouldn't have felt bad losing to her. "Delta Dawn" was quite a record. Tanya looked so cute that night, and I fussed over her the whole time, fixing her hair, making sure her slip straps didn't show. It tickled me to death to see her there so excited to meet all the stars. She said the first song she ever done onstage with Ernest Tubb was one him and me had out on the charts, "Sweet Thang."

I still try to mother Tanya. Just this year, she come out to help me open my new museum at Hurricane Mills. We done a big show and Tanya was on the stage with me, dancing around in a flippy little skirt. I could see she was just itchin' to flip it up a little too high. So I eased over and whispered, "Do it and die, Tanya." She laughed her little butt off. But she didn't flip that skirt.

✦ ✦ ✦ ✦ ✦

I can't leave this section without mentioning my sister, Crystal Gayle. I was always hoping to help my family get started in the record business, because so many of 'em had so much talent. Jay Lee was playing guitar and fiddle out on the road at the same time I was on the road singing. My sister Peggy Sue was a wonderful singer and songwriter. Both of them made some good records, too. Jay Lee charted three songs on Decca between 1967 and 1971. But the one who had the biggest success was Crystal, also known as Brenda Gail Webb. Her music was different from mine, because her background was different. Crystal grew up in Wabash, Indiana, not Butcher Holler. We don't sing anything alike and we don't talk anything alike. I helped Crystal get on Decca, and wrote her first hit song, in the 1970s, "I've Cried (The Blues Right Out of My Eyes)." She moved over to United Artists a few years later and started having more hits, like "Wrong Road Again," "Somebody Loves You," and her first number one, in 1976, "I'll Get Over You." Crystal had hits all through the 1970s and 1980s on several labels.

Here is one of the sorriest things about the music business: time is too often the enemy. Crystal's music was always pop or torch. Now that she's no longer on a major label, most of the women working are singing pop music, and Crystal ain't on the charts. She sings that music better than anybody out there right now, and nobody is playing her.

One idea I have is for me, Peggy Sue, and Crystal to record an album together. We'll see what happens, though. Crystal wants to cut a bunch of pop songs, and I want to stay country. Finally I went out and bought $600 worth of CDs with the kind of songs I thought we could do real good together. I said, "All right, Crystal, you and Peggy pick out fifteen songs you want to record and we'll be in the studio before you can say 'fried baloney gravy'."

Fourteen

Hello, Darlin' . . .

THE SAME YEAR THAT TAMMY came into my life, I met the person who would become my best male friend of all time; my duet partner, business partner, father confessor, and soul mate. And I could have said all that in front of Doolittle Lynn without him pitching a fit, because he loved Conway Twitty as much as I did. Conway loved Doo, too. It still seems strange that them two hit it off so big. Doo usually liked to hang out with the drinkers, and believe me, he could find plenty of 'em in Nashville during the seventies. Conway didn't touch a drop. But both of 'em had a sense of humor, was hard workers, and was honest in their business dealings. Even with their honesty, or maybe because of it, both of 'em had seen plenty of their businesses go belly-up. And maybe that was something they understood about each other, too.

It was Owen Bradley that introduced me to Conway, but it was Doo and Conway that bonded and got us started recording together. It all started in 1965 when Owen signed Conway to Decca. Owen knew that Conway was one of my heroes because I'd told him about that poster I had in my bedroom back when I was a fifteen-year-old housewife. So one day I stopped by the studio and Owen said, "How would you like to meet Conway Twitty?" You could have knocked me over with a chicken feather.

"Well, turn around," Owen said. And right there in the room was the man in that poster. I barely knew what to say except that I bet I was the world's biggest Conway Twitty fan. We got along real well, but that wasn't when we started talking about recording together. That came on a trip to the 1967 Wembley Festival in England. Doo and me was fussing at each other, like always. There was an empty seat between us, and Conway come up and sat down in it, probably to keep us from working up to a full-fledged feud.

I never seen anything like it. Doolittle was on a roll that whole trip. He was telling Conway jokes and stories and outright lies, and Conway was loving every minute of it. I can still hear him laughing and so could everyone else on the plane. They hung together through the whole trip, and on the flight back, Doo told Conway more tall tales. By the time we got to Nashville, it was a done deal. Conway and me was gonna make a record together.

There was only two problems: Ernest Tubb and Owen Bradley. I wasn't sure if me singing with Conway would make Ernest feel like he'd been traded in on a new model, and if that had happened I couldn't have stood it. I shouldn't have worried, though. Ernest had been in this business a long time, so a duet partner singing with someone else wasn't any big deal to him. Besides, doing duets with Conway didn't mean I couldn't still travel with Ernest from time to time and sing our songs. He gave me his blessing.

Owen Bradley was another story. He told Conway he was dead set against it. Owen had seen what happened with Dolly Parton and Porter Wagoner when they was recording as a duet for RCA. They started squabbling and it durn near rocked Music Row. Owen didn't want no mess like that at Decca. We finally convinced him we wasn't gonna squabble our way across the tabloids, and he agreed. Now Conway hadn't had a country hit when we first started thinking about duets, and some people in Nashville thought it was strange I'd want to sing with a rock and roll singer. That never entered my mind. A great singer is a great singer.

It didn't matter anyway, because by 1971, when our first song together was released, Conway had proved he didn't have to take a country backseat to nobody. In just 1968 and 1970, Conway had five number one songs, and had spent ten weeks at the top of the charts. Our debut, "After the Fire Is Gone," sat on top for two more weeks. Everybody was tickled, and nobody more than Doolittle Lynn. And we won our first Grammy for it, too.

My friendship with Conway was so loving, so great. He became like a brother to me. I would go to him with my problems, including the ones that involved Doo. Since he was friends with both of us, he never took sides. He'd just let me talk, try to put things together, and give me whatever advice he could. He never once said, "Leave that dog." What he would say was usually something like this: "Well now, Loretta, you know how Mooney is. You've lived with him all these years and you two have a long history. I know you love each other. So just hang in there and be tough. Things will get better. I promise."

Conway was right. Doo and me had a history. For better or worse, it was our history. And a long time ago we'd promised to hang in there for better or worse.

After I got free of my deal with the Wilburns, Conway and I started the booking agency I mentioned earlier, United Talent. And Conway and me were united; we were a team. That's how we felt, anyway. That partnership lasted for twenty years, and wouldn't have ended except for Conway's death. But before we started it we sat down and had a long talk about a woman and a man partnering up. We promised we'd never, ever let ourselves get romantically involved, even if we was inclined, which we wasn't. We promised to treat each other with respect. We started out equals. Conway wasn't making me a star, and I wasn't making him one.

Conway run interference between me and Doo any time he could. He'd talk to me or Doo and try to find some solution. Sometimes, though, he just had to laugh. There was this one time when we was all staying at the same hotel, and we all arrived back from the show at the same time. Me and Doo got into a fight in the parking lot, with Conway right beside us, getting his things out of his car. Doo was sitting in our car, and I was standing by his open window, when he up and called me a bitch. I reached my arm in the window and started beating him on the head with my purse. Well, Conway just run as fast as he could, heading for the hotel. I stomped off, leaving Doolittle there yelling. I got into this one elevator with a bunch of other folks, stood right in the front, muttering to myself about how I'd probably get a whupping when Doo got back to the room. All of a sudden I heard all this noise in the back of the elevator. I turned around and there was Conway, laughing so hard tears was falling down his cheeks. Who knows what them folks in the elevator thought.

I got back to the room, and within a few minutes the phone was ringing. It was Conway. "Now, Loretta," he said. "Don't you and Doo keep on fighting!"

"Why not?" I asked. "We fight all the time."

"So there's nothing I can do?"

"Nope," I said. "Just stay out of it."

That time he did stay out of it, and Doo didn't whup me, anyway.

The next morning Conway asked me what happened.

"Not one thing," I said. "Doo just come on up and went to bed."

Conway just smiled and shook his head.

Me and Conway never once come close to any affair, even though half of Nashville thought we did at one time or another. A lot of fans thought so, too, because it was hard for them to hear them songs and not think something was going on. I thought it was funny, and one time even embarrassed the tar out of Conway.

We was signing autographs after a big outdoor show in the early eighties when some man walks up and says, "Ain't you and Conway married?" Before Conway could jump in and say "no" I says, "We're just living together." Well, he turned red as a beet, threw his pen in the air, and walked off. I laughed till I thought I'd pee my pants. He wasn't mad, though. Just embarrassed.

In fact, the only time Conway Twitty ever got upset enough to jump all over me was because of my looks. Here's how that come about. In 1985, I decided my eyes was beginning to droop. Well, everybody I knew was having something done to their faces, so I decided to have some plastic surgery while I was at the home Doo and me had bought in Hawaii. I talked to the doctor and told him I wanted the tops of my eyes brought up and the wrinkles smoothed out some. I didn't want no complete face lift, just enough to drop a couple of years off me. I got to look good in public after all, and I wasn't no twenty-year-old chick. We set it up to get it done in his office, and he said it would be so simple that I could just be an out-patient. I wouldn't even have to be put to sleep; just take something to kill the pain. I warned him that I get blood poisoning awful easy, and he brushed that right off.

I laid back on that table and he started cutting on the top of my eyes. I'll tell you what I *could* feel; I could feel blood rolling down the sides of my face. It dang near did me in.

"Oh Lord!" I said. "This is killing me! I can't do this!"

This doctor just smiled and said, "Oh you aren't feeling any pain, just think about the water coming in off the waves."

Shoot. All I could think about was the blood coming down the sides of my face. I thought, "You son of a gun, you think of the danged ocean!"

He finished up, sewed my eyes back together, and sent me home. But it was obvious to me and anybody who saw me that something was wrong. There was a big red splotch coming on my nose that wasn't no bruise. I went back to the office in a panic, and he acted like it wasn't no big deal. He shot me up with some drugs and said he'd take a closer look. All of a sudden he's scraping the skin back off my nose. All told, I went back four times, and the last time I had it out with him. Not only had I gone through hell with this "listen to the ocean" outpatient stuff, my eyes was all screwed up. They was pulled up and slanted till I looked like one of them geisha girls.

"Oh, sure," he says. "That's the Oriental look. Everyone likes that these days."

I said, "You so-and-so, if I was meant to be Oriental, I'd 'a been borned in Japan! I just wanted some of them droops lifted."

Well, talking to that man didn't do no good. So I healed up and come back to the states for a concert tour with Conway.

The minute Conway saw me, he stopped short.

"What in the world have you done to yourself?" He looked like somebody'd kicked him

"Well, I got some of the drag outta my eyelids," I said.

"That's terrible!" Conway shot back. "You looked just fine! How could you let somebody do this to you?"

"Well, you just don't know how worried a woman gets about aging," I tried to explain. But Conway wasn't hearing none of that. He hated my eyes, and wouldn't talk about it till they drooped back enough that he didn't notice. That took a couple of years. I decided right then that I wasn't going to get my face cut up again to try and look younger. If I drag, I drag. If I droop, I droop.

Fifteen

And the Winner Is . . .

AWARDS IS FUNNY THINGS. Somebody like Conway Twitty, a man who had more hits than anyone, and did as much as anybody in the business for country music, can be overlooked for years. Then somebody else can come along with one hit, and get covered up with trophies. I like to think Conway and me worked for ours, and we got quite a few over the years.

They all meant a lot to me, especially fan-voted ones like the *Music City News* awards was. For one thing, getting an award will go a long way to make up for the times you *wasn't* appreciated. I well remember one of my first shows with the Wilburns. That was back in the days when I was still trying to sing like Kitty Wells. One old boy at the show proved just what he thought of me when he throwed a potato at the stage. He missed me, and knocked the breath out of Don Helms, who was on steel. Trust me, goin' up onstage and having somebody hand you a trophy is a lot nicer than having some old boy throw you a potato.

The first award that liked to drop me to the floor happened in 1972 when I was the first woman to be named the Country Music Association's Entertainer of the Year. Shoot, I was the first woman they even nominated.

By 1972, I had recorded six number one songs in ten years on Decca Records. I'll be honest, a number one record really makes you happy. I think the reason it's so important to an artist is that the public, people who work hard for a living, spend their money to buy enough of your records to say they think you're the best. To this day I can't believe that somebody would like my singing enough to pay $14.95 or more for a CD.

I was thrilled to be considered for the grand prize in 1972, and that's putting it mild. I got telegrams and letters of congratulations from fans, disc jockeys, the President, movie stars, including my favorite, Gregory Peck. Dick Clark sent words of encouragement to me, too. A lot of the country music stars in Nashville sent me congratulations and said they was pulling for me.

No one, especially me, had the foggiest notion that I'd win "Entertainer of the Year." I was going against some great artists, like Charley Pride, Johnny Cash, and Willie Nelson. I'd had some big hits in 1971, like "You're Lookin' at Country," "I Wanna Be Free," and

"One's on the Way," but them other folks had hits on the charts, too. For one thing, Charley Pride had three big songs in 1971, including "Kiss an Angel Good Morning." And all the people nominated was out there touring as hard and fast as me. I was up for several awards that night, and the best I hoped for was just one. Any one of 'em would do.

The night of the CMA show and my "Entertainer of the Year" shot finally arrived. The show, carried by CBS, was held at the Ryman Auditorium, and lots of reporters from around the world came. I've heard some of the old Nashville stars say it's just another night to them, but I don't believe one bit of that. If you can't get excited about all the excitement at the CMA Awards, you're either in the wrong business, or you're dead and don't know it.

I planned on being a good sport that night. By that, I mean a good loser, and I'd be doing it alone, since Doo wouldn't go. He went off hunting. He hated awards shows and any of the other fancy things that went along with the music business. Usually I just shrugged it off and went alone. But this time I couldn't shrug it off. He said he was going to go hunting because I didn't stand a chance of winning anyway. I didn't think I did either, but I wasn't used to Doo outright discouraging me.

So the producers had first one person, and then another, sit in the seat next to me, so there wouldn't be an open chair when the television cameras panned the audience. Well, the night turned good right off. When the

"Female Vocalist of the Year" was announced, I won! I had won back in 1968, and then got it again in 1972. Twice in five years. I can't tell you how proud I was to think that all the people in the CMA, about 5,000 members, thought I was the best female singer in all of country music.

They announced the "Vocal Duo of the Year," and I waited for Porter and Dolly to collect. By the time of the 1972 awards show, me and Conway had only released two singles, "After the Fire Is Gone" and "Lead Me On." They was both number one songs, but our big run of duet hits that started with "Louisiana Woman, Mississippi Man" didn't start until June of 1973. Porter and Dolly had five singles go up the charts during 1971 and 1972.

"Loretta Lynn and Conway Twitty," said the presenter. I almost fainted. Me and Conway walked to the platform to get our trophies, but I done all of the talking. He never did talk much. I talked too much, but I always do when I'm excited.

Man, I thought to myself. I'm having a field day. Two awards in one show! I felt plumb embarrassed.

The CMA Awards show is done live. There is no editing. If there is a mistake, millions of people see it, and that's just fine with me. I don't mind making my mistakes in public. That's better than trying to cover 'em up.

I remember watching the last commercial for the

show on the auditorium monitor. It was for Kraft Cheese. Then they started reading the nominees for "Entertainer of the Year" and I looked at some of the other artists, expecting them to win. The clock was ticking. The show would be off the air, and most folks would soon be watching their local news.

"And the winner is Loretta Lynn!"

I never won the Entertainer of the Year award again, but I'll remember that night forever. I think the thing that made it the most exciting was that people said it made a difference for women artists. I can't give enough thanks to Lorrie Morgan, Tanya Tucker, Shania Twain, Reba McEntire, Wynonna Judd, and other women singers, who have publicly said that I broke ground for women in country music. I sometimes have to chuckle at my twins, though. Somebody'll tell 'em that I opened doors for women in country music, and either Patsy or Peggy'll say, "Opened 'em? Nah, she kicked 'em in."

The thing I remember most about my acceptance speech was thanking Doo. I said that people ask him what it's like to be married to a famous woman, and I stressed that I wouldn't be famous if it wasn't for him. "He's the one who pushed me, who forced me through the doors, and I wouldn't be standing here tonight if it wasn't for him," I said. "He deserves this award as much as I do," I said, then added, "but he's gone huntin'."

Doo not showing up for the biggest night of my career hurt me as much, maybe more, than anything he ever done. I cried during my acceptance speech. Everybody thought I was shedding tears of joy. I was. But I also cried because Doo wasn't there with me.

There was all kinds of parties and things going on after the show, but I told the people from Decca and from the CMA that I had to get on back home. Them things always involve a lot of drinking and I wasn't in the mood for it. So I drove home alone in our pickup truck listening to the deejay on WSM brag on me and play my records. I finally turned the radio off. I wasn't feeling all that excited anymore.

And I wondered whether Doolittle Lynn was huntin' four-legged or two-legged game.

When Doo got home, he said he'd been watching the show in a bar, celebrating the win with his buddies. And the truth is, I know he was proud as punch about that night. He just didn't understand how much more it would have meant if he'd come along.

Of course, there was one award, an award that meant more to me personally than almost anything, that even I missed. That was in 1983, when I was inducted into the Songwriters Hall of Fame. I was on the road for that one, and Owen Bradley picked it up for me. Honoring me as a singer or entertainer was great, but as a writer— well, that was unbelievable.

There's another award I want to mention right here, because it was another one that meant the world to me. This time, though, the person I wanted to go with me did go with me. And she won the award, too. This one happened when I got a call from President Jimmy Carter.

"Loretta, I'd like you to select your favorite teacher of all time," he said. "We are going to honor teachers of famous people from all over the world, and one of them will be named Teacher of the Year."

Well, that blowed me away. "Why me?" I asked. "I only got to the eighth grade."

"Why not you?" President Carter asked. Then he told me to stop and think who taught me the most in this life. "You tell me who you want to honor, and you'll both be my guests at a White House ceremony."

I'd had teachers in school, a lot of 'em. Sometimes I had four or five in one year, and it's hard to get close to 'em when they change so much. I did like Miss Bessie a lot. But I sat there thinking about the fact that it wasn't Miss Bessie who taught me to read. I knew that before I started school. It wasn't Miss Bessie who taught me about herbs and healing and about loving people or trying to do good in this world. That person was my mommy.

Mommy didn't have much education, but believed in bettering herself; she believed in learning all you could in this world. When Daddy's health was bad in Wabash, Indiana, Mommy was the one who stepped in, working first as a waitress, and later in a nursing home. She didn't have no real education early in her life but she later went to school and learned to nurse people in the homes.

Them folks couldn't have loved nobody more. She treated them with such care and respect. She treated them not just with medicine, but with love and laughter. She'd dance, and tell jokes, and carry on something fierce. And their lives was better for it.

Mommy loved to josh people. One time I went to the home to visit her, and there was this one old lady wearing a big old patch between her eyes. I asked what was wrong with her and Mommy grinned, "Why, Loretta, she's wearing that patch so she don't get no wrinkles on her face. She's only ninety."

That was the kind of thing I wanted President Carter to understand. That there's lots of ways folks teach. It don't all come from books or colleges.

"The best teacher I ever had was my mommy," I finally answered. "She learned me more than anyone else in this world. If I come to that White House thing, I'll be bringing my little mommy."

He told me he hadn't known anyone who'd made that kind of a nomination before. Most folks picked a schoolteacher. He said he'd call me back. Then, he called and said, "Honey, you bring your little mommy to the White House. We'd love to honor her."

It was hard for Mommy to get out and do some things. Her health wasn't all that good. By that time, them doggone three packs of unfiltered cigarettes she smoked every day had already claimed one lung and was ready to take the other—and her life. But Mommy was as happy as I ever seen her when I told her about it, and she loved going to the White House.

We all sat there and waited for the announcement of the Teacher of the Year. Other artists was there with their favorite teachers. Shoot, there was people from fancy universities in that room. My little mommy, who never graduated from grade school, won it. She was all flustered when she was asked to come onstage. Mommy was a shy person when it came to things like public speaking.

"What should I say?" she asked me.

"Just say thank you," I whispered.

And that's what she done. I saw her cry for the second time in her life—the other time was when Daddy died. I watched her walk across the oak floor in the White House, and thought about the fact that she'd been born in a shack and raised in the mountains. Mommy had lost her own mama by the time she was five, and her daddy, my Grandpa Ramey, didn't pay no attention to his kids. He just let 'em root around for their own food, and for places to stay. It didn't take long before her little brother died, and then a sister. I once asked Mommy what they did about a funeral for 'em. She said they didn't have no funeral. She just wrapped 'em up, dug a hole, and buried 'em herself. That is starting life out hard.

She raised eight children in our little old place in Butcher Holler, not more than a shack. And there she was accepting an award in the White House. Later, when Mommy was looking at the table where President Franklin Roosevelt had signed the bill for the Works Projects Administration into being, I thought about the fact that it was because of the WPA that Daddy had once found work to put food on our table. That was before he got work in the mines.

I'll bet Mommy remembered when her and Daddy went to vote when Roosevelt ran for President. Daddy was a Republican, because his daddy was one and his daddy before him, too. But Mommy was a Democrat, and she voted for Roosevelt. She loved him and thought he was a real friend to the working people of this country. There was always a big show around our house when it come to elections. One time when they went to vote, Daddy ran down to the school first and cast his vote. I don't have any idea who the Republican was that he was voting for, but I do know that Mommy would run down to cast her vote and meet him coming back.

"Clary," he said. "You're just gonna kill my vote if you run down there!"

"That's just what I mean to do," Mommy said.

And that night at the White House, there stood Mommy looking at a table where the man she stood behind in every election had once sat.

I couldn't speak much that night, because I was too emotional. But every performer had been asked to perform, whether it was to dance or sing opera or to sing country music. So I had brought my guitar and was prepared to sing. "Coal Miner's Daughter" had been a hit several years earlier, but it was about to be revived because of my book coming out. I thought it was a fittin' tribute to Mommy. I have sung that song thousands of times and hope to live to sing it a thousand times more. But that is the only time I had tears running down my cheeks the whole way through.

I consider myself lucky to have known six United States Presidents. I can even count two of 'em as friends: President Jimmy Carter and President George Herbert Walker Bush. I used to say politics and music didn't mix, so I was stayin' out of elections, but I did campaign for George Bush and I want to help little George—well, I guess I better say George W. Bush. I'm also going to Florida to campaign for Jeb Bush. I plan on going through Florida like a dose of Epsom salts.

I'll tell you some stories about the presidents I've known later, including a funny story on Doo, Jimmy Carter, and Ronald Reagan. And aside from the Teacher of the Year award for Mommy, there is an award I got in Washington, D.C., that just might be the biggest honor of my life. But if I ever felt like I was a woman out of place, that was the night.

This happened ten years after my Entertainer of the Year award. George H. W. Bush was President. There is an organization called the American Academy of Achievement that gives an award called the Golden Plate to people who they believe serve as role models to young people looking for ways to achieve their dreams. In some of the papers they sent me they even call these folks "heroes." I sure wasn't feeling like no hero the night I went to Washington, D.C., for the ceremony!

Since they said it was a formal dinner, I put a long gown on, and got myself all fussed up. My manager at the time, Dave Skepner, was with me, but they only allowed the folks being honored to sit at these certain tables. So after he brung me inside, I sat down, and it was among some of the strangest-looking folks I ever seen. Now, some people may think hill people looks different. I'll tell you, look to the scientists and other geniuses and then tell me a hillbilly looks funny! One of the men I was sitting with had curly, fuzzy hair sticking up around a bald spot, glasses wore down low on his nose. They looked like they might have their minds on something a million miles away, and they probably did! I tried to start up a conversation by asking what these men did for a living.

The first one I asked said his daddy had founded Johnson & Johnson. I then turned to an old man on my other side and asked him what he did. He said he split the atom. Well, I was between an atom-splitter and the head of a huge corporation. The fellow from Johnson & Johnson asked me what I did, and I said that the real thing to know, was what I was fixing to do. I was *fixing* to crawl out of that room under the tables because I sure didn't belong in no room with people who could split atoms!

'Course, I didn't crawl out. My long gown wouldn't

have allowed me to do much crawling, anyway. I stayed and accepted the award, and I will tell you that it is one of the things I am most proud of in my life. The Golden Plate award is now located in my new museum at Hurricane Mills, Tennessee. Which brings me to another point.

The Teacher of the Year award that Mommy got is located in my sister Crystal Gayle's home in Nashville, Tennessee. I asked Crystal to bring it out to my museum so I could put it in a tribute section for Mommy. But Crystal ain't done it yet. So Crystal, if you're readin' this book—you better hustle that award on out here. Remember, I was a pretty good sneak thief back in my watermelon stealin' days. And for any of my friends and fans readin' this: if you hear I am in jail for breakin' and enterin'—could you come on to Nashville and go my bail?

CHAPTER

Sixteen

Doing the Television Circuit ...

MY CAREER WENT INTO high gear after I won Entertainer of the Year. I even got me a publicist. Here's an example of why I needed one, and some examples of some of the television shows I got booked on in the next years.

Doo still hated the road, and he usually stayed home. But one time Doo come along on a trip, and when we was walking through the Los Angeles International Airport, I seen a magazine on a news shelf.

"Lookie there, Doo," I said, inside the airport. "That there is the magazine that done an interview with me. I forgot that it's supposed to be in this month's issue. Let's buy it and see what they wrote."

It was the first issue of *Penthouse* magazine.

I didn't know what kind of magazine it was. I had

done an interview with a magazine filled with naked women! And their poses made *Playboy* seem modest. My name was plastered all over the cover next to some woman with boobs about to fall out. She didn't wear nothing but a smile, and I was embarrassed to death.

Doo hit the fan. It wasn't long before I had me a publicist to advise me about what magazines to get in. But the *Penthouse* article was real good.

A young fellow named David Brokaw was working for the public relations firm in Los Angeles that represented MCA Records, my label at the time. Before Decca Records was folded into MCA, the label had put out what they call a "bio" on me, a paper that gives some history of the artist. David was about twenty-four when he read it. When he saw the lines about me being "married at thirteen, mother of four by eighteen, grandmother at twenty-nine," he like to fell over. But my story interested him and he wanted to start representing me. It was David who first started talking about a book or a movie or some story about my life.

He wasn't no hillbilly, that's for sure. He had a college degree in political science, and was one class away from another degree in English literature. He quit his job, and school, and started his own business.

Here's what he told me one time: "I went from reading Shakespeare and Keats to the lyrics of Loretta Lynn." I had heard of Shakespeare, but I didn't know anybody named Keats.

David's first three clients was me, Lou Rawls, and

Ricardo Montalban. I got Mickey Gilley to join with us and Mickey and I are still with David's agency all these years later. Sandy, his brother, joined David at the publicity firm. Today, they have one of the largest and most successful publicity firms in the entire entertainment industry.

I love those boys like family.

The first thing David Brokaw did for my career was to book me on network television. But in 1972 he had a tough row to hoe with that job.

"We don't use country acts on this show," the producers kept telling him.

I might have been doing good in the rest of the country, but Hollywood still wouldn't have me. They thought I was too country—too hillbilly.

One of the first shows I got on was the *Dinah Shore Show*. Dinah was from Nashville and she had two network shows that together ran for ten years, one for six and one for four. I got lucky and was a hit on both programs.

In fact, every time I had a new record I performed the song on one of Dinah's shows. Dinah Shore, in the 1970s, was about as powerful as Oprah Winfrey became in the 1990s. Dinah's show could sure help a record. The first time I worked her show I did "Here I Am Again" and the song shot to number three in *Billboard*. Later that year, I did the show again and sang a song a few days before it was released. It was called "Rated X," and it even got crossover play. That means the song was so popular that its airplay crossed over to radio stations that didn't usually play country music, but played rock or some other kind of music, like disco, which was popular at the time.

Through them years, me and Doo made mighty good friends in Fred Tatashore, Dinah's television producer, and Fred's wife, Marianne, who did fashion tips on Dinah's shows. Now, Fred is a practical joker, and so was I in them days. I still like a good prank, as long as no one gets their feelings hurt, and no other harm is done. So Fred come to me and said that his wife had made a special belt for me. I told him I thought it was a beautiful thing for her to do.

"Oh, yes, and it's a beautiful belt," he said. "But when she gives it to you on camera, I want you to tell her it's the ugliest thing you've ever seen."

I agreed to play along, because I thought we'd have our laugh and Fred would edit it out of the tape before he put it on television.

So Marianne gave me a beautiful belt with sequins and other sparkling things. She gave a big buildup about how hard she had worked to make it by hand, and how it was the only one like it in the world. She handed it to me and kept waiting for me to say something. Dinah sort of glared at me, also waiting for me to say thank you, and to talk on about the belt.

"This here is the tackiest-looking belt I ever seen," I said.

I could see Fred off-camera laughing his head off, but

Marianne didn't think it was a bit funny. She grabbed the belt and she threw it at me.

I confessed to the joke quick, thinking she was durn near ready to whup me. Then we all laughed, and I thought that was the end of it. But Fred left it in the tape, and it went all over the nation. I'm sure that for a few minutes folks all over the nation thought I was the rudest woman in the world.

Fred said I played Dinah's show thirty times. I don't doubt that one bit. The most popular part of Dinah's show was called "Cooking with Dinah." One of my favorite shows was a real blowout. Dinah was making potato soup, and we was both standing behind the stove in our aprons. She let the fire get too hot and the lid blew off a pot. Soup flew all over me, all over her, and all over the set. The pot didn't just boil over, it blew.

"Is that explosion part of the recipe, too?" I asked Dinah.

After Dinah, it seemed like every television variety show in Hollywood wanted me. Kids today don't even know what a variety show is, because modern network television is mostly situation comedies or dramatic series or all sex. But in the 1950s through the 1970s, there was variety shows that featured all kinds of acts—singers, dancers, comedians, musicians, acrobats, jugglers, trained animals, and more. *The Mike Douglas Show,* *The Ed Sullivan Show,* and *The Merv Griffin Show* were just a few.

There's another few stories from national television

that I like to tell. One of 'em starts with a fellow named Greg Garrison, who started out in the fifties producing the *Kate Smith Show*. Greg later became producer of *The Dean Martin Show*, another hit variety show that ran during primetime for ten years. Greg was one of the first producers to believe country artists were good television guests. He used to book Johnny Cash and the Carter Family on both Kate's and Dean's shows, and knew us country artists could draw a crowd, even in the cities. So Greg called June Carter Cash, and asked her to recommend another entertainer from Nashville. He said June gave him my name.

Greg took June's word about me. I was booked on Dean's show.

Dean Martin was the sex symbol of the day. He had young girl dancers on his program called "The Golddiggers," and they used to rub against him and make eyes and flirt. Then he'd cuddle with his female guests when they sang duets.

You'd think he'd come to rehearsals to practice his show, but Dean Martin never came to rehearsals. His guests and his orchestra would rehearse all week. Then he'd come in at 9:30 on Saturday mornings and do what he was told. If he messed up, which he often did, Greg left it in the tape 'cause Dean's audience liked him just the way he was.

I rehearsed my parts all week, including the duet I was supposed to sing with Dean. I think Greg sang Dean's part with me during rehearsals. Come Saturday,

Greg said, "Now when you get to the end of your song, Dean will swirl you around and sit you on his lap."

"The heck he will," I said. "My mommy didn't even sit on my daddy's lap, and I ain't sittin' on no man's lap."

I'd'a walked off the show before I'd'a set in Dean's lap.

"Do you know how many women would give anything to sit in Dean Martin's lap?" Greg asked me.

"No," I said, "and I don't care. Get them down here and let them sit in his lap. I ain't gonna do it."

I sang my duet standing next to Dean and we never touched.

Greg was set plumb back by my spunk. I walked into my dressing room on that Saturday after we taped the show and there was no room to move. Hundreds of bouquets of roses were all over the place.

The show's producer introduced himself. He had sent the flowers.

He said he never came to his own show, but had to come down and see the little girl that wouldn't sit in Dean's lap.

After *The Dean Martin Show* finished its run, Greg had another idea. He wanted to do *The Dean Martin Celebrity Roasts,* where Dean would have celebrities make wisecracks about other celebrities each week. He sold the idea to NBC. Not long after, Greg asked me to be at a roast for Jack Lemmon.

Well, I'd never heard of a "roast." I thought Dean

Martin was inviting me to dinner with his Hollywood friends. So I dressed up real nice. They made a special dress for me out of material flown from Paris, France. I couldn't understand why they wanted me to eat in that fancy dress. They made me read from a Teleprompter and I was scared to death and told Dean I don't read so good. But I didn't have a choice. I was stuck. Making me feel still worse, I started in saying the most awful things about Jack Lemmon. I didn't know they was jokes. So each time I said something, I turned to Jack and said, "I didn't mean that, honey. I don't even know you. I'm just saying what's on that there card."

When I was finished, I sat down next to Dean.

"I'm starving to death," I whispered. "When are we gonna eat?"

"What do you mean, eat?" Dean said.

"Well ain't we gonna have a roast?" I said. "I didn't eat any lunch because I thought we was gonna have meat and potatoes."

He like to have fell out of his chair laughing, and the studio and television audience wondered what in the world was so funny.

When it come his turn to talk, he told that story on me. Maybe he thought I was putting him on. I wasn't.

You can't mention Dean Martin without thinkin' of Frank Sinatra. So I'll tell you about one time in 1973 when I was on one of his specials. Frank was another one who didn't show up at rehearsals. They gave me this song he wanted us to sing called "All or Nothing at All," and try as I might I just couldn't get it to where it sounded right. Finally I told the piano player I thought it was the worst song I ever heard. When I run into Frank I told him that, too. Then I said I thought we should sing the song that me and Conway had out right then, "Louisiana Woman, Mississippi Man." "Now, there is a song," I told Frank.

"Well, little girl," Frank said, " 'All or Nothing at All' was my first hit, and this show is called *Frank Sinatra and Friends*. When you have a show called *Loretta Lynn and Friends*, you can sing any song you want."

I'm surprised with all them goof-ups producers kept asking me back, but they did, and I was on almost every variety show television had to offer in the 1970s and into the 1980s. I couldn't have asked for no better publicity, neither. Going inside Americans' living rooms through television established me more than anything. You can do one network show and get more exposure than you can from hundreds of one-night concerts. It was the Brokaws, the television shows, the newspaper articles, and the awards that was behind me writing *Coal Miner's Daughter*, and ending up seeing my life put in the movies.

It seemed to me that the only dream I didn't have was a dream house, like ones you read about in books or seen in the movies: big old Southern mansions. So when Doo and me run up on one outside Nashville, one that had a whole town attached to it, we up and bought it.

Seventeen

Hurricane Mills

I LOVED HURRICANE MILLS the first time I saw it, and I still love it. I love the old mill that has been on the property for a couple hundred years, the western town, the streams and rivers that run through it. Even though Doo and me eventually had homes in Hawaii and Mexico, the house that first done me in was that big old Southern mansion at Hurricane Mills. It looked like a hillbilly's dream. We put so much work in on the house, and it was so costly, that we could have had three mansions in Madison or Goodlettsville. And the cost of fixing things up meant I had to work twice as hard out on the road. That caused a problem I couldn't tell you about when Doo was alive. With me out working all the time, Doo got bolder about bringing women around. By the time I was fixing to move into the big house at Hurricane Mills, Doolittle had already had a girlfriend out there with him.

He never got away with nothing when I was on the road. I had people—both friends and not friends—who was only too happy to report back to me about Doo's doings. I'd get phone calls at some motel or some concert hall. I'd have folks waiting for me to hit the city limits, only too happy to pass along bad news. So by the time I was ready to move in, that house was ruined for me. I'd look around at all that work me and Gloria, our housekeeper, had done, at the wallpaper and paint and pictures on the wall, and all I could think was that this other old gal had been there first.

I never felt too comfortable in the house, and when you seen me and Doo looking to build another place at the end of my movie, this other woman problem was as big a part of it as anything, although I do believe the house is haunted. Jack seen a Confederate soldier standing there big as you please one time. And there was this one spirit that got real possessive about the albums that I had framed on the walls. If somebody messed with 'em, he'd nudge 'em back.

We never did build a house on that site you seen at the end of *Coal Miner's Daughter*. That is the part where the twins say Doo and me rode off into the sunset. Now one of the twins thinks she'll build up there. And I hope that sunset works for her, 'cause it didn't for me. Doo started building a house behind the big house with the columns, and I finished it after his death. That's where I live now.

In many ways, I started to feel like a visitor in my own house back in the seventies and eighties. The farm was expensive to run, so slowing down was not an option. I'd come in for a few days, and feel like I was almost an outsider. The family had a routine that I often didn't fit into. My kids' friends wanted to come around to see their "star mom," so I couldn't even hang out in old clothes without no makeup, which is the way I like to be when I'm home. I even got so I'd want to stay in Nashville if I was only home for a night. If Doo picked me up at the airport, he'd stop on the way home and pick up a bottle. I'd say, "Honey, I ain't home but one night. Don't get drunk." That would fire him up, and he'd pop the bottle and drink while we was driving home. By the time we got there, he was ready to pass out.

He also built what he called a "rec room" out behind the big house. What it was, was a big old party room right next to the swimming pool. It had a long old bar that Doo kept well stocked, and his pals purely loved that. He'd have big parties, and I'd come home to find the place strung with liquor bottles, and women's panties from one end to the other. I'd even find watches layin' around, from when them men decided to take 'em off and jump in the pool. If I hadn't known Gloria was keeping a close eye on them twins, I wouldn't have been able to sleep a wink on the road, knowing what was going on at home. And even Gloria couldn't always keep 'em under control. They was wild as billy goats.

Once Doo got the farm going out at Hurricane Mills, he pretty much devoted his energies to it and gave up on rodeos, hunting lodges, and the like. And once we had us a working ranch, we decided to open a dude ranch at Hurricane Mills. You see, Hurricane Mills actually was a little old town, so we had places to put in shops and a place to display things like my doll collection. It's worked out good, and now, in 2001, there's all sorts of things going on out there. We've got trail rides, canoe rides, family campgrounds, fishing, concerts, and, the most recent addition, my new museum. We host the National Moto-Cross Championship every year, and you should see the crowds for that! I had to laugh this year, because my grandson, little Ernie, who is a nineteen-year-old, good-looking guy, come in the house during them Moto-Cross races and said, "Me-maw, I got to rest awhile. There's too many girls to chase this week!" He's just like his daddy, Ernest Ray.

Doo worked hard to make Hurricane Mills a place where families could come on vacation and not break the bank to do it. On the other hand, living at a tourist spot has its problems. The lack of privacy really got to be a problem after *Coal Miner's Daughter* come out in 1980. I'm not sure some fans understood that I still lived a certain way, the way I growed up understanding. That way sometimes involved blood, sweat, and tears.

Here's one example. One day I was out in the yard with the kids, killing chickens to clean and freeze. The kids and me had an assembly line going. Jack Benny would wring the chicken's neck, Ernest Ray would dip the bird in scalding water to loosen the feathers, then Betty Sue and Cissie would pluck 'em. I had the final job of gutting them, cutting them up, and getting them ready to freeze. I was looking purely awful. My hair was a mess, no makeup on my face, and blood all over me, even in my hair. All of a sudden we was surrounded by a group of tourists with cameras. And just when they walked up to us, Jack Benny let loose of a chicken whose neck had just got wrung. If you know what happens when you wring a chicken's neck, you can appreciate the next scene. That chicken flopped all over the yard, right onto this one woman's foot. This old gal fainted deader than a doornail, and I bet her and her husband ain't been to Hurricane Mills since. Over the years we learned to fence off our private quarters, and of course, now I have a house built behind the original one. And I ain't had anybody wring a chicken's neck in a long time. But the memory of Loretta Lynn that them fans has is pretty gruesome!

Even after I moved into the second house, we still had some privacy problems. One day I was cleaning house, and noticed some women wandering around looking things over in the other room. I thought they was friends of Gloria's. I also thought they was being awful nosy. I sure wouldn't have been picking up things and looking 'em over at somebody else's house. They never did come in and say anything to me, and finally left. When I saw Gloria, I mentioned that her friends seemed a little weird.

"What friends?" she asked. "I didn't have any friends in here!"

I don't know who they was or what they were doing.

Doo loved meeting fans who come out to the campgrounds. He'd take pictures with the women and flirt some with 'em. He'd drink with the men and good-ole-boy it up with 'em. They loved him, and he loved them.

Usually.

One time, though, we had a visitor who would probably be considered a stalker nowadays. I think you'll appreciate Doolittle Lynn's answer to stalkers.

Here's what happened. Me and Doo was working outside one afternoon. I was down on my hands and knees digging weeds out of the garden, when some man pulled his car into the drive, walked over to me, and asked me what I was doing.

"Working in the garden," I said. That seemed real obvious.

Then this fellow started telling me how he was my biggest fan and he loved my singing. He also made a statement that pulled me up short.

"I like you personally," he said, in a kind of strange, quiet way.

Since he didn't know me personally, and his tone of voice got weird, I didn't answer. I just kept right on pulling weeds. By this time Doolittle had noticed the man, and the man had noticed Doo. This fellow then did the strangest thing of all, and it was the thing that made me know he was crazy. He walked right over to Doo and told him he was in love with me and that he had come to get me. I was surprised Doo didn't coldcock him. Instead, he invited him to sit down and have a drink with him! Doo pulled out a bottle, and them two sat there talking about me for the longest time. Doo would pour hisself a pop, and he'd pour this man a pop. Well, ain't nobody I ever knowed who could go drink for drink with Doolittle! The man got drunker and drunker, sweatin' like a pig. Pretty soon the guy passed out cold.

Doo dragged him over to his car, stuck him in the passenger seat, then drove into the barn lot, right into a big pile of manure that hadn't got shoveled out yet. Then Doo rolled down the windows of the car and left him there. Big piles of manure and sweaty men attract some of nature's meanest little flying things—barn flies. They are the bitingest flies you'll ever run into. Doo and me went back to the house and locked ourselves in. The next morning the stalker was gone, probably with whelps and rashes that was drivin' him crazier than he already was. But he never come back. Somehow I don't think he was my biggest fan no more, either. After Doo died, I finally put up a big metal fence and security system. I hated to do it, because most folks who come see us are wonderful. The fence is for the very few who ain't.

For example, one time I was signing autographs and this woman wanted me to sign her shirt. I said, "Ain't that something, that shirt looks just like one I got." She says, "It should. I got it off'n your clothesline!"

You can run into some strange ones anywhere. I remember one time when I was at a book signing for *Coal Miner's Daughter*, a fellow showed up in his pajamas. The cops come running in and started to arrest him, and take him back to the sanitarium, where they said he'd escaped from earlier that day. I said, "Well, he's got a book, ain't he? I better sign it before he goes!"

Another problem with the ranch was the fact that Doo never believed the kids should play a big part in running it. Well, Betty Sue and Cissie are now running the ranch, and doing a dang fine job of it. In fact, I believe Betty Sue and Cissie could do almost anything they set their minds to.

The silly thing is, Doo thought them kids should all take complete responsibility for their lives, but he didn't trust 'em enough to give 'em jobs to do so they'd learn.

There was work Jack could have done on the ranch, could have supervised, if Doo had given him the chance. But Doo never seemed to have confidence in our boys. Jack would work on something for a time, then Doo would bring somebody else in to head up the project. I know that hurt Jack a lot, because it didn't take much to hurt my first-born son. In *Coal Miner's Daughter*, I wrote that working on the ranch was too much responsibility for Jack. That was Doo's opinion, not mine.

Now, Ernest Ray is a different story. It takes a heap to hurt his feelings. He's always been a pistol. Of all the kids, he's the one who'd actually make his daddy say "I love you." Doo could barely say them words to anyone, including me. Ernest Ray would force 'em out of him. Ernest Ray got interested in music as a little boy, and he started traveling with me before he was a teenager. I used to try to keep the band from using cuss words around him, or talking about the women they was running with. Then one day, when Ernest was about fourteen, I heard a lot of laughs coming from the back of the bus. I went back to see what was going on and one of the band members told me that Ernest had just told them the dirtiest joke they ever heard! I don't know where he was picking up that stuff, the band swears it wasn't from them.

That wasn't the worst time, though. Once, in the late seventies, we had just stopped at a truck stop to gas up the bus, and was going back down the road, when I heard the band hooting it up. I looked out the window and there was a big semi, with a guy's bare bottom mooning us! I walked up to the front and asked, "Boys, when did Ernest Ray get in that truck?" They couldn't believe I knowed it was Ernie. But who else would do a thing like that? He wasn't putting nothing over on me.

Cissie, who is really named Clara Marie, after my mommy, was the one who was always easy to get along with, and she almost never got yelled at by Doo, like the older three. Like Ernest Ray, she started singing when she was still a little girl, and I also took her out on the road from time to time. But school was also real important to her, so the road would have to wait. Cissie made good grades, too. I was real proud of that.

Jack and Ernest Ray both signed up for the military right after they got out of high school, probably to show Doo they could make it on their own. Ernest was a marine, and Jack was in the army, stationed in Korea. Jack was married when he signed up, and maybe the time he was gone hurt the marriage, I don't know. But they ended up getting a divorce and it like to killed both me and Jack. Cissie's marriage didn't work out, and neither did Betty Sue's first marriage. Ernest has been divorced, and so have my twins. I guess their parents staying together didn't have much influence over any of 'em. Or maybe it did.

Over time, me and Doo kind of split the duties, split who was the boss of what at home. He ran the farm, and I ran the dude ranch. It was either that, or get a divorce.

The thing is, after a decade and a half of being a good wage earner, I had changed. Them feelings that started when I was picking strawberries in Washington state, the ones that made me think I could pick up and leave, had come to full fruit. Back then, I saw money as a way to do the actual leaving. But I still didn't know how I could live without Doolittle. I couldn't picture me without him in my life.

But a lot of things had come into play over them

years. I learned that it wasn't just Doo that believed in me. I knew men like Ernest Tubb, Owen Bradley, and Conway Twitty, who didn't think I was an ignorant hillbilly. I had women friends like Patsy Cline and Tammy Wynette, who loved me and believed in me. Then, there was the fans who came to hear my show, and applauded, showing me unconditional love I didn't feel I always got from my husband. Doo wasn't the only towering figure in my life. And while I knew I loved him and I didn't *want* to live without him, I could do it.

Here's what happened at Hurricane Mills's version of the gunfight at the OK Corral:

When the American Bicentennial came around in 1976 and they had that big wagon train going all across the country, Doo decided he was gonna take Patsy and Peggy and make the trip. On the one hand, I thought that was great. What an experience them two girls would have. On the other hand, that was going to happen during the one month I'd taken off to work out at the museum we was putting together in the old mill on our property. I only had one date to work that month, at Sunset Park, in Pennsylvania. I was wanting to get the museum at the ranch ready for business, and Doo was bailing out. Hermalee, my brother Herman's daughter, come out and helped me. I'd sleep until about eleven every day, then get up and work the rest of the day and through the night. It was hard work, but we were getting it done.

Well, the truth come out while Doo was still on that

trip. I was in the old church where I'd stored some things, with my head down inside a garbage can, when this woman walks in and tells me she is here to run the place. I asked her how she figgered that?

"Doo sent me," she said, real sure of herself.

I wonder just how dumb her and Doo thought I was. All it took was her attitude confronting me like that, and I knew she was one of Doo's girlfriends. It made me madder than hell.

"Well, Doo ain't in charge of this here store," I said. "I am."

"But he give me the job," she ups and says.

"He ain't got the right to give you the job," I said. Then I run her off the ranch.

She must have run straight to Nashville and called Doo, because he showed up at the Sunset Park show madder than the devil.

"What's the matter with you, Loretta?" he yelled. "I sent that girl down to run the store, and she said you wouldn't talk to her."

" 'Course I wouldn't talk to her," I said. "I run her off the place."

He was so mad he was shaking. "You'll answer to me for that, Loretta Lynn!"

"No, I won't," I said. "I don't answer to you. This dude ranch belongs to me. The Western store belongs to me. You have the farm. You run that. But I ain't answering to you for one thing in the dude ranch. You want to give your girlfriend a job, put her on a tractor."

Eighteen

Hello, Country Bumpkin—
My Little Crush on Cal...

DOO GOT HIS JABS IN AT ME, too, when it come to suspicions, and I sometimes played right to 'em. He was busy running that ranch, but not too busy to stay jealous of me when I was on the road. Sometimes I'd get a little mad, and other times just plain mean as a snake. I was capable of leading Doolittle right on in the suspicion department.

This one time, when I come in off the road, I was mad at Doo about something, and decided to stay in Nashville and let him stew over where I was, and what I was up to. So I went home with the bus driver, Jim Webb (no relation), and his wife, and stayed a week. Jim come back one day and said he'd seen Doo in town, packing a gun. So I finally called him, and was awful happy that I could prove that the bus driver's wife was standing right there next to me. She could stay with me because I asked her to take the week off, and paid her twice her salary to do it! But again, it kind of tickled me to be putting one over on Doo. He sure never checked in with me when he run off here and there.

I later found out that Doo was so mad he gave Ernest Ray $500 and sent him to Nashville in his Bronco to find out who I was with. He picked the wrong boy for that job. Ernest Ray got drunk, wrecked the Bronco, spent the money, and come home with nothing to report.

Now, if Doo had been jealous of Teddy and Doyle Wilburn, I wish you could have heard him on the subject of Cal Smith! I'd had a crush on Cal since he tuned my guitar that night at Ernest Tubb's Record Shop. We toured together first with Ernest, and later as part of a United Talent lineup. It came about because Conway believed he and I did too many shows together during our duet days. One day he sat down and explained to me that he was afraid people would start to think of us only as a duo and not as solo artists. "You take some of the United Talent people on your tour, and I'll take the others," Conway said. And when we started dividing up the talent, Cal Smith, who'd signed with us, come with me. Aside from the fact that I had that long-time crush on Cal, I loved having him on the road with me because nobody could ever tune my guitar as good as him.

Doo knew durned well that I had a little crush on Cal. In fact, every so often I'd tease him that if I ever started stepping out on him, it would be with Cal. He got so that if we was listening to the radio and a Cal Smith song come on, Doo would jump up, run to the radio, and turn it off. Then he'd look at me as if he'd done something big. I secretly got a big kick out of it. Now, I don't know if Doo was talking behind my back, or whether it was just the Nashville gossips, but people in the business started whispering things about me and Cal. Rumors about me had been floating around clear back to the time folks thought I'd slept with an Opry official. Then came the Wilburns, then Conway. And they finally settled on Cal. We didn't care. Maybe it's because we are both Aries, and a little flighty. I always heard about the rumors almost as fast as they got started. Like I said, lots of people in Nashville was only too willing to give me news about the state of my marriage. Cal and me thought they were funny. He was just as married as me.

Rumors aside, Cal and me had ourselves a ball out on the road. He is one of the best people I ever met, and funny, too! He did love to kid me about my lack of general knowledge, but he never done it in a way that made me feel ignorant. I remember once when we were still out on the road with Ernest Tubb, we all decided to go to this golf tournament in Portland, Oregon. Ernest and Cal was gonna play, and I was gonna watch. Since I'd never seen a golf game, Ernest had insisted I go. I wasn't sure about it, but Cal said, "Loretta, get your little tail ready. We are gonna play us some golf!" So we got to the golf course, and I looked over and saw the sand trap. "Look at that, Ernest!" I hollered. "Somebody had gone and dumped a load of sand on this beautiful green grass! Why in the world would they do that?" Ernest and Cal just laughed their fannies off. But they never made fun of me, at least not in a mean way. Cal and me cut up so much at that tournament that Ernest finally looked at us out of the corner of his eye and said, "You two are having way too much fun, in my opinion."

We got so full of ourselves that we decided to play it out a little more, especially since it was right in between our birthdays and we wanted to celebrate. Mine is April 14th, and Cal's is April 10th. That evening we went down to the bar at the Holiday Inn where we was staying. My band, the Coal Miners, and Ernest's Texas Troubadors was all hanging out in there, drinking and raising the dickens. Ray Griff was on that tour, and he was in there, too. Ray was a Canadian singer who had hits like "The Mornin' After Baby Let Me Down" and "If I Let Her Come In." He was a good looker, too. Doolittle Lynn didn't know how lucky he was that I didn't run around and that all of the gossip was just that—gossip!

I hardly ever went into the bars in hotels, and I don't think Cal Smith did either. I never knew him to be much of a drinker. But we got to talking toward the end of the tournament and decided to really stir things up some. So we walked right in that bar, arm in arm, and took us a little table for two. Our original plan was to hold hands and coo over each other a little. Then we'd see how fast it took for somebody to call Doolittle Lynn. We'd sat there a little while, giggling at the looks on them band members' faces, when up comes the waitress for our order.

I didn't even know that many drink names. Doo always had that jug of whiskey, and I sure wasn't gonna ask for one of them. Cal suggested a sloe gin fizz.

"I'll have me a sloe gin fizz," I said, real loud, so those boys across the room could hear me. They heard me all right. Their heads popped around so hard they could have broke their necks!

Cal just shook his head. He ordered a drink, but I'm not sure what it was. When the waitress left, I said, "Cal, we are gonna start us some rumors this time!" He just smiled and shook his head again.

Well, I sipped along on that sloe gin fizz until I felt plumb drunk. I can't hold liquor at all, and the drink tasted more like Kool-Aid than liquor. Finally I said, "I better have me another one of them things!"

"Well, hon, I think this bar is about to close," Cal said, sounding so much like Ernest Tubb it would scare you. He'd traveled with Ernest so long he'd started talking like him!

I hollered up to the waitress and asked if they was closed.

"We ain't closed, but we're fixing to be," she hollered back. All them boys at the bar rubbernecked at me and Cal again. You could just about hear the gossip they was storing up. In fact, Ray Griff looked so upset that I thought he was gonna jump up and whup somebody. Neither me nor Cal wanted anything to do with that, because everybody knew that Ray was a karate expert.

That didn't stop me, though. I hollered at the waitress, "If it's closing time, bring me a pitcher of that stuff." I was rollin' by that time. So off we went, Cal hangin' on to me and me hangin' on to the pitcher of sloe gin. Them boys in the band jumped right up and followed us, trying to act like they was getting kicked out because the bar was closing. They followed us down the main hall, and some of 'em even jumped on the same elevator. Me and Cal got off at the same floor, and some of them boys did, too. We just wobbled on down toward my room, and finally the boys couldn't stand there no longer without looking completely foolish, so they ducked and run. Then Cal went to his room, and I went to mine.

Doo got all that information straight away. But the part he didn't hear was this: I went to my room laughing to beat the band, then sat down all alone and started writing a song about drinking sloe gin in Portland, Oregon—"Portland, Oregon and a sloe gin fizz, if that ain't love, then tell me what is." I was probably writing that song at the very minute Doo's ears was burning from somebody's phone call.

Doo took action, then. Without me knowing anything about it, he installed a taping system at the house. He was sure he was gonna catch me and Cal Smith—or me and *somebody*—spoonin' over the telephone. Now, there is a real big problem with a drinker trying to be a spy. They forget what they are up to. That's what finally happened to Doo. He got drunk, and got sloppy. Instead of him catching me messing around, I caught him! One day, right when I come in from a tour, I noticed an unlabeled tape on the bedroom dresser. I thought maybe somebody was pitching me a song, so I took it downstairs and put it into the tape player. There was Doo sweet-talking this girl! He taped his own self and then forgot to destroy the evidence. The worst part of it all was this: the girl was a girlfriend of Jack Benny's. It fired me up more that he betrayed his son than that he'd put in a tape player to spy on me. I flung all that in his face, but he just shrugged it off.

And that's how we lived. Even with the career and more money than I ever dreamed about, we wasn't living anything close to the family life I'd seen all them years ago on that little black-and-white television in Washington state. In fact, in the years after my autobiography come out, and then the movie, things got worse, if anything.

Nineteen

Doo's Dry Out . . .

DOO DRANK MORE THAN EVER in the years after *Coal Miner's Daughter*, the time when we was supposed to have rode off into that sunset. Today, the kids tell me about some wonderful Christmas memories they have, from their childhood and afterwards. Betty and Cissie swear that they remember lining up and singing Christmas carols for their daddy, and how he loved the holidays. They say that they'd all have to sing carols before they opened their presents. They remember Doo letting each one open a present at a time and saving the biggest, best present for last. Of course, the big things sometimes backfired, like the time I bought Doo a brand new Chevy pickup and had it customized with a fortune in chrome. It even had a horse trailer hooked up to it. Doo went outside, looked at it, and said, "Well, it's a beauty, but I'm a Ford man." I like to have died.

I'm glad the kids have good memories of the holidays, but mainly, I remember drunken brawls. Anybody who lives around a big drinker will tell you that holidays seem to bring out the devil in 'em. Worse yet, Doo's drinking had spread. Ernest Ray and Jack Benny was doing it, too.

Almost every Christmas or Thanksgiving was predictable. I'd get up early in the morning and start cooking a turkey. I'd bake pies or cakes, or both, and get out some of the vegetables I'd canned from the summer garden. I made everything from scratch, from pies to gravy. And every time I started cooking in such a fine kitchen, I remembered back to Butcher Holler, when we had to rely on Lee Dollarhide for chickens and candy, and Mommy and Daddy had to scratch for even the littlest gift. I remembered them days even more fondly when the men in my house got up later in the day. The first thing they done was almost always to start drinking whiskey. I'll never know why so many people likes to celebrate the birth of our Lord Jesus by getting dog drunk.

By the time we'd eat, my husband and sons wouldn't have knowed if I'd served 'em TV dinners. Then one would say something that somebody else took wrong. Or Doo might insult Jack Benny. Another would argue— argue about nothing. The third would take one's side, and the arguing turned into shouting. Then they'd jump up from the table, sometimes kicking back their chairs so hard that they fell over. I'd try to break up the fight, knowing I couldn't, and crying the whole time. I saw a few Christmas dinners where Doo turned over the dining table. Food and drinks, of course, went in all directions. Me and Gloria would spend the rest of the day cleaning food from off the floor and walls. It didn't seem like we'd come very far from the green bean throwin' days in Washington state.

Sometimes, the men's behavior turned violent, and fists started to fly. The men were punching and kicking and cussing and my daughters were screaming. The men might throw plates or vases at each other. I've seen them knock each other into the Christmas tree, and I've seen it fall and most of the decorations break into pieces.

Our Christmas Days, for years, were free-for-alls. And they made them old poverty-stricken holidays at the Webb cabin in Butcher Holler seem like heaven.

That is why I silently thanked the Lord when one day, in the early eighties, Doolittle come up to me and said words I never thought I'd hear from his lips.

"Loretta, I think I'm an alcoholic. I know I drink too much, but I just can't seem to stop."

There hadn't been no one incident that brung it on, so I guess Doo must have been thinking about it on his own for a long time. I was never so proud of him. I couldn't say a word. Tears was flowing down my cheeks. I hugged him. And except for the time when he was sick and dying, and I feared life without him, I never loved Doolittle more than that moment.

He'd already made the decision to go into a rehab center, and of course, I was behind the decision one hundred percent. I hated it that the doctors at the Betty Ford Center in California said I couldn't stay there with him, but I understood that it was something hc had to do by himself. The doctors said they'd let me know when to come back. So I left Doo there to face his problem, and went back on the concert trail.

These days, some of my grandkids and me have a joke "saying" we throw at each other. Maybe I'll do or say something and one of them kids will say, "Me-maw, you need 'thurpy'," meaning therapy, of course. Sometimes we mean one sort of therapy, like when my grandson, little Ernie, was working construction, fell three stories, landed on his head, and after he had surgery, needed physical therapy. And sometimes, when I say something the kids thinks don't make sense, it's meant to be mental health therapy. Here's something I learned during Doo's stay at Betty Ford—our whole durned family needed thurpy.

After a while the doctors told me to come back and bring the family. So we headed to California. We all got to the hotel and settled in, scheduled for our family time with Doo at Betty Ford the following day. I didn't know it until later, but Jack Benny and Ernest Ray started right in drinking the minute they got to their rooms. By the next day, when we was supposed to show up to family therapy, they was both nowhere to be found. I done everything except put the police out after 'em, but nothing worked. I couldn't find 'em nowhere. It turned out they'd hightailed it out of town. Maybe they just couldn't take the pressure. It was pretty clear that they needed a good dose of thurpy, themselves—and Ernest Ray still does!

The girls and me finally got to the Center, and I had to tell the doctors what had happened to the boys. Dog drunk and missing in action.

"Is everybody in the family a drunk?" this one guy asked.

I didn't even have an answer. And that's about the last thing I remember from the whole day. My girls remember it, though. They said it was about as painful as anything they ever saw. They wouldn't say nothing bad about their daddy, and the counselor kept pushing them to tell all the ways he'd hurt folks when he was drunk. None of us wanted to say nothing, according to the girls. And when the counselor got pushy about the girls not talking, they say my mother hen side showed up. I jumped up and told her to leave 'em alone. They also say that it broke their hearts when their daddy had to say these words in the therapy session: "My name is Mooney Lynn, and I'm an alcoholic."

I think my mind sometimes tunes out what it doesn't want to deal with, and I think that day was one of them times. I do, however, remember what happened when I got back to the hotel. I walked in looking like a hag. I'd been crying most of the day, and if I'd started out with any makeup, it was all cried off. And however bad I looked, I felt five times worse.

There, in the center of the hotel lobby, was the last thing in the world I expected—a newswoman and a team of cameramen. I honestly don't know how she knew I was there. Maybe somebody at the hotel tipped her off. Maybe somebody in Nashville tipped her. But she knew exactly why I was in California. Somebody shoved a microphone in my face and I heard them cameras start to roll.

I can't remember her exact words, but the question that she put to me had something to do with me having a demanding schedule, and an alcoholic husband. I started crying all over again, and that's how they put me on television. If I thought getting caught back at Hurricane Mills with chicken blood on my apron was an invasion of privacy, I knew then that it was nothing compared to what could happen. The next thing I knew, Doo was calling me, raging about the tabloids. There was stories all over 'em about my drunken husband. Doo demanded a divorce, swearing that I had to have give 'em the story. It took a while, but I calmed him down, and underneath, I have to believe he knew I'd never tell the tabloids nothing bad about him. But if he'd been able to prove I had, Katie bar the door!

Jack and Ernest Ray finally showed back up in Nashville. They'd parted company in Los Angeles, and Jack ended up passed out in the Memphis airport. Them boys was in a lot of messes like that, most of 'em caused by drinking. One time, when they was on the road with me, Jack put the money from concessions in his boot and flew home. He must have got drunk at the airport bar, because he woke up and found out he'd not only missed the plane, but he was missing the money boot. It was his—or my—bad luck that our friend, Max McMullin, didn't run into him. Max works for Delta in Memphis, and more than once he found one of my sons drunk at the airport. He took 'em home to his wife Mary, and she put 'em up in a spare bedroom. Now that bedroom has a bunch of posters of me on the walls. So the first time Jack woke up in it, he jumped out and said, "My God! Mama's *everywhere*!"

Doo had stayed in rehab for five weeks, and stayed sober for five more weeks when he got out. When he started drinking again, it was worse than ever before. Them tabloid stories was his excuse. Since everybody and his dog knowed Doo was a drunk, he might as well go back to being one. The publicity had been a license to drink. I knowed he was in a pitiful stage of alcoholism when I woke up one night and heard him peeling back a paper bag to get a sip of vodka. Right there in bed. He'd woke up and that was the first thing he wanted. I heard that sound many times over the next years. I remember once telling a reporter: "I wouldn't live my life over again if you handed it to me on a silver platter."

Twenty

Friends in the
White House...

'COURSE, THE MINUTE I SAY something like I wouldn't live my life over again, I remember some of the special folks who have made me feel like I was living the perfect life. Meeting United States Presidents fit into that category. That is one of the things that makes being an entertainer so interesting—the people you meet. I was at the White House right around the time President Nixon was involved in Watergate. I well remember how silly I felt that night, because I wore this Victorian dress. I thought you was supposed to dress old-fashioned at the White House. I was really "country comes to town" that night. When we ate, I sat between Mrs. Nixon—Pat—and a black gentleman who was from General Motors. I looked down at all of them forks and asked him which one of the forks I was supposed to use for the salad. He just grinned and said, "Well, at home I only use one. So I'm not going to worry about it." That put me at ease, but I still watched him and tried to use the same forks he did.

And I well remember how President Nixon left suddenly, looking worried. I asked Pat if Richard was all right, and she just smiled and said nothing was wrong. I also asked her what kind of cream she used to clean her face, because she had the most beautiful skin I ever seen. She said she just used soap, nothing special.

The press heard that I called President Nixon "Richard" to his face, instead of President Nixon. When we got off the airplane in Chicago the next morning, I saw three cameras, and a bunch of reporters come running toward the plane. I stood aside to see what movie star or other important person was gonna get off the plane. Shucks, the first one run up to me and said, "Loretta, why did you call the President by his first name?" It shocked me that they asked such a question. I looked at him for a second and said, "Well, they called Jesus, Jesus, didn't they?" That ended the interview and they took off in a dead run.

Not long after that Watergate broke out in all the newspapers.

I'd knowed Jimmy Carter before he was President. I got to know him and his mama, Miss Lillian, in Georgia, years before he was running the country. They come to my shows. I loved him, and I loved Miss Lillian. She was a character! That is one woman who said just what she thought. I remember one time when I was mad at Merv Griffin and said I wouldn't do his television show. He called back and asked, "If I get Miss Lillian, would you do it?" Well, I couldn't turn that down, so I done it and we had ourselves a ball.

Doolittle used to tell folks about his visit to the Carter White House. He was upset that he wasn't being served whiskey fast enough. So he sneaked into where the kitchen staff was, and said, "Boys, I know somebody's got some whiskey stashed." One of 'em left and brung him back a glass of Jack Daniel's. He stayed with the cooks for the rest of the event.

But if any President ever made me feel like I was special, it was President George H. W. Bush. And if any woman alive is my hero, it is Barbara Bush. George Bush was the only candidate I ever compaigned for, and I worked hard for him both times he ran. Barbara is one of the best first ladies in the world, too. She shamed me into tryin' to take some classes and get my G.E.D. I still ain't got it, but I'm studying.

As to my continuing education, I've thought hard about Barbara Bush's encouragement, and I hope to get that GED someday. Waylon Jennings got his some years back, and I know it made him proud. Tanya Tucker has said that's a goal of hers, too. I'm gonna try to do it. And if I have my say, I'm gonna figure out some way for Barbara Bush to give it to me, or at least be there when I get it, since she inspired me to try.

The thing I love about President George H. W. Bush,

and First Lady Barbara Bush, is that they're real. There ain't a phony bone in either one of 'em. Doo and me was visiting them one time, and I came into the room to find the President and Doo on their hands and knees, studying a desk. "Look here, Loretta," Doo said. "This is quite a desk the President made." And he had made it himself, too. One of the finest rugs I ever did see is one Barbara made, needlepointing all of her kids' names into it.

I remember that Barbara was showing me the White House kitchen when her daughter stopped to say good-bye. She said she had to leave because she had to make some cookies for her little girl to take to school the next day. Barbara said, "Well, maybe we can have it done here. How many cookies do you need?"

"Seventy-five," her daughter said.

"Oh dear!" Barbara said, shaking her head. "That's too many for the taxpayers to have to pay for."

Anybody else wouldn't have given a second thought to baking 1,000 cookies in the White House kitchen. But not Barbara. I'll never forget her worrying over seventy-five cookies, and I've told the story many times, even onstage.

Let me tell you how most folks are. At President George H. W. Bush's inauguration, there was a party at the White House. I attended with a bunch of other artists. We all had us a White House glass, with a drink in it. I finished my coke, and turned my glass in to the bartender. The other artists had already left—gone out the door. When I handed my fancy glass back to the bartender, he said, "God bless you, honey. You are the only one who didn't take the glass with them!" Well, that's just the way I am. Taxpayers pay for the glasses, too. But let me tell you, Barbara Bush would'a turned her glass in, too, if she had been in my shoes.

Every time I see President George H. W. Bush, I talk politics, my idea of politics. I got all kinds of worries— about health care, poor folks, and nursing homes. I got me a list started for President George W. Bush, too. I wasn't sure just when I'd get to see him to give him my concerns, but the new President Bush recently asked me to serve on the Presidential Advisory Commission for the Performing Arts. I bet I take advantage of this to give him some advice on a few other things, too.

I'm not usually on a soapbox, but right now I am climbin' right up on one to say that President George H. W. Bush was one of our greatest Presidents and he hasn't got enough credit for it. I got no gripe with Ronald Reagan, but every time I hear folks saying that another airport or highway ought to be named for Reagan, I ask why ain't they naming a bunch of things for President Bush? After all, he was there for eight years advisin' Reagan, and then four more successful years. Our economy was pulling out of a slump by the time he left office, too. It griped me half to death when folks throwed it up to him that he raised taxes after he said he wasn't gonna do it. Shoot, you show me a President that hasn't had to make a hard decision, whether he wanted to make it or not.

I'm not sure I could find the words to describe how I felt when the events of September 11, 2001, happened. I was just numb. And I was in California, where I was supposed to play a show in San Francisco. It got canceled because of security worries. We drove all the way back to Tennessee, and I still couldn't take it all in. Pure evil, is what it was. But even if I can't fully describe the feelings of loss and heartache for our country, I can easily say this: I was glad that George W. Bush was in the White House, and that he had a daddy like George H. W. Bush. The country is pulling together, and our current President learned from the best, his daddy.

Twenty-one

She Kept Folks Smiling . . .

SPEAKING OF MOMMIES and daddies, whether they are presidents, first ladies, or mine, some folks has the idea that I was closer to my daddy than my mommy. I was a daddy's girl, all right, but I loved my precious mommy more than anything. And like I mentioned earlier, she was my finest teacher. Mommy was no hillbilly shrinking violet either, not quiet like she seemed in the film. She could really be something, Clara Webb. She sang and danced, winnin' Charleston contests right and left. I use some of her Charleston routine and mix it up with some other steps in my show.

I remember once when I had a show in Las Vegas, and my opening act was a wrestling match. Mommy purely loved wrestling, and went to one of the shows with my sister Crystal Gayle, and my daughter Cissie.

But by the night they went, I'd already learned that it was all a fake. I couldn't believe it! Them boys was backstage plotting the whole thing out! So I told Mommy all about how it was fake.

"That's a lie!" Mommy said, firmly.

"No, it ain't no lie," I said. "I heard 'em as plain as day."

Mommy was having none of it, and when she got to the show that night, she was ready for blood. She wasn't as big as nothing. A big wind could have blowed her across the yard. But she sat there yelling at them big ole men, anyway. "You S.O.B.! Don't you hit him again!" Every time one of 'em did something somewhat dirty, she'd jump up and yell at 'em. And she never did believe that it was all for show. She was durn near mad enough to whup me for even suggesting it.

Mommy danced and sang and always loved a good joke. She was one who didn't mind a little off-color joke, too. When she was in the hospital, she had me call her every night before my show, and she'd tell me a joke to tell the audience. I remember the last one she ever told me. "Loretta," she started out. "Have I told you about this old man who was walking down the road and found a little boy crying?"

"Tell me the story," I said, amazed that as sick as she was, she was still telling jokes.

"Well, this old man stops and says, 'Little boy, what's the matter? Why are you cryin' so hard?' The little boy stops crying long enough to explain. 'I just learned I cain't do what the big boys do.' And that old man sat down and started crying, too."

She even got drunk one time. I surely don't want to make light of drinking and the problems it can cause, but it is a true fact that when I was about five years old, Clara Marie Webb got drunk on her way from Van Leer to Butcher Holler. This was before Daddy got work in the mines or WPA work from the government, like so many men did during the Great Depression. Mommy pulled her weight by walking to Van Leer every day to do people's washing and ironing. She could earn fifty cents a day, and it came in handy.

One day, when it was real cold out, Mommy was starting to walk home when who should come up the road but—you guessed it—Cousin Lee Dollarhide.

"Clary!" he said. "You look like you're freezin'! You better have a little moonshine to warm you up."

Mommy said she guessed she better. She took a little drink, and went on toward Butcher Holler. Then somebody else come up the road, a brother-in-law of my daddy's named Ferris Castle. He said about the same thing, and she took another drink. She was feeling a little warmer by then, so she speeded right on toward home. Sure enough, before long, another one of the Dollarhide boys, Charlie, seen her, and *he* offered her a pop. Mommy wasn't feeling no pain when she come through the door of our cabin. I thought she was sick. I put two chairs together and propped a pillow on one of 'em, so she could rest. When Daddy come home, I told him Mommy was sick and I couldn't do nothing with her.

He leaned over and looked at her with surprise.

"She's not sick," he said. "She's drunk as hell!"

Well, the next morning Mommy just laughed it off. "Maybe I did have me a couple of drinks," she told Daddy, with a grin. "But I was freezin' to death. You're lucky I made it home."

Mommy never had no drinking problem, though. Her addiction was cigarettes, and it was some kind of addiction. Sometimes, when she was out of tobacco, she'd send us kids down to the road to look for cigarette snipes, which is what we called cigarette butts, so she could get enough to roll another one. She smoked all her life, and it finally killed her at the age of sixty-four.

I was playing Harrah's in Las Vegas, in the late seventies, when I first heard she had lung cancer and was about to be operated on for it. She was still living in Wabash, Indiana, and was taken to Indianapolis for the surgery. Harrah's was wonderful about it, and got John Denver to fill in for me so I could come home.

Mommy made it through, but losing one of her lungs weakened her a lot, and we decided she should move to Tennessee. I had the house at Hurricane Mills, and wanted her to come live with me. But Mommy didn't like the ponds and rivers out at my place. She was always awful scared of water, and maybe that's why I always have been, too. One time during her sickness, I got to thinking about how scared of water Mommy was, and I started worrying that she'd never been baptized. I told her I would get a preacher to come and sprinkle her. She looked at me like I was nutty.

"I've been baptized," she said.

"When was that? And why didn't I know about it?"

"I was baptized when I was sixteen years old," she announced. "You didn't know about it because it wasn't none of your business."

I had to laugh. That was the hills coming out in Mommy.

Here's another way the hills came out in her: she predicted to me that I'd lose a child to the water. And I eventually did.

I ended up buying a house in Nashville, and offered to move her in there. But I couldn't find a housekeeper to help her, so Mommy decided to stay at Crystal's house in Nashville. Crystal already had a housekeeper. During the time Mommy had left to live, Crystal and me waged a little war over how to take care of her. I don't mean a fighting kind of war, but we had different ideas about how to keep care of Mommy.

I do not believe in pain if there is any way around it. I don't understand it when doctors and nurses withhold pain medicine from people who are sick and dying. If I was dying of cancer, I'd steal pain medicine as fast as I stole the watermelons all those years ago. I also don't see any reason sick folks can't eat whatever they want. Every time I visited Mommy in the hospital, or at Crystal's house, I'd sneak her a Snickers bar, or whatever kind of treat she wanted. And when them hospitals was giving her such a pitiful amount of pain medicine that I could see the hurt all over her, I'd pitch a fit. Crystal didn't think she should take as much pain medication as I did, and she always left instructions for the nurses to give her half of a 5 mg Valium, which ain't nothing.

The nurses was always telling me that they had to follow Crystal's orders.

"But, Loretta, Crystal said—" they'd start to say.

"Crystal ain't here," I'd say. "I am. And she needs more medicine."

I'll tell you something else. If I had it to do all over again, I'd never have let no doctor take away Mommy's cigarettes after she got that cancer. She loved 'em, and she missed 'em, even though she knew what they done to her. By then, it wouldn't have mattered, anyhow.

Mommy lived about a year after the night we attended my movie premiere together. Once, toward the end, folks was trying to prop her up in bed, and talk to her, and comb her hair.

"Oh, just lay me back down," she finally said. "I'm hurting so bad, I just want to lay down." Then she looked up and grinned. "You know, even God rested on the seventh day." That's how she was. She kept folks smiling.

Mommy believed in the Happy Hunting Grounds, just like most Indians. Don't get me wrong. She was a good Christian. She believed in God, and Jesus and Heaven. But, philosophically, she also believed in the spirit world. She once told me that Indians didn't think they was going no particular place when they died, they was just leaving this old place behind for a better one. Their spirits went to the hunting grounds and traveled wherever they wanted. She also believed, like her Indian ancestors, that people had to take care of the earth, for all the new folks that comes along after the old ones go on to the spirit world.

I'll tell you something now that I never told nobody before. The reason is that whenever I get started telling stories about spirits, or about me or Mommy having "the sight," it usually ends up in the tabloids and I sound crazy. But I will tell you this, and it is the God's truth.

I was with Mommy when she died. Four years after her first operation, she got so sick the doctors said she might not pull through. I was working at another hotel, not Harrah's, this time. When I went to tell them I had to go home, that my mother had cancer and might die, they just blowed me off. The attitude was: mommas are always dying. Maybe they had heard that before, as an excuse from some entertainers or workers, but it flew all over me. I said, "Well, mine dies just once, and if it's now, I'm gonna be there with her." Then I turned around and left for Tennessee. They got Helen Reddy to fill in for me.

She was so weak when I got there it shook me to the

core. I knew we were losing her, but I still couldn't face it. I didn't know what I'd do without her, how I'd get the strength to see it through.

I was sitting there with her when I seen her eyes start to roll back, and felt her start to slip away. I grabbed her and tried to keep her from going. I'd never seen nobody die, but I knew what was fixing to happen. I hollered for the nurses. They run in, but there wasn't nothing they could do. Mommy was gone. I fell down on a cot we had in her room and felt like I was dying, too. Everything was a blur, then I heard something like waves, like strong ocean waves. And I felt something strong and alive surrounding me. Then it was gone, but the strong feeling stayed inside me. I believe that her spirit put its arms around me and filled me with her strength. I think Mommy knew what was coming in the very near future, and left me every bit of strength she had to fight back. Because I was going to need it.

Twenty-two

Losing Jack . . .

THIS CHAPTER IS ABOUT the darkest time in my life.
And it begins like most times have done in my world,
with a tour. By 1984, Doo was still constantly telling the
press that he wished I would slow down, spend more
time at home, do less personal appearances. Of course,
he'd been saying that for years. But I couldn't slow
down, and booked still another long tour of one-night
shows.

I had done the last concert of the tour, and that night,
I fell into bed more exhausted than I'd ever been. At the
time, my office manager and friend, Lorene Allen, traveled with me, sleeping in the same bedroom on the bus.
She woke up suddenly, and realized I was breathing
funny.

She called to my driver, Jim, who had pulled into a

gas station to fuel up. Jim took one look at me and said he believed I was having a seizure.

"I'll get her to Nashville as fast as I can," he said. We were about five hours out.

"No," Lorene said, "there's gotta be a hospital nearby. We're not going to leave her in this shape for all the time it takes to get to Nashville. She'll be dead!" Fortunately, there was a hospital right beside us. When we arrived, the emergency workers came out with a stretcher and took me off the bus. It's hard to believe, but someone took a picture of me on that stretcher. Lorene threw a rock at him.

I stopped breathing three times, and was "brought back" three times by the doctor and his nurses. A seizure specialist just happened to be there for the first time that late. I wish I could tell you I saw Mommy and Daddy standing there welcoming me to the light, but I don't remember nothing from that night.

Lorene called Doo, who said that he wouldn't be able to come right away. The reason, he told Lorene, was that there was a mystery happening on our ranch. And then Doo said something she'd never heard him say. He said he was scared. Jack Benny was missing. Workers and searchers and my other children had started looking for him when he didn't come back from a horseback ride, and when they found him three days later, he was dead.

As soon as Doo learned our son was dead, he called Lorene back. When he told Lorene the time a coroner figured Jack had drowned, it chilled her. The time of

Jack's death was the same time I had gone through my seizure. I firmly believe the two were related. Somehow I knew he was gone.

"Do you want me to tell her?" Lorene asked Doo.

"No," he said, "I'll tell her."

"Shall I put her on the phone?" Lorene asked.

"No," Doo insisted. "I'm coming up there. I'm going to tell her myself, and I'm going to bring her home."

Lorene told me that Doo was on his way, but I couldn't understand where I was, or what was happening. I thought he had come to see me on my tour. I still didn't realize that the tour was over, or that I was sick.

Doo walked into my room looking downright haunted.

"What's wrong, honey?" I asked. He stood there looking like death hisself.

"Jack Benny is dead," he finally said. "We've lost our boy."

I was speechless. I couldn't take it in.

"It can't be true," I said to myself, over and over. Then I started sobbing from some horrible, scary place deep inside me. I started screaming so loud that the nurses shut my door, so I wouldn't disturb the other patients.

Doo tried to restrain me as I bolted from the bed, but he wasn't strong enough. What's that stuff that makes you instantly strong, adrenaline? It must have pumped instantly into my system, and Doo was no match for me. In the end, he put me back in bed and had to lay on top of me to keep me there.

Then he began to call me "baby" and said over and over that everything would be "all right." But I knew that everything wouldn't be all right. My baby boy was dead at thirty-three. When I finally stopped screaming, I started firing questions at Doo.

"What happened?"

"Was he alone?"

"Where did he die?"

"How did he die?"

At first, Doo didn't answer. He just kept trying to comfort me. The more he did, the more hysterical I became.

Finally Doo started piecing together what he knew about the events surrounding Jack's disappearance and death. He started by saying that Jack was crossing the Duck River, on our ranch, when he fell from his horse and hit his head on a rock.

"How do you know?" I yelled. Jack Benny, like all my kids, liked to ride horses. He was an excellent horseman. He even rode broncs and bulls in rodeos. He raced horses and won. How could this have happened?

"That's what the coroner said," Doo answered. "He found a bump on Jack's head, and his scalp was torn. The fall on the rock knocked him out and he drowned."

I told Doo to tell Jim to start the bus. I was going home to my son.

"We don't need no bus," Doo said. The doctor had arranged a hospital plane.

The doctors put me in an ambulance, and me and

Doo were driven to a tiny airport. They made me lay down, and they put my feet in the air, off the floor. A doctor flew with me all the way to Nashville and held up my feet. I don't know why, and I don't care. I would have flown standing on my head if that's what I had to do to get home. But even though I went back to Nashville, the doctors wouldn't let me go home, and they wouldn't let me see Jack's body. But the doctor did say that I could go to the funeral, if I was returned to the hospital as soon as the service was over.

I decided to go to the funeral, but I don't remember one thing about it. I can't tell you who preached it, I can't tell you what songs were sung. I can't even tell you where it was held. I was completely in a haze throughout Jack's entire service. I was "out of it" simply because I was grieving so hard I didn't see or hear a thing that was happening around me. I do remember that someone dressed me in a light blue suit that I thought was white. I wondered why anyone would dress me in white for a funeral.

Jack was buried, but I didn't even ask where. For a solid year, I didn't ask to visit the grave. Finally I asked, and was told Jack was buried at the campground. I thought it was foolish to bury him in a tourist spot. After Doo died, I moved Jack to a family graveyard in the hills near Hurricane Mills. I wanted Jack to be near his daddy.

Betty Sue was as crazy as me when Jack died. Them two had been so tight you couldn't have got a slip of paper between 'em. They'd been through a lot together. Betty Sue says that if Jack had five dollars to his name, she knew half was hers for the asking. And he was that way with almost everybody. But him and Betty Sue was always a team, being the oldest kids. After Jack died, she used to go to his grave to rake the leaves away, and she'd rant and rave at him for leaving her. Then one day, she was cleaning off the grave, and found a little black plastic horse. She took it up to her house, and wondered about it. Then, the next time she went, she found a little toy Jeep, like one her daddy had. She took that back, too. It was like things that meant something to Jack were waiting there for her each time she went. Now, she says, she doesn't cuss him so much for dying. But she don't miss him any less.

Jack had not lived an easy life. Doo often acted as if he didn't like him, and he wouldn't let me help Jack financially. But that was the way Doo believed. Your kids have to make their own mistakes and learn to live with 'em. He'd done the same thing to Betty Sue, and with Cissie. It seemed crazy to me. Me and Doo was living in a mansion, and some of the kids was living in places I thought looked like shacks. I'd call home and have Gloria or Lorene sneak 'em some cash. He said they'd have to "make it on their own just like we did."

I was angry at Doo for years about that, and Doo knew it. After Jack's death, he had a lot of guilt about the way he had treated Jack. He wouldn't talk about it unless he got real drunk. But he blamed hisself for not stopping Jack from riding that evening. He said he knew the river was too high to cross the day Jack died. In his own way, I think Doo tried to kill hisself after Jack's death. Oh, he didn't pick up no gun or take no pills. But he tried by working and running hisself to death. He'd run as fast as he could for hours in the July heat on our ranch. And there was times he said he wanted to die.

I don't believe that Jack died the way the coroner said he did. Every time anyone brought up that theory about Jack hitting his head and drowning, I argued. I knew something had been going on out around the ranch, and I kept badgering Doo about it. Finally he said, "Shut up, woman. You'll get us all killed."

I later learned that there was some bad folks wanting to use some of our property for something to do with drugs. I never learned what they wanted, whether it was a hidden place to make drugs, or a place to land planes, or what. They was purely evil folks, though, and I found out Jack knew about 'em, knew what they wanted, and was scared of 'em. He even talked to Doolittle about it. Nobody knew exactly what to do, because there was some threats involved. What I believe is this: them folks killed my baby boy. He wasn't having nothing to do with their idea, and they killed him. I don't know for sure who they was, and they better hope I never find out. And they must have dropped their plans, because me or Doo never heard no more about it.

In all honesty, some of my kids thinks I am nutty to believe this; that it ain't so. But I know what I heard.

Jack's death was the greatest tragedy in my life, up to that point. Losing a child is something so terrible that words cain't be used to describe it. I learned something from it, though: God doesn't give a mother her children. He loans them to her. They're His, and He'll call them home when He decides it's time.

I do know that Jack Benny Lynn was a child of God, and that he was saved. I know it because of something Jack once told me.

Jack's place on our ranch was nothing more than a shack. He called it a cabin, but it was a shack. The roof leaked, and the place was falling down. After Jack got out of the army, he never did quite find himself because his wife had left him. He'd help at the ranch, but he was always broke. Just thinking about it makes me mad all over again. Mad at Doo for not helping Jack when he needed money, and mad at myself for not insisting on it.

Nine months before Jack died, he came to me and said he was going to stop drinking once and for all. I have to admit that I questioned the sudden decision, even though I applauded it. "Jack," I said, "don't say it if you don't really mean it." But he did mean it, and went on to tell me about something that had happened to him.

He said that a man showed up at the cabin recently, and introduced hisself as a preacher. He said that he was supposed to become the pastor at a little church house, "somewhere around here." He described the church house, and asked Jack if he knew its location.

"Sure I do," Jack said. "I'll take you there. Won't you come in for some coffee first?"

The preacher went inside with my son. They had some coffee, and made some small talk. Then, out of the blue, the minister asked Jack if he would like to pray.

"I don't know how to pray," Jack admitted.

"I do," said the preacher. "You repeat after me, if you mean what I say."

The preacher prayed, and asked the Lord to forgive him of his sins, and to come into his heart forever. Then the preacher told Jack to pray, and he did. The preacher said he never heard anyone say a prayer so well. The words just flowed from Jack's mouth. From that day forward, my Jack Benny was a sober and changed man. He was converted.

Strange, ain't it? The preacher had been lost in a physical sense here on earth. Jack had felt he was lost in a spiritual sense. Jack could lead the preacher to the road to find his church, and the preacher could lead Jack to the right road to find God. The Lord does work in mysterious ways.

But even though I came to terms with Jack's soul going to God, my heart was tore up. It took every bit of my own strength and Mommy's, too, for me to get out of bed every day. I lost my will to do much of anything, except just what was required to keep my family afloat financially. After Jack's death in 1984, and for the next decade, I could hardly bring myself to face my own career. I had tours already booked, and couldn't get out of that. But I barely recorded a lick.

Twenty-three

The Hardest Battle of All ...

WHETHER YOU WANT IT TO OR NOT, life rolls right on after tragedy. I couldn't imagine being able to sing, to entertain anyone with the dark, heavy cloud that followed me around after Jack's death. A lot of them shows must have got done on automatic pilot, 'cause I don't remember much about 'em. But I had bookings and financial commitments, so me and the band went right on with our personal appearances, including extended engagements and one-night shows, throughout the 1980s.

I have always been able to get bookings, no matter what was going on with my records, and I'm sure thankful for that, because between 1984 and 2000, I only had five songs to hit the charts. Like I said, my heart just wasn't into making records. Plus, once MCA decided I couldn't have Owen Bradley as my producer, everything changed. I did as most of the MCA artists did, and stayed on the label and with its new president, Jimmy Bowen. I don't know about nobody else's experiences with Bowen, but he never showed up much while we was recording. He was there for the first one, but that was about it. I will say this—Jimmy Bowen was a recording genius. He just wasn't Owen Bradley. I made three albums for MCA after I left Owen, the last one in 1988, *Who Was That Stranger*. After that, I left MCA and never looked back. I loved being on Decca, with Owen. But with all them mergers and consolidations, and whatever was behind the companies getting so big, the family feel of it was gone.

In 1988, I was inducted into the Country Music Hall of Fame. Back then, the CMA didn't announce the inductee ahead of time like they do now, so it came as a surprise to me. I was sittin' in the audience with Minnie Pearl. When they said they was gonna announce the new people in the Hall, Minnie leaned over and said, "You're gonna get this one tonight."

"Oh, baloney," I said. For one thing, there was folks like Faron Young and the Wilburn Brothers, who wasn't in yet. Why would I go in ahead of them? Willie put it best a few years later when he suggested they induct a bunch at once to catch up. And that's what they done this very year.

Minnie grinned real big when Johnny Cash come out and started talking about a coal miner's daughter. I knowed it had to be me, and jumped right up outta my chair. After he finished talking, I run up on the stage and jumped right into Johnny Cash's arms. Ain't that funny? I refused to sit on Dean Martin's lap, but I'd hop into Johnny Cash's arms.

Maybe it's because he was like family. One time back in the early days, I picked up a *Billboard* magazine in the Wilburns' office and saw a full-page picture of Johnny and me. "When was that picture took?" I asked. "That ain't you," one of the Wilburns said. "That's June." I didn't believe it until I saw that the woman was wearing a dress I had never seen before. And, when I first come to Nashville, the Carter Family thought I ought to join up with them, 'cause I looked so much like June. I turned 'em down, 'cause I knew I couldn't harmonize the way they wanted with nobody but myself.

As usual, Doolittle refused to show up at the awards the night I was inducted into the Hall of Fame. I truly believe that he got to where he knowed he'd get drunk, and didn't want nobody from the music business seeing him. I don't think I was all that mad at him for it by that time. It was just another little hurt. Even if I was, I didn't have long to stay mad, because the following year, everything changed.

In 1989, Doo began what would be the hardest battle of his life. He got up from the breakfast table to get to the telephone to call the office, and couldn't seem to dial the phone. Audrey, Betty Sue's daughter, was living with us at the time in Hurricane Mills, and she finally dialed the number for him. When Doo got Louie, my office manager, on the telephone, all he could say was "corn," and he was slurring the word.

Louie called an ambulance from nearby Waverly, and had Doo brought to Nashville. They arrived from the ranch at our Nashville house at the same time I came in from the road.

"What's going on?" I asked.

"Doo's sick," Louie said.

I looked at Doo and knew that something was very wrong.

"I think he's had a stroke," Louie said.

We went right over to the hospital to check him in. The nurse asked, "Mister Lynn, how old are you?"

"Twenty-six," he said.

"Who is the President?" she then asked.

"Eisenhower," Doo said.

"Don't get smart with me," the nurse said, for some dumb reason.

"He ain't gettin' smart with you, but I'm fixin' to," I said. "I'll answer them questions for him."

But underneath my words was a bone-chilling fear.

I kept trying to think straight, to figure out what could have caused this. Of course, I knew his drinking had got even worse after Jack's death, and I knew he was half trying to kill himself with work from guilt. Also, Doo's mother had recently died, and he was grieving. I figure that had something to do with the stroke. I don't know.

Doo's doctors did something called an MRI, and discovered that his carotid arteries, the two arteries that lead from the heart to the brain, were clogged. They done surgery to clean out the arteries, and they probably saved Doo's life. But the damage from the stroke couldn't be totally repaired. He spent two weeks in the hospital that first time.

Later, Doo would still try to work on the ranch as hard as he once did, but he didn't have the stamina he'd had all of his life. That must have hurt a proud man like Doo. But I'll tell you something. He didn't lay around complaining or feeling sorry for hisself. Doolittle Lynn was a man's man in so many ways. You can go through hard years with a man, maybe even question your feelings about him, yet if the love was ever strong, it's gonna come rushing right back when he's sick. For the first time in my life, I felt protective of Doo. I knew he needed me more than he ever had, and it made me realize all over again just how deep my feelings for him had always been.

Doo come with me a few times when I had shows to play. One time, in Las Vegas, our old friends Rosie and Chuck Hamilton come to see us from Phoenix, Arizona, and got a firsthand view of just how serious Doo's problems still was. He'd try to say a word like "apple" or "orange," and all he could say was "ball." He knowed he was saying the wrong words in front of our friends, and I could tell it dang near killed him.

It got obvious after a while that Doo wasn't gonna

be able to come with me, but since I had no choice but to work, we tried to come up with another answer to his health problems, my career, and our need for an income. Finally, in 1992, we started thinking about doing the same thing so many artists had done: taking the show to Branson, Missouri.

Branson became a popular place for country artists to locate after Roy Clark built a theater in the remote area of the Ozark Mountains in Missouri in the 1970s. Pretty soon, other veteran Nashville entertainers began to build Branson theaters. As you may know, Roy Clark and Buck Owens started *Hee-Haw*. I believe this show helped country music as much as any show ever did. People loved that show, thanks to folks like Sam Louvello and Elmer Alley.

Me and Doo talked about it, and decided that building a Loretta Lynn Theater in Branson would be a good idea because it would help us slow down, and we'd be together more. We could move to Branson, where I could do two shows a day, then go to a house, not to a bus. Best of all, I could sleep in a bed every night next to my husband. It sounded good in the talking stages.

We had planned to have meals together and live more "normal" than we had since Doo worked manual labor back in Washington state. That never happened. The reality of it was far different from our dreams. I wound up getting five hours off between shows, not enough time to get home and back because of traffic. By the time I got home from the 8:00 show, Doo had gone to bed.

When I'd leave for my first show the next day, he'd be out working, bulldozing and clearing some land we bought in the area. The way shows in Branson are scheduled can be hard on you. When your shows are so far apart, through the day and into the evening, you never really relax. I don't know how entertainers stay there for years and years without burning out.

I played at a temporary theater in the beginning, planning to move into my own place when it got built. I never did like the temporary place. It had been a bowling alley, sat at the bottom of a hill, and folks could hardly see it from State Highway 76, the main road back then to the Branson attractions. I always sold out my shows, but artists who played there on the few days I took off didn't. I think their smaller crowds had something to do with the theater's location.

Doo's health continued to go downhill. In addition to heart problems that were starting, he was diagnosed with diabetes, a disease we never even thought about, and sure didn't know much about. He eventually had to take insulin shots, and soon began to give them to himself. Doctors said he'd have to stop drinking. Alcohol had been a part of Doo's life for almost half a century, and giving up booze didn't come easy for him. But after he got on insulin, he knew he'd pay a heavy price if he went on a bender. Finally, Doo quit liquor completely. I never thought I'd see the day, but with God's help, Doo weaned hisself. He got down to three beers a day. Three beers affected Doo about as much as three glasses of

Kool-Aid. He said he only drank the beer because it helped him sleep. As he got worse, he even had to quit the beer.

The insulin slowed down the diabetes, but it didn't stop it. And then, Doo had a heart attack. That was a big wake-up call, and after it happened, I decided Doo needed me more than my fans. I told the guy booking the shows that I was not going to work anymore—period. I told him I was gonna spend every night and day with Doo, whether he was in the hospital, or inside our home. I wasn't gonna work fourteen shows a week no more.

The guy pitched a fit and said he was gonna sue me. I didn't care. I wouldn't put a price tag on the care I could give Doo, or the need he had for me.

Lane Cross, my then manager, went to Branson three times with lawyers, and got it straightened out.

Doo ended up having open-heart surgery in May of 1993. I stayed at the hospital with him. There was a walkway at the hospital that connected to a hotel with rooms for family members. I got rooms for all of us; anyone who could come and stay close. My routine was that I'd only leave when I absolutely had to do it, to use the bathroom or take a shower. Maybe to bring some food up to the room. One day I left to take a shower, and had just put the key in my door when I heard a voice over a loudspeaker.

"Will the Lynn family return to the hospital immediately!"

The request scared us to pieces. Me and the kids was running into one another as we scrambled across the walkway from our rooms to Doo's.

We couldn't believe what we saw. It looked like Doo's heart had exploded. The doctors, of course, had put stitches into his chest after his heart operation, and he'd busted wide open. Towels soaked in blood were all around his bed. Doctors and nurses was flying around like crazy.

I don't blame anyone at the hospital for his chest busting open. In fact, I can't praise them Springfield doctors enough. It was the greatest hospital that I had ever been in. They rushed Doo back into surgery and sewed him back up, making some more repairs, as I understand it. But, they said, more damage had been done. I don't know the particulars of what had happened, from a medical sense. I just know that Doo was near death that day.

When Doo was wheeled back into his intensive care room, one of the kids was told he probably wouldn't live through the night. Nobody told me, and they was smart not to do it. I think the Lord was with Doolittle that night, but there was something else that helped him pull through. Ernest Ray said that Doo was "leather tough." Five years later, after his daddy died, Ernest got to thinking about it all, and put it this way: "Anybody else would have give up and died, and you cain't blame them. But not the old man. He just hung on and on."

When they brought him back from that second heart

operation, his chest was held together by metal. It was covered with things that looked like giant staples, and they sunk deep into Doo's chest. So he not only had pain from the surgery, but the pain of all that metal sticking in him.

They kept him shot full of morphine for pain, until he found out he was being given morphine. Then he ordered the doctors to stop the morphine. He would suffer "cold turkey" until he got well, he said. I think he thought painkillers was for sissies, and he also didn't want to get to a place where he depended on them. He also thought they was a form of dope. Doo didn't mind drinking himself into a stupor, but he was dead set against any kind of dope. I stood by his bed hundreds of times during the next years and saw him waller and sweat from nothing but plain old pain. The only painkiller he ever took was Tylenol III, and he didn't realize he was taking that. I sneaked it into his pill box. It helped, but not much. It was about like trying to put out a forest fire with a water pistol. But that's the best I could do.

Twenty-four

Seeing Conway
for the Last Time...

DOO HAD GONE INTO the Springfield hospital in May, and was still there in June, when I learned that Conway Twitty was planning on paying him a visit. Conway was also playing Branson off and on during the early 1990s. On a Friday afternoon, Conway finished up a show, and was leaving on the bus for Nashville, when he collapsed. They was already headed for the hospital, but instead of walking in and visiting with Doo, Conway was carried into the emergency room by his band members.

I remember looking out the window of Doo's room and seeing the bus turn into the hospital.

"Look'a here, Doo," I said. "Conway's come to see you. I'll run downstairs so he don't have to look for the room."

I saw two band members carrying him in. He was bleeding from the mouth and his eyes was crossed. They told me later that Conway had a stomach aneurysm, and bled to death from inside. He was put in intensive care after an operation, but he never woke up, as I recall.

Conway was my best male friend. When we toured together, his band sometimes rode on my bus, and my band sometimes rode on his. We ate at the same truck stops. We had toured the United States, Canada, and overseas together. We had sold millions of records, and played for millions of people. I knew his kids by their first and middle names, and he knew mine just as well. If my band had a problem that my road manager couldn't get to, Velton Lang, Conway's road manager, handled it as a favor. My road manager did the same for Conway's bunch.

Doo loved Conway as much as I did, and he had been touched that Conway had planned to stop and see him on his way home. Doo knew as well as me how badly an entertainer who's just finished a tour wants nothing more than to get home. Nonetheless, here came Conway to spend time with Doo. Of course, Conway had no idea that he'd become a patient himself. He never saw Doo. The chaplain at the hospital come up and told me that Conway was in the emergency room, and he was in trouble. Doo couldn't stand it because he couldn't get out of the bed to see about Conway.

I practically wore a path running from Doo's room

to the waiting room where Dee, Conway's wife, was waiting with his band. Dee thought everything was going to be all right, and I sure never told her no different. But one of the chaplains had earlier come to me and said, "Loretta, if you want to see Conway for the last time, come with me." Then, the chaplain asked if I wanted Dee to know that Conway was about to die.

I didn't tell Dee how bad things were, but I told the chaplain I wanted to take her with me. I figured she was about to be hurt bad enough, the way things was.

Dee and me went in the room, and I spoke to Conway. I don't know if he could hear.

"Conway," I said, "you love to sing, so don't you die. You know you love to sing too well."

Then Dee talked to Conway, and told him he'd been through bigger battles than this. Of course, she didn't really know what a battle he was facing.

Meanwhile, I was still praying that Conway would live, even though I'd been told different.

Death is the final rest, but it's an ugly rest to behold.

I'd always heard, from the time I was a little girl in the mountains, that until a person's spirit leaves the body, a person ain't truly dead. I was hysterical, and determined that Conway's spirit not get out of his body. If I could keep it there, or if I could get it back in there, Conway would come back to life, I honestly believed. When I leaned over Conway, his body was so warm, I became convinced that his spirit was still there. I told his spirit to stay inside him, and when I feared it had gone, I looked up and told it to come down and get back inside him.

"Oh God, don't let him be dead!" I yelled. "Oh God, bring this here body back to life. Come on down Conway, and get back in your body."

"He's already gone to Heaven," the chaplain told me.

I remembered the Bible stories of Jesus raising people from the dead. I remembered the scripture that said, "Jesus Christ, the same yesterday, today, and forever."

"God's gonna heal him!" I kept yelling, completely hysterical. They finally gave me a shot—a sedative—and took me out of the room. The sedative had started to work by the time I got back to Doo's room, but I still had to turn my head to the wall, so he wouldn't see me cry.

Death seemed to be 'a stalkin' us. A week after Conway passed, my oldest brother, Junior, fifty-nine, caught a cold and went to the hospital in Fort Wayne, Indiana. The doctors later decided he had pneumonia. He was put on a respirator, and died a week later. Junior hadn't ever been in a hospital before, so it became his first and last trip. I flew out to his funeral, and returned to Doo as soon as the service was over.

I lost another brother in 1996, three weeks before Doo died. My brother Jay Lee, who had traveled so many miles with me during my career, was diagnosed with cancer of the pancreas. He was dead three months after the cancer was discovered.

Conway's death left me numb. The world just moved around me, and I was mostly unaware of anything that was going on, with one exception: my husband's health draining out of him.

Twenty-five

How Do You Get Ready
for Death?

DOO TOLD BETTY SUE, my oldest daughter, that he made his peace with God when he was hospitalized in Springfield. I cain't tell you how much that pleases me. But, he told Betty Sue, even though he was ready to meet the Lord, he couldn't leave this here earth for at least a year. He told her he thought he needed that long to get me ready.

How are you going to get somebody ready for death? How do you prepare for some of the things that lead to death?

Not long after Doo was released from the Springfield hospital, we moved back to Hurricane Mills. Doo's health was on a downhill path, but he was determined that we have a life as close to normal as possible. We'd started taking some trips together—just the two of us—

in the mid-eighties. Doo bought a fifth wheeler, and insisted we do it. When we first started taking 'em, he was still well, but even when his health got worse, he wanted us to hit the road from time to time. We traveled all over through the Northwest, with him driving, and me "backseat" driving. I drove some, and he started to feel proud of me for being able to handle a big vehicle, and even admitted it. His proudest moment was seeing me able to hook up the trailer to that truck. We had us some great times on the trips, even though he was in pain a lot of the time. We camped, and Doo would sit on a riverbank and watch me fish. He'd laugh and joke. He was nothing like he'd been during them bad old day trips in the early years of our marriage. It's a shame that dying can be the thing that brings out the best in a person. I think Doo insisted on the trips to start saying a long goodbye, to help prepare me for life without him. But while the trips was wonderful, they didn't prepare me for the rest of the battle, or the way it ended.

I had family and friends close, but the ones I came to lean on most were our two old friends from Arizona, Rosie and Chuck Hamilton. In June of 1995, Chuck retired from the trucking business he owned, and when they learned how bad things was with Doo, they got in their motor home and headed to Hurricane Mills. By the time they got here, Doo was in terrible shape from the diabetes. I had a bed set up in the living room, and I slept on the couch right next to him.

One of his legs got to hurting him so bad that he

would have done anything to stop it. Anything except take drugs, that is. Doctors said there wasn't much they could do for the pain without his consent. Doo could have taken Demerol or some strong pain medication, but he was still dead set against it. I finally signed papers authorizing the doctors to give Doo the badly needed pain medication. He didn't know I did it, and he didn't know he was on the medicine. It made him "high," and he had hallucinations.

During one hallucination, Doo ordered me to get out of the way before he ran over me. He was hollering that from his bed, thinking he was driving a bulldozer. Another time, when he was at home, he tried to call the law and claimed that I had stolen all of his clothes, and that he was being held hostage.

Seeing him like that made me almost sadder than seeing him in pain.

The pain medication didn't help all that much, anyway. Every step he took was like walking on hot coals. Finally he told the doctors that if they didn't cut his leg off, he was gonna shoot it off hisself. He made the decision on his own. He never talked it over with me or any of the children. My husband's leg was cut off below his knee.

It meant the world, having Rosie and Chuck there. It was almost impossible for me to help Doolittle by myself, once the leg come off. One time, when I was trying to wheel him outside for some fresh air, the wheelchair tipped on a rock step and he slipped out. Chuck come running to help me get Doo off the ground, and, I have to admit, we all laughed at what the tabloids would have printed if they'd seen that: "Loretta Dumps Husband" would have been the headline.

It was after he lost the first leg that Doo took my hand and apologized to me for the years he spent drinking. Like I said at the first of this book, when he said he'd have ended up in the gutter without me, I told him he was crazy to say it. It wasn't no time to be havin' guilty feelings. And Doolittle Lynn would have never ended up in no gutter.

When he had only one leg, he nonetheless insisted that me and him go for drives. His eyesight and physical skills had been limited by the diabetes and the mixture of medications he was taking, although none, as I've said, included painkillers at that point. I didn't especially want to ride with him because with his physical limitations he was a worse driver than he realized.

He'd drive on our ranch, which has many asphalt roads and hills. Me and him would travel seven miles into Waverly, Tennessee, and cross the interstate highway onto other winding and hilly roads. But he couldn't see too good by then, and there was times he drove right to the edge of a cliff. I'd grab the steering wheel in the nick of time to save us from an accident.

Ernest Ray would take Doo for jeep rides, and Doo would insist on wearing a pair of cowboy boots. At that time, he still had one leg. He'd try to get a boot on the stump that was the remainder of his leg. The boot wouldn't go on, and Doo would get aggravated and throw the boot. The important thing is he wanted to go for a ride, not lay in the bed feeling sorry for himself, and he wanted to dress the way he always had—awful. Ernest thinks the medicine prevented Doo from realizing that half of his leg was gone, and that he didn't realize he had no foot. Maybe so. Doctors said Doo would have phantom pain—that his leg would hurt and itch, even though it was gone. I think he tried to wear that boot because he forgot he had a missing leg; it didn't feel like it was missing.

I think Doo would have tried to wear both boots whether he realized he only had one leg or not. Doo would have tried to wear gloves if he'd had no hands. He fought to be normal, and to regain his life, right up until the second he lost it. But Doo's reckless driving and the rides with Ernest Ray and all the rest that was his life stopped when diabetes took his second leg. After that, he couldn't even turn over alone.

Doo talked to Chuck and Rosie and asked them to consider staying on, as a sort of companion and assistant. Mainly as friends. Rosie says they thought it over hard, because, as Chuck told Doo, sometimes mixing friends and work don't make for a good situation. But Doo convinced them to stay, and they are with me to this day. Chuck keeps the yard up, and helps me do a lot of different things. Rosie works part-time in my new clothing shop, and is a full-time friend.

During the last years of Doo's life, we made a lot of

changes. I hardly worked, and didn't record. But I did take a few dates, because even with insurance, I was running out of money. My manager arranged for me to work about five days a month, just to cover household overhead.

I had to take my band of twenty-seven years off salary, and pay them only for the handful of shows they worked. That hurt me something awful, because I knew they counted on them jobs. But my record and songwriting royalties were not enough to keep the family going. The older country artists such as myself were not getting radio airplay in the early 1990s in the country music industry. Me, Merle Haggard, Tammy Wynette, Johnny Cash, Charley Pride, Willie Nelson, Waylon Jennings, and others were almost never heard on American radio as the 1990s rolled on.

I'd fly to a show, and fly back the same night so I could sit up with Doo all night. By then he was so sick, he often didn't even know I was gone. I told you I slept sitting up, but "slept" is a poor choice of words. There was many a night when I didn't sleep a lick. And neither did Doo. I slept when he slept, which wasn't much. More and more, he talked less and less. His pain was so intense that it was probably all he could think about. And he wasn't about to talk about pain.

One night he looked up at me and said, "Loretta, I can't hear the music anymore."

Twenty-six

Death Carries Forgiveness . . .

DOO HAD A FIGHTING SPIRIT. He just wouldn't take no for an answer. That's how it was when he knocked on the doors of disc jockeys back in 1961 to try to get them to play "Honky Tonk Girl." That's how it was when he knocked, unannounced, on the door of the big shots at the Grand Ole Opry in 1962 when Doo insisted they put me on the show. And that's how it was when death knocked on Doo's door. He refused to die for a long time, even with heart trouble, diabetes, losing one leg and then another.

But there wasn't any getting around it; he was dying, and we both knew it. I tried so hard to stay strong for him that it affected me physically. One night, about three weeks before he died, Doo woke me up yelling "Loretta! Get the nurse!" I jumped, because I thought something awful was happening to him. "Are you feeling worse?" I asked, scared out of my mind. "The nurse ain't for me," he said. "It's for you! Look at yourself!" I was broke out all over my body. Big old welts. And my face, arms, and legs still breaks out. Me, who never had a pimple, fights break-outs all the time to this day. Your body will only take so much.

Doo didn't have much of an appetite during the last days of his life. A man who had demanded three hefty meat-and-vegetable meals a day didn't even crave a cracker. He was also having a problem with dehydration, and to get fluids in him, I started serving watermelon.

"Baby," I said, on the day he died. "I'm going to eat a piece of watermelon. And each time I do, I want you to eat a piece too."

We finished the watermelon, and he looked up at me and smiled. It was the last smile that I'd see on his lips.

I had just gone outside to cry, when Doo began to choke. His lungs was filling with fluid.

One of the nurses went to get Rosie.

"Go find Loretta!" the nurse said to Rosie. "Tell her Doo is dying!"

That's exactly what Rosie did. I ran to Doo's bedside. His skin had changed color. I could hear him choking. He shook with every cough.

I screamed for somebody to do something. Nobody did much of anything. Maybe there was nothing they could do. Maybe, if he'd been in the hospital, something could have been put down his throat and into his lungs to drain the fluid. Maybe. But he wasn't in no hospital.

He was in God's hands, and God was tightening His grip.

And then Doo's head turned toward me, and the remainder of his near half-body lay still. His eyes locked squarely with mine. I prayed and kept on praying. And Doo kept watching me. His lips didn't move, but his eyes smiled. They gave a shine directly at me. And they spoke silently. They said that everything was going to be all right. Doolittle Lynn was soon to be at peace. There wasn't a sound in the room, but I believe that he could hear a choir of angels. Finally, I knew I had to tell him it was going to be all right.

"Just go around the corner, honey, and wait for me," I told Doo. "I'll catch up to you."

Doo's was the prettiest blue eyes I'd ever seen since I was thirteen years old. They turned immediately to gray with one breath, his last. It was August 6th, 1996.

I got a little crazy when they said he was gone. Finally, I went to my bedroom to be alone for a while. The nurses had give me a shot to help me.

When I returned, Doo's body was not there. Ernest Ray had him taken to the funeral home for embalming without my consent. Later, I found out that Ernest had gone to our family graveyard with a backhoe and dug Doo's grave three days earlier. I pitched a fit because

Ernest had taken his daddy away while I was in the bedroom. I know now that Ernest did it intentionally, because he knew I would have not agreed to it.

I slept that night on the couch where I had been sleeping next to Doo's bed during his long illness. Rosie and my granddaughter Taylor stayed with me. At daylight, I called the funeral home and told them to bring Doo home. I wanted to sit up with the body, like my people in Kentucky had done for so many years. I thought my kids would join me, but they never did. It was the longest night of my life.

His body lay inside a coffin, where his bed had been before his passing. It lay there all day and all night. I was alone with Doo during the last night he spent in his coffin in our house. I sat by him, and I talked to him. He didn't wear no suit or necktie. I knew he'd want to be buried in what he wore most every day of his life, so I picked out one of his favorite shirts. Our house, the one he was building when he got sick, has a glass roof. The moonlight leaked into the dark room. It was the only light on him, except for the natural glow that I'll swear he somehow put there even in death. For one last time, I sat up all night with Doolittle.

Neither of us ever dreamed it would end this way, not this soon. There was just so much I wanted to say before he would be put beneath the ground.

I'm sure his spirit heard me. I kissed his lips about every half hour and I like to think he kissed me back. Some people told one of my friends that the notion of a dead man kissing me back was crazy. I don't care what anybody says. I'm gonna continue to believe that he kissed me back and heard every word I said.

It was pitch black outside our home, seven miles from the nearest town. It was hot, and the only sound was that of summertime wildlife.

Doolittle Lynn was no saint, and neither am I. He wouldn't want me to make him out to be one now. But nothing bad that he ever did came to my mind that night. That night, if anybody had brought up any of that stuff and said a bad word about my Doo, I'd 'a whipped them. I would have, right there beside his body. Doo probably would have got a kick out of it.

Death carries grief. It also carries forgiveness.

People has seen me and Doo argue and throw punches. They'd seen him drunk, and so had I. I've been embarrassed many a time at the way he behaved in front of folks with me right there in the room. But none of that mattered. Doo, who wasn't no angel, looked like one that night.

It was *our* time together. Its memory will last me for a lifetime. On the day of the funeral, they took Doo's body from our house to the church. I was still in my bedroom, dressing for Doo's service, and the light came on. But I hadn't touched the switch. Then it went off. Then on and off again and again. No one touched the switch. And there wasn't no electrical short.

I believe it was Doo's way of telling me he was home. To me, Doo's funeral was a lot like Jack Benny's. I don't remember much about it. The church was filled, and the crowd overflowed into the yard. Some of the veteran members of the Grand Ole Opry was on hand, but I can't remember which ones, except for Johnny Wright and Kitty Wells.

I've often wished that I had given Doo a military funeral, since he had been in the army. I wasn't thinking at all. I was just going through the motions.

Ernest Ray has been the most misbehaved child I ever had. He's had his scrapes with the law and more. But I'll tell you something: he loves his mother, and he was right by my side. Me and him argues, and he says awful things about me. But I'd pity the poor soul that ever said anything bad about me to Ernest Ray.

I don't remember a word of what was said at the funeral. I do remember leaving the church afterwards, when me and the kids got into what they call the "family car." It slowly followed Doo, whose body lay inside a coffin on a horse-drawn carriage.

The preacher said a few words at the graveside while people stood with hands folded and eyes lowered, the way they do at them type of things. The only other sounds, once again, were the sounds of nature. The birds sang; the wind blew. The earth went on as if nothing was wrong.

Nothing was wrong in my world either. At that moment, I didn't have no world.

The children vented their grief in their own ways.

They don't like to talk about it to me, or to anybody else. I never seen a family like ours. We love each other, but we don't share everything. There are things about me that my kids don't know to this day, and vice versa.

The cemetery, as I said, is hidden from tourists. There is a locked gate at the bottom of a hill that seems to lead to nowhere. You can stand on that hill and hear what people say down below, near our home.

After Doo passed, I was alone in the big house that Doo was building for him and me. People who worked at the ranch came and went, but without Doo, I was alone. I told Rosie I couldn't stand it, and I went to my Nashville home to get away from all the memories.

Before I left, me, Rosie, and Doc Turner and his wife from Kentucky sat at the kitchen table one day and she looked up at our glass roof.

Leaves had stacked so thick on top of the roof that they was beginning to block the sunlight.

"Now how are we going to get them leaves off the roof?" Rosie said.

We couldn't crawl across it. We'd fall through the glass.

"I wish a strong wind would come along and just blow them leaves away," Rosie said. But there was no wind blowing.

She had just spoke them words when a gust came from nowhere. Not one leaf was left on the roof.

I think Doo heard Rosie, and asked God for a favor— to send me some wind.

Twenty-seven

The Long Road Back...

AFTER DOO DIED, I MOVED to my house in Nashville, and stayed there for a year. I was so out of touch with the world right then, I thought I'd only been away from Hurricane Mills for a couple of months. But it was a year before I saw the ranch again.

I just couldn't take looking at anything out there. Doo's presence was in the house and on the property. It was like he was out there on one of his tractors, a bulldozer, or just ridin' around in his pickup truck, checking to see that things was getting done. I had spent years trying to figure out how I could live without Doo if the day come when we divorced. The idea of me living without him because he was dead hadn't entered my mind until the end was near.

When I started losing Doo piece by piece, I lost half

of myself. I got myself back together in stages, in pieces. At first, I holed up in Nashville with Rosie, sometimes sleeping for days, sometimes going days without sleeping. The rash I'd got when Doo was sick got worse. It would come on like a fury, then retreat, then come back again. I wish you could 'a seen me. Well, no, I don't. If pictures of me would have got out during that time, I swear I don't know what people would have thought. Maybe that I'd been taken over by an alien. I know I was going through depression, but when you consider that rash all over my body, and the amount of stress that it took to keep it around for months, you got to figure that I had a nervous breakdown. Talk about somebody needing thurpy.

Time didn't have no meaning for me, and neither did money. I couldn't have told you the day, the month, or even the year. And I done some foolish things, like buying a full-length fur coat when the temperature in Tennessee was still in the ninety-degree range. The coat cost a lot of money; money I didn't really have after all Doo's doctoring was paid for. On top of that, it wasn't a good color on me, and I needed it like I needed another hole in my head. But I bought it.

By December 1996, the rash could at least be covered up with stage makeup, and my manager, Lane, reminded me that I'd committed to play the Grand Ole Opry. It really hit me when I picked up a newspaper and seen the show advertised. Then the radio stations started making a big deal out of the fact that this would be my first appearance since losing Doo. They was making it sound like some kind of a comeback performance, even though I was only supposed to do one song.

The more I thought about that one song, the more anxious I got. I'd start shaking, and feeling sick—workin' myself up to a full-blown anxiety attack. I had performed sick many, many times, sometimes singing long concerts with migraine headaches that almost blinded me. But thinking about one piddly ole song at the Opry froze me.

Hours before the show, I told Rosie to get Lane on the telephone and tell him I was canceling. Lane run right over. I heard him coming up the stairs, and every footstep upset me more. I guess he knowed how I'd be, because all of a sudden the footsteps stopped. What he done, was take his shoes off. He walked in on quite a sight. Rosie and Jackie, my hairdresser, was sitting there watching me pace the floor, crying and saying I couldn't do it. They wasn't able to get through to me at all.

"You call the Opry and tell 'em I ain't coming," I said, the minute he walked in.

Lane didn't say nothing. He didn't argue one bit. He handed the phone to me. "Here, Loretta," he said, real polite. "I'll dial the Opry manager. You tell him yourself."

"You're my manager!" I yelled.

He shook his head. "And you are the person who promised to do this show. You'll have to be the one to tell them you're backing out."

I yelled and carried on for almost an hour. I knowed things was getting out of hand, because by that time television crews would be arriving at the Opry House, getting set up for interviews with me. I knowed that as well as anything. Finally I give in.

"All right," I said. "Don't nobody call nobody. I'll go do the show." And I did just that, although I can't tell you to this day what I sung. Shoot, I couldn't even tell you who introduced me. Some time after I done it, I told somebody that Acuff introduced me that night. They looked at me like I was goofy.

"What's the matter?" I asked. "Acuff did introduce me that first night back."

"Not unless he done it from his grave," the person said. "Acuff's been dead over four years."

But I will say that going to the Opry that night helped me to start getting back into show business. It's a good thing, 'cause the music helped me to start feeling like I was alive again.

I didn't jump back into the business, though. I more or less crawled. In February of 1997, I done the Statlers' television show, and later that month a Florida promoter called and asked if I was up to doing some shows in Florida. I thought long and hard on that, and finally said I'd do it. It was danged strange to be thinking about being on the road, the way I was doing right then. I had done thousands of one-nighters, getting back on the bus after the show, riding through the night to get to the next stop, then playing another show and starting it all over again. All of a sudden, that seemed impossible.

In the years before Doo died, I took him with me, no matter where he was. If he was at home, I thought about him. I'd wonder whether he was working on the farm, drinking with some fellows at the campgrounds, running with women—you name it, I wondered and worried about it. Now I was going out with the knowledge that he was not doing any of those things. He was buried on the hill. The main thing I worried about that winter, was whether Doo was cold up there in his grave.

I worked with Ernest Ray and my keyboard player, Gene Dunlop, to get together a band, since I'd let mine go when Doo was sick. That led to a situation I regret. Some of the boys from the old Coal Miners was available, and some was working for other folks. I will not ever try to hire a musician away from somebody else. There's lots in the business who'll steal a good picker from you in a minute. I ain't one of 'em. Ernest Tubb taught me that; he wasn't one to steal musicians, either. In the end, there was at least one musician who wished he'd been asked, no matter what he was doing at the time. I hated the idea that he felt overlooked, because that wasn't the way it happened at all. But the new Coal Miners band was real good, and I reckon they'll be with me as long as they want to play.

I was as nervous as a long-tailed cat in a roomful of rocking chairs, but we played them Florida shows, and I think we done a good job on 'em. You can work whether you are heartsick, or not. And work, especially when you have fans in your corner, can pull you back together.

One person who made a big difference in them days is my granddaughter, Tala, Ernest Ray's daughter. She's always upbeat and mischievous, just like her daddy. In the months after Doo died, me and Tala become more like girlfriends than grandma and grandbaby. I took her on the road, and she sang a couple of songs with the band.

Owen Bradley died in 1997. He'd been in the hospital with some flu symptoms, but they must have thought he was doing better, because they released him. After he come home, he got real sick all of a sudden, and that time he didn't make it. Now they got a little park in Music Row that's dedicated to Owen. He was one of the best this town ever seen.

The first time I come back to a recording studio after Doo's death was in March of 1997, to do a gospel album that Heartland Records had been after me to do. God is on my mind a lot, and especially in the year after I lost Doo. Because of touring, I never got settled into one particular church, but there's many times the bus roared down the road seventy miles an hour, with me prayin' along the way.

Jerry Kennedy produced the album, and it was almost like having Owen Bradley back again. Jerry has produced so many great people over the years: Tom T. Hall, the Statler Brothers, Reba McEntire, and Johnny Rodriguez. Jerry was from the old school, like me and Owen. Doing them sessions brought my spirits back up considerably.

My twins was having success with their careers, too, and that was good to see. They signed with Warner/ Reprise, and put a self-titled album out. Them two girls have a lot of talent. They wrote eight of the songs on that album, and they're strong songs, too. I got to say that they done it without my help. They started playing shows down at Tootsie's Orchid Lounge, the little bar that become legendary during the early years of the Opry. All them Opry stars and songwriters hung out there—Hank Williams, Faron Young, Willie Nelson, Roger Miller, Harlan Howard. Doolittle Lynn hung out there, too. And once the twins come along, he'd take 'em in with him. By the time they was three years old, Patsy and Peggy was singing and dancing on the bar. Tootsie would reward 'em for their show with Coca-Colas and gum.

The girls felt they was practically raised there. So when they got serious about their careers, they started playing at Tootsie's under the name "The Honkabillies." That's so nobody would know they was my kids. I suppose some folks realized it, but it wasn't known all over town, and a lot of the record people was new. One night a representative from Warner/Reprise come in and got real excited about this new duo. The girls not only put on a show with their music, they kid around a lot, tell jokes, and really entertain.

They was offered a deal before the label realized they was second-generation show business. Even though the label knew their names was Lynn, they didn't make the connection. It was just like the girls to drop the information into the conversation kind of sneakylike. This one person at Warner/Reprise was tellin' the girls all about the label, when one of 'em up and says, "Oh, we know about the label. Our aunt was on it for years."

"Who's your aunt?" the fellow asked.

"Crystal Gayle," they said.

That's when it started dawnin' on the fellow. "Then who is your mother?"

"Loretta Lynn."

The guy like to fell off his chair. I bet he was surprised they hadn't tried to use the name to get their break, or have their mama call the label, or something. But that ain't the way them two operate. They got a lotta me, and a lotta Doolittle, in 'em. Patsy and Peggy look exactly alike. But the minute they start to talk, you can tell 'em apart. Peggy is the oldest, and she'll speak right up on any subject you want to mention. Patsy started out more bashful, but now she's quite a go-getter. She writes songs, produces, and between her and her husband, Philip Russell, has seven children! She makes raisin' 'em look easy, too. Peggy is married to Mark Marchetti, who works for my publishing company. Him and Peggy are expecting their first baby.

They've seen both sides of show business. Back when I was doing commercials for the Crisco company, they was in 'em. Cissie, too. The downside to it was that kids at school made fun of 'em every time Crisco showed one of them commercials. The upside was that they stopped making fun of 'em about the time the girls saved up enough of their Crisco money to buy new cars!

I have to admit, they won't listen to me about the music business. I got lots of advice about radio, and record labels, and managers. They don't want to hear none of it. They didn't back then, and they still don't. Usually. There is one thing I told to all my girls, and they listened. That bit of advice is this: if you slide into show business on your back, you'll slide out on your belly.

Cissie was another one that didn't listen to me when she was out on the road. She got herself a backer, and got a bus. Cissie done pretty good, too. She's another one with a great voice. She toured all over, and was doing great until the backer dropped out. I think that hurt her feelings and her confidence bad, too. I think I mentioned before, that you dang near cain't hurt Ernest Ray's feelings. He could have been a major star, if he'd stopped his drinking and hell raisin'. He just loves going out and playing shows with me. The twins started going out with me, too, even though they don't pay no attention to anything I say.

I'd fight a bull for any one of 'em.

Maybe the girls are afraid I'll do something like I done to Crystal a lot of years back. I not only come up with her name, I gave her the idea of having long, straight hair as her trademark. I never knew she'd grow it to the floor. I was thinkin' more waist level. But her hair did set her apart. When I first come up with the idea, I told her we'd start makin' her hair soft, so when it got real, real long, it would be the most gorgeous hair anybody ever saw. I got out a jar of mayonnaise and slathered the whole thing on her head. I will stand here and tell you that Crystal's head stunk for about a month. She never did trust none of my tips after that.

I finally moved back to Hurricane Mills. Going back to the place where Doo lived his last days was very difficult, because there I faced the reality of being a widow square in the eyes. There was memories everywhere I looked. Even the road reminded me of Doo. I remembered the time we was driving along in the jeep, and I saw an old dead snake in the road. It had been flattened by something. I told Doo I wanted to stop and see what kind of a snake it was. He stopped, and I jumped out. But when I got right up to the snake, it reared up and went for me. It was a danged cottonmouth. But it didn't get me because Doo pulled his gun and shot it in a split second. I told him I couldn't believe he'd been able to do it, 'cause everyone knew I was the best shot in the family.

Little by little, I started realizing just how much Doo done out on the ranch. Things wasn't running like usual. Oh, Ernest Ray was able to get on a bulldozer like his daddy done. But Ernest Ray would rather be out playing guitar than plowing or bulldozing. I saw just how much of the county's work Doo had done all them years, too.

He'd been keepin' up the roads, and a lot of things the county should 'a been doing. Putting Betty Sue and Cissie in charge of the town and the dude ranch helped a lot. But the farm needed somebody strong to keep everybody working.

Another friend come back into my life on a much closer basis during this time, and started helping me finish the renovatin' Doo had started on the house. That's the one behind the one with the big old columns. My dressmaker of twenty-five years, Tim Cobb, moved to Hurricane Mills, and he is with me to this day. I've come to depend on him for so much. He runs the household now, and he's the one who designed my new museum. Tim and me is like family. We fuss and squabble at each other, but it don't mean nothing.

One of the things I done was fix up a room in the front of the house where we could have company in any old time, and it would look just perfect. It's real elegant, with an organ and fancy furniture and artwork. The room where we hang out and watch television is more casual, with a lot of Indian art—bowls and statues and pictures. I added some extra bedrooms, too. Doo had always said this new house should just have one bedroom, because all the kids was growed up. I decided my kids and grandkids should have a bed waitin' for 'em if they needed one.

A strange thing started to happen as we got to finishing the house. I realized that it was the first thing that I felt was mine, mine alone. Every other place we lived seemed to take on Doo's personality. This time I was putting my own into it.

I was plenty glad Tim and Rosie and Chuck were out at Hurricane Mills, because the kids didn't come by as often as I'd like 'em to. They were busy doing a lot of things, I guess. But I wanted to see 'em more. Friends and family ought to stay in close touch, 'cause you just never know what's waitin' around the corner. I learned that over and over in my lifetime. And I was reminded of it again in April of 1998, when my sister Crystal called me with the news that Tammy Wynette had died. I dropped the telephone and almost couldn't pick it back up to hear the details. Death just kept walkin' through Nashville and grabbin' folks I loved.

Nineteen ninety-eight was also when I finally had surgery to remove a breast implant I'd got years earlier. It was back in 1973, around the time a lot of women in the entertainment field decided to get 'em. That was one of the dumbest dang things I ever done. By 1998, that thing was leaking into my chest cavity and under my arm. It had got to the point where I was getting scared. Then I signed up for the surgery. If I hadn't got them things removed, I would have died. I come out at the time, warning women about 'em. If you got 'em, get 'em out. They can be real dangerous.

There was still another milestone that year. In 1998, I recorded my first solo album in twelve years. A lot of the tunes was written by staff writers for my publishing company, and some was written by me. Remember that line Doo used, when he got so sick? "Baby, I cain't hear the music anymore." That statement confused me at first. I thought he was saying that he didn't want to hear no music in the house, that it somehow bothered him. But I finally realized that Doo was slipping away to a place where he really couldn't hear.

I tried to write a song about that, but couldn't collect my thoughts enough to suit me. So I told one of my writers, Cody James, about my idea and how I couldn't get it finished. After giving him my ideas, him and a friend, Kendall Franceschi, come back the next day with a finished song, "I Can't Hear the Music Anymore." We put it on the album, and it is one of the songs I love more than anything.

The album, *Still Country*, came out in 2000 on Audium Records. If you listen close, you can hear me cry a tiny bit on that song about Doo. The fact is, what you hear is the result of many attempts by me to get through that tune. I'd break down and cry and the producer, Randy Scruggs, would stop the session. I'd regain myself, get a few lines, and we'd have to stop again. It took us days to get bits and pieces of the whole song.

Randy done a wonderful job producing. I picked him for the album because he is a genuis, and I've known him since I came to Nashville. We grew up together in music. His daddy is Earl Scruggs. Him and Lester Flatt was one of the most famous bluegrass duos of all time. Randy's mama became a good friend and handled the early bookings of my shows. Randy was a master guitar player by the time he was twelve. I remember Owen Bradley used to write notes to Randy's schoolteachers, asking that they let him out of class to play on recording sessions. And since his daddy was Earl, there is no arguing that he came by his talent honest.

Randy picked the players for my album, and I asked if he had picked his daddy. I don't know why he hadn't. So I insisted that Earl play on a couple of cuts. On the album, you can hear me say, "Aw, that's Earl Scruggs" when he takes a banjo break. The other musicians thanked me for insisting that Earl play. They said that playing with Earl was the greatest thrill of their life.

The album has a cut called "Country in My Genes." That was the first single release. I first sang it in public on May 12, 2000, at Billy Bob's Club in Fort Worth, Texas. Billy Bob's is the world's largest honky-tonk. At least that's what the owner advertises. I sang a line about being more comfortable in my Wrangler jeans than in the finest gabardine. The cowboys hollered and threw their hats in the air. I knew I had a winner.

Even with a few shows here and there, I didn't really get back to a real tour schedule until the spring of 1998. By that time I knew I wanted to, *had* to get back on the stage full-time. We'd had lots of offers coming in. Now I started taking 'em. I kicked off one of the first tours on May 8th at Lowell, Massachusetts. When word got out that I was serious about getting back into the business full force, the papers wrote quite a bit about it, and I got a lot of support from fans and country artists.

I well remember that show in Lowell. There was twenty-one dozen roses waiting for me, a welcome back present from Garth Brooks. I've heard people blame Garth for how country "changed" to a more pop sound, and to concentration on sales. That's plain silly. All of us worth our salt is interested in selling records. Anybody who says they ain't is kidding themselves or lying to you. And anybody talkin' about my boy Garth is in danger of a whuppin' from Loretta Lynn.

In the spring of 1999, I had played what some folks in the music business call a "career date." That means it's an important show where you get lots of press attention. Mine was in New York City in the heart of Manhattan. I hadn't played Manhattan in years. Something funny happened at that show. I was singing a love song, and was lost in the words, the way I intentionally get deep into my music. Some man in the crowd got my attention. It was obvious he wanted me to sing the song to him. I try to do anything fans ask, within reason. I even let people come onstage and sing with my band— people I've never heard before in my life.

Anyhow, I sung my heart out to this here man. I finished the song and don't remember how I found out that the man, who got my song pledge of love, was actually a woman. I'd heard about the cross dressers in New York. The band thought it was hilarious that I was fooled. I don't care. He, rather she, enjoyed it, and so did the audience. Doolittle Lynn would have got a big laugh outta that one.

As I got started back in the music business, I realized just how much I had relied on Doo's thoughts. He was one of the most logical thinkers I've ever known. You'd give Doo a problem—one that seemed real complicated—and he'd cut through all the parts that didn't mean nothing, and come up with an answer that should 'a been obvious from the start. What I wouldn't give to have Doolittle come home and tell me he'd decided to buy some danged old hunting lodge someplace so hard to find that it was doomed from the start. I'd be right in on it with him.

Back before Doo passed away, we used to watch Pastor Arnold Murray on television. He was teaching instead of preaching, and I liked that. I like learnin' things about the Bible. But me and Doo always called him "the preacher." You can find Pastor Murray on television twenty-four hours a day if you have a satellite dish.

"Your preacher is on television," Doo used to holler. I'd run to the television with my notebook.

I met Pastor Murray in 1999, and I've learned more about the Bible from him than from anyone else. I was watching the pastor's program one morning and I had a question about something he said. I was tempted to try to call him, but I was too shy. So I made Tim do it. Tim asked the question for me, then went and told the preacher that I thought I was too country to bother a man with a national ministry. The next thing I knew, Pastor Murray sent me some spiritual material and two pictures of himself. One is just a head and shoulders photograph that hangs in my bus. The other was a picture of him riding a mule named Pearl.

"This is a shot of Pearl and me," the preacher wrote. "Pearl is the mule. I'm just country, too."

I thought that was funny as the dickens. Pretty soon, we was talking on the telephone. Doo had been dead for three years at that time, and Pastor Murray's wife had been dead for two. Me and him had both been married more than forty-seven years to our mates. We took up right off over the telephone, and the preacher come to see me perform on the Opry.

I took the pastor with me to the Grand Ole Opry in the summer of 1999 and introduced him to the audience. The flashing cameras never stop going at the Opry. One of them pictures of me and the pastor was sold to a tabloid, and it made up a story to go with the picture. It said the pastor and me was in love. Directly, another said we was going to get married. I swear, them tabloids! 'Course, I read 'em as much as the next person. I apologized to the pastor for any embarrassment I caused him or his ministry, but he took it in stride.

I went to see him in the late fall of 1999 in Gravitt, Arkansas. He lives there, and he videotapes his television programs there, too. I got to know the preacher's sister-in-law Martha, who was practically raised by him and his wife, her older sister. Me and Martha got to be great friends on that trip.

The Battle of Nashville was one of the most famous ever fought during the Civil War. Each year, men dress in uniforms just like the original Union and Confederate armies wore, and reenact the battle at my ranch. The pastor filmed it in 1999 for a documentary that he produced. At the reenactment, me and him dressed in formal costumes that went with the day and time of the Civil War. I have pictures of us dressed that way displayed on the mantel in my Nashville home.

I got letters from fans saying they hoped I was falling in love. Others just wrote that they hoped I was happy. Well, me and the preacher are still good friends today. We don't see much of each other, because we are both so busy. But when we do we have a good time. My kids like him, too. He likes them, although that mess of an Ernest Ray played a terrible practical joke on him.

When he come to see me one time, I was gonna be busy for a few hours and needed Ernest Ray to be host to the preacher, maybe take him to dinner. I should've asked Betty Sue and Cissie. Now, there is plenty of fine restaurants in Nashville. But where did Ernest take the preacher? To Tootsie's Orchid Lounge.

Pastor Murray is a tall man, and stands out in a crowd. Ernest Ray told the pastor he'd lead him through the shoulder-to-shoulder crowd, and the preacher followed Ernest close. You know what Ernest done to the preacher? He went through the crowd pinching girls on the butt. The preacher couldn't see that. Each girl whirled around in time to see the pastor, and thought he done the pinching. Because his television program goes all over the nation, I'll bet a lot of them recognized the pastor, and thought he pinched them. That's what Ernest wanted them to think. One woman even went to get her boyfriend to confront Pastor Murray. I just know he got the reputation of being the "pinching preacher" that day, thanks to Ernie. I was plumb furious at Ernest Ray, but the pastor just laughed it off.

Somebody asked if I compare Pastor Murray to Doo. I didn't speak my answer. I yelled it. "No!" One of the good things about our friendship is that we talk about my late husband and his late wife. Neither one of us is jealous of the feelings we still have for 'em. That kind of honesty feels real good.

Right after Doo died, I got into some business deals I shouldn't have. But by the year 2000, I was touring hot and heavy, and things were looking up. I toured more than I had in the past fifteen or so years, and loved every minute of it. We finished up the Coal Miner's Daughter Museum at Hurricane Mills, and held a big grand opening, attended by several thousand people. Naomi Judd come, and George Jones, Tanya Tucker, Jett Williams—they all helped me kick off the camping season.

As I was wrapping this book up, trying to remember some specifics, I started thinking about things in general. I'd like to tell you about this one night, and how I come to put some things in perspective.

Twenty-eight

Still Woman Enough

ALL THESE YEARS OF LIVING on a bus has left me with a sleep problem. Sometimes I fall asleep at 7:00 in the evening and wake up at midnight, or 2:00 in the morning. Sometimes I can't get to sleep until the early morning hours, and then I sleep late. A lot of the time, when I can't sleep, I get up and watch television. I'm a news addict, and could watch TV news all day and all night. I'll get up and fix myself a sandwich, or find some leftovers, and turn to one of them twenty-four-hour news channels. Usually it works, and I can get back to sleep in an hour or two. But there was this one sleepless morning, around 3:00 A.M. in the summer of 2001, when I couldn't get interested in the news.

It had been a week when I was getting up around 5:00 in the morning. I'd been putting in a new rose garden, and wishing I could find a place to buy some more Patsy Cline roses. I had some once, a whole row of 'em, and wanted some more. There's almost nothing I like better than getting my hands in the dirt, planting flowers or vegetables.

I decided to walk around outside and look at my handiwork. The moon was bright, it was warm, and I had a lot on my mind. So after I checked all the new plants, I started off down the road.

The past five or six months had brought a lot of change for me as well as a health scare. The health problem happened in April, just a few days after I filmed an Arts & Entertainment "Loretta Lynn by Request" special. The show went great, and I was proud that people said I sounded in top vocal form. That means a lot to me. I hate to ever shortchange my audience.

But after the special, when I was hugging folks in the audience, I must have picked up a bug, because three days later I come down with bacterial pneumonia. I dang near died several times over the next few weeks. In fact, my grandson, little Ernie, almost died, too. That was when he fell three stories from a construction site, and ripped the back of his head half off. He come to my house when he was released from the hospital, and we tried to get well together. Every time we turned around, we was telling each other we needed thurpy.

But I felt fine by the time I took that moonlight walk. I walked away from my newer ranch-style house, through the property where I could see the front of the big house, where tourists still visit. Doolittle loved that house so much, and I thought back to the time when, after we bought it, Doo **got** down under the house and seen how close to falling down it was. He said he lay down there and cried, thinking about how much work was gonna have to be done.

Standing there in the moonlight, the memories of Doo's taking a woman there before I could move in seemed far away. Not forgotten, but somewhere long gone and not too important. My husband was one who thought having more than one woman is a man's right. It ain't, of course, but that don't mean them men don't think it. It don't mean women got to put up with it, either. But, like I said, when I seen Doo sick there at the end, the hurt of his womanizin' washed out of me. I forgave him for anything he ever done. Forgiveness had already set in, anyway, because I forgave myself before I ever forgave him. The way I done it was by giving up all the guilt I felt all them years. Like a lot of folks, I blamed myself for everything—the cheatin', the fightin', and the drinkin'. The only way I could grow was to come to terms with the fact that I wasn't the cause of it. If a person can't get past guilt, they ain't going nowhere.

While I was thinking about Doo, I reminded myself that I want to plant one of them old-fashioned lilacs up by his grave. He'll like that.

Then I walked on down the road, past the pond where we know that an old fox is a-catchin' my ducks, and havin' 'em for dinner. He better hope I don't come up on him doing it. I quit wringin' chickens' necks a long time ago, but I might just grab that fox by the throat.

Then I went on over the bridge to where the old mill stands, the one built in the 1700s, where I got my doll collection, and a gift shop. That building has been a woolen mill and a grist mill, and I'm proud we kept it up for folks to visit a little part of Tennessee history. Right across from the mill stands a replica of our old house in Butcher Holler.

Every time I look at that house, I am reminded of how lucky I was to have lived the first thirteen years of my life with such a loving family. Love you get as a child, and a strong family life, will give you something to keep you going through almost anything. I don't mean just the love I got from my mommy and daddy, either. My sisters and brothers meant the world to me. When I look at that old cabin, I can see 'em and hear 'em.

My oldest brother, Junior, died of the same kind of bacterial pneumonia that dang near got me in 2001. Like mine, it come on fast, and hit hard. Lord, I loved my big brother. He took such good care of me, always makin' sure I got home from school safe, keepin' them big old boys at school from botherin' me. 'Course, he wouldn't play with me himself, 'cause he thought that would be a sissy thing to do. That's a big brother for you—they'll love you at a distance when they're kids. One thing I respected most about Junior is the way he took care of his family, working three jobs at a time if he needed to. I admire hard workers more than almost anything.

Next come my brother Herman. He and I have always been really close, even though I did have one of the worst fights with him I ever seen. It was back when Doo throwed me out and I come home, fourteen years old and pregnant. One day I was crying and Herman starts sayin', in this singsong voice that brothers and sisters tease each other with, "I know why yer cryin'—it's Dooooo-little, Dooolittle." I run after him, and when I caught him, I slapped his face. Then he run after me. Mommy come in the yard and was almost ready to whup Herman, when she seen the slap marks on his face. Then she turned to me and said, "Loretty, if you wasn't pregnant, I'd let him beat the snot out of you." It's funny what stories you remember and get a kick out of, ain't it? Herman and me talk on the phone all the time these days. And I ain't had to whup him in years.

Jay Lee come along three years after me, and we spent a lot of hours together in our adult years, since he drove the car and played guitar with me for a long time. Jay Lee was a nervous guy, and he got them sick headaches, like me. One thing about Jay Lee—you always knew where you stood with him. If you made him mad, he'd tell you off in a second. Didn't matter who it was that made him mad, neither. Could be me, or Doo, or the Wilburns, or the night clerk at the hotel. He was what you could call an equal opportunity honest man. I miss him awful.

Next along in our house was Donald Ray. Now, Herman looked a lot like our daddy, but Donald Ray acts more like him. He's a real lovable person, with one of the sweetest personalities. He *loved* being the baby—before Peggy Sue grabbed his spot in the family. I'll never forget one year when Mommy had us an Easter egg hunt, the *only* year I remember us doing that when I was still home. She squashed pokeberries in a bowl of water, and put boiled eggs in there until they was kind of a light wine color. After she hid 'em, us kids went down to the lowlands to find what we could. I only found one danged egg, and little Donald Ray found three! I guess nobody should have been surprised that, like Junior, Donald turned out to be a hard worker.

Right after Donald Ray come *my* baby, at least the one I laid claim to—Peggy Sue. I considered her mine to mother, and carried her around till her feet was draggin' the floor. I bathed her, diapered her—all Mommy had to do was breast-feed Peggy Sue. I remember coming through Wabash one time, and Peggy was writin' a song about drinkin'. She and I put our minds to it, and come up with "Don't Come Home a'Drinkin' (with Lovin' On Your Mind)." She's a dang good writer, with or without me. And she sings her tail off. She loves to have fun, and, like Mommy, will tell you a joke at the drop of a hat.

I was gone for a lot of the time when my littlest sisters, Betty Ruth and Crystal, was being raised. But I can tell you that there was some things I figgered out about 'em from the time they was young. Betty Ruth will let you know where you set with her just as fast as Peggy Sue will tell you a joke. Betty Ruth is a lot like our Grandpa Webb when it comes to talkin' right up. And I always knowed Crystal was a great beauty and a great singer. I saw her talent long before I saw mine.

I don't know what my bein' gone on the road so much done to my own kids. It couldn't have been good for 'em. Even though Betty Sue and Cissie wasn't babies when I got started, they both say it hurt them awful every time I got on the bus to leave. I wish it could have been different. Me and Doo's original plan was for me to work a few years, buy a farm, and retire with our kids. We didn't know just what it took to keep a farm going.

Lord knows, I wanted to mother hen my kids. I am the world's biggest old mama hen, no matter how you slice it. Shoot, one cold winter night some years back, I had a whole bunch of hens' and ducks' eggs waitin' to hatch in the kitchen. A storm come up and knocked out the electricity, which meant them babies was gonna freeze right in the eggs. I put 'em all in a basket and hauled 'em to the bedroom, throwed back the covers, and stuck 'em all in our bed. Then I crawled in under the blanket, so my body heat would keep 'em warm. But them babies was warm and hatched out three just fine that night. So when I call myself a mother hen, I really mean it.

But nowadays, when I think about my kids, I try not

to think about what I could 'a done better. I try to think about what I wish for 'em from now on. I got me a kids' wish list. For one thing, I wish Betty Sue would start writing songs again. She used to write a lot, and I think she's got some songs that could be hits. She's happily married now, and her husband Sonny is a real addition to Hurricane Mills. He's one of them guys you can always count on. Betty Sue's doing a good job at the ranch, along with Cissie. And along them lines, I wish to see Cissie happily married again. And singing. Cissie is so pretty, and was such a good singer. She still would be if she can just quit them danged cigarettes. Betty Sue's quit now, and I'm hopin' Cissie will follow her example. Cissie's had a lot of heartache in life—her divorce, and career getting snarled up—but underneath it, she's still as sweet as she always was. She just tries to hide it at times. Now we come to Ernest Ray Lynn. He may look like my daddy, but he sure don't get his personality from Ted Webb. That comes straight from the Lynn side of the family. He's a joker, a drinker, and—yes—a womanizer. I want him to quit all them things except the jokin'. I'll even let him moon the band bus, if he'll just lay down that bottle. I worry about Ernest Ray. I still miss Jack every day, but I don't worry about him, because he's in God's hands. But it sure ain't natural for a mama to bury her baby, no matter how old he is.

The twins ain't exactly like the Lynns or the Webbs. They are their own selves in this world, maybe a little of both, but not really either one. They'll say anything, though. Sometimes they'll get to squabbling onstage, and one of 'em will get huffy and say, "Well, at least I know who my daddy was!" They're jokin', of course, but sometimes I think their record company didn't always know it. Them girls have been known to pass along a smart comment I made to 'em, too. So I got to be careful what I say around 'em.

The twins left their record label before this book got finished. There's times when, as an artist, you just got to pack it up and go, and this was one of 'em as far as I could see. They got other labels wantin' to sign 'em, but I wish they'd give their mama a chance. I'd purely love to put 'em on my little record label, and run their careers. I'll bet I could do it, too. But them girls would barely let their mama run them to town, let alone run their careers.

I got some things I'm plannin' for myself, too. For one thing, I got me a couple of ideas about the dude ranch, and I thought about them when I was walking through the Western Town just about dawn. Jesse James lived in a little cabin that still stands on our property. We got papers on it and everything. I'm thinking about having it moved to Western Town, and turning it into a honeymoon cabin. Shoot, Las Vegas ain't going to have nothing on us. Folks could get married here, and even spend their wedding night in Jesse's home. I like that idea. I might even let 'em spend wedding nights up at the big house, in me and Doo's original bedroom. I don't know if anybody's got the nerve for that, though.

I've been a writin' fool in the past year, and I want to write more next year. I got a lot of songs to make up for. I had hundreds of lyrics in a bag in my bedroom, and when we was renovating the house I live in, somebody walked out with 'em. They took quite a bit of other stuff, too, including some pictures and mementos that I got sent back to me, all put inside a scrapbook. But they ain't sent back the songs.

I am chompin' at the bit to get in and make that trio record with Crystal and Peggy Sue. There ain't any two women better to sing with. And I want to make a record with my whole family—brothers, sisters, kids, grand-kids. I got grandbabies that makes us all sound like we can't sing a lick.

I am ready to sign up for a USO tour, too. I was the first country artist to hit the Middle East during the Gulf War, and seen some scary things over there, missiles flyin' and bombs bombin'. But I am ready to go back, and I'll go there on an airplane, too. This whole country, from its young kids to its grandmas, is tough as a pine knot, and some folks is getting ready to find that out.

There's more personal sorrow to face, I know that. My dear friend Lorene Allen is real sick. Lung cancer, like Mommy. She's been a part of my life ever since I met her at the Wilburns' office. She come with me when I left, and here she stayed. One of my old managers, David Skepner, died early this fall. Some tabloid called my manager, Keith, and asked him if Skepner hadn't mishandled some funds and that's why he left Loretta

Lynn Enterprises. Can you believe the nerve? Skepner was a big old Boy Scout, he never mishandled none of my money. And shoot, he's been gone from my company for fifteen years.

I do have one career worry, and I hope my fans will understand. After me getting that bacterial pneumonia, my doctors said my lungs was real scarred. I've just had too many bouts with that kind of thing. They said I don't dare take the chance of signin' autographs late into the night. So I'm gonna listen to 'em, for a change.

I wish I had Doolittle to listen to these days. I'd like to know what he thinks of my idea about Jesse James's cabin, and if I had the nerve, I might even bring up the idea of letting folks sleep in our old bedroom. He might just shake his head, and say, "Loretta, you are one ignorant hillbilly." I wish I could hear him say it one more time. Livin' with him was often hard; livin' without him is worse.

I think Doo would be proud of me, though. He worried so much about what would happen when he died. He worried that I'd just wither up, and of course, I did just that for about a year. He didn't know if I'd ever be able to have a career again. But I've done it, with the help of managers like Lane Cross, with the help of my staff, and friends like Rosie, Chuck, and Tim. With encouragement from my kids. I'm always surprised to find that with or without a record on the charts, I can still sell out almost any venue. And I am gonna keep right on doing it. You can take that to the bank.

Doo also thought people was gonna take advantage of me, and I'd end up in the poorhouse. That ain't gonna happen. The very day Doo died, just before he went into that silent, loving stare at my face, he warned me to be careful of my business, of people taking advantage. I am paying attention to what's going on. Close attention.

I think he'd also be proud that I am trying very hard to stay in touch with the real world. That was always one of his biggest concerns back in the early days—that I'd start thinkin' like a "star" and forget what was important. That's why, when I come in off the road, he'd drag me out on the tractor to look at the corn crop, or stop at the stables to see a new colt. He don't have no worry there, I know that new life still stands for what's important in this world.

And for each life, it's important to keep going through thick and thin, to never give up, and to make peace with yourself, no matter how long it takes. I always kept on going, but it took years to come to peace with myself. I had so much to learn, so much to give, and to give up. I had to give up guilt, give up blame, and know that when it's all said and done, that I am the person responsible for my own self. Not a husband, or a manager, or even my children. Just me—and the Lord, of course.

That is what "still woman enough" means to me: taking responsibility for what you feel, for what you are. That's why I'm still woman enough: I know you are what you give—to your husband, your family, your friends, your fans, and yourself. Yes, that's why I'm still woman enough.

Then, of course, just to show you I ain't always too serious, I got this one thing to say about bein' still woman enough. Folks like to say that behind every great man is a woman. I'll go 'em one better. Behind every great man is an even greater woman. Women think faster, move faster, ARE faster. And that is the dang truth.

I'll add one more thing, with a little grin on my face, a twinkle in my eye, and a world of affection in my voice: Doolittle Lynn would 'a whupped me for sayin' that.

æ L O R E T T A   L Y N N æ

"The Most Awarded Lady in Country Music History"

A W A R D S   A N D
D I S C O G R A P H I E S

Awards, Honors, and Achievements

1960
Billboard—Ranked as #4 Most Promising Female Vocalist

1961
Billboard—Most Promising Female Vocalist

1962
Becomes a Member of the Grand Ole Opry
Cash Box—Most Promising Female Vocalist

1963
Cash Box—New Female Vocalist of the Year (singles)

Awards, Honors, and Achievements compiled by Rick Cornett; Discographies compiled by Rick Cornett.

1964

Billboard—Favorite Female Vocalist
Cash Box—Most Programmed Female Vocalist
Female Vocalist of the Year (singles)
Music Business—Female Country Singer of the Year
Record World—Top Female Country Vocalist

1965

Billboard—Outstanding Achievement Award
Billboard—Favorite Female Vocalist
Cash Box—Most Programmed Female Artist
Cash Box—Favorite Female Vocalist, Favorite Female
Vocalist (singles)
Record World—Top Female Vocalist

1966

Billboard—Outstanding Achievement Award
Billboard—Favorite Female Vocalist
BMI—Citation of Achievement for "You Ain't
Woman Enough"
BMI—Citation of Achievement for "Dear Uncle Sam"
Cash Box—Most Programmed Female Artist
Cash Box—Female Vocalist of the Year
Country Song Roundup—Favorite Female Artist
NARM—Best-Selling Female Country & Western Artist,
Best Country & Western Vocal Performance
Nashville Music Industry Award—Outstanding Achievement

1967

Billboard—Top Female Vocalist
BMI—Citation of Achievement for "You Ain't
Woman Enough"

Cash Box—Most Programmed Album (*You Ain't
Woman Enough*)
Cash Box—Most Programmed Female Artist
Country Music Association—Female Vocalist of the Year
Country Music Hall of Fame—Walk of Stars
Country Song Roundup—Favorite Female Artist
NARM—Best-Selling Female Country & Western Artist
National Songwriters—Outstanding Achievement Award
Record World—Top Female Vocalist, #1 Record of the
Year "Don't Come Home a'Drinkin'," Favorite Female
Vocalist (albums)
TNN/*Music City News*—Country Female Artist
of the Year

1968
BMI—Citation of Achievement for "Fist City"
Cash Box—Favorite Female Vocalist
Cash Box—Most Programmed Female Artist
TNN/*Music City News*—Country Female Artist
of the Year

1969
BMI—Citation of Achievement for "Fist City"
Country Song Roundup—Favorite Female Artist
England—Female Vocalist of the Year
National Songwriters—Outstanding Achievement Award
TNN/*Music City News*—Country Female Artist
of the Year
WSM's Opry Star Spotlight—Top Female Vocalist

1970

BMI—Citation of Achievement for "To Make a Man"
Decca Records "Country Choice"—Proud to launch a
new decade by proclaiming January 1970 as
Loretta Lynn Month
England—Female Vocalist of the Year
National Songwriters—Outstanding Achievement Award
SESAC Award—"I'll Still Be Missing You"
TNN/*Music City News*—Country Female Artist
of the Year

1971

Academy of Country Music—Vocal Group of the Year
(with Conway Twitty)
Academy of Country Music—Female Vocalist of the Year
Billboard & Record Mirror—Top U.S. Female Singer
Billboard Country Awards—Best Duo/Singles (with
Conway Twitty)
BMI—Citation of Achievement for "Coal
Miner's Daughter"
Cash Box—Favorite Female Vocalist, New Vocal Duet of
the Year, Vocal Group of the Year, Vocal Duet of the
Year (singles)
England—Female Vocalist of the Year
Grammy—Best Country Performance by Duo/Group with
Vocals (with Conway Twitty)
Outstanding Kentuckian Award
Record World—Top Female Vocalist, Top Vocal Duet
TNN/*Music City News*—Country Vocal Duet of the Year
(with Conway Twitty)

TNN/*Music City News*—Country Female Artist
of the Year

1972

Billboard Country Awards—Best Songwriter/Female
Billboard Country Awards—Best Female Artist/Singles
Billboard Country Awards—Best Duo/Singles (with
Conway Twitty)
Billboard & Record Mirror—Top U.S. Female Singer
BMI—Citation of Achievement for "You're Lookin'
at Country"
BMI—Citation of Achievement for "I Wanna Be Free"
Country Music Association—Vocal Duo of the Year
(with Conway Twitty)
Country Music Association—Female Vocalist of the Year
Country Music Association—Entertainer of the Year
Crossroads Music Park—Entertainer of This Decade
Davidson County, TN B&PW Club—Woman of the Year
England—Female Vocalist of the Year
Nashville Women of the Year (selected as one of the five)
Record World—Top Female Vocalist, Top Vocal Duet
(singles), Top Female Vocalist (singles)
TNN/*Music City News*—Country Vocal Duet of the Year
(with Conway Twitty)
TNN/*Music City News*—Country Female Artist
of the Year
United States Air Force—Honorary Recruiter

1973

Academy of Country Music—Female Vocalist of the Year
Billboard Country Awards—Best Female Vocalist

Billboard Country Awards—Best Duo/Albums (with
Conway Twitty)
BMI Citation of Achievement for "Rated X"
Cash Box—Favorite Vocal Duet
Country Music Association—Vocal Duo of the Year
(with Conway Twitty)
Country Music Association—Female Vocalist of the Year
NARM—Best-Selling Female Country & Western Artist
Pageant magazine—Country Entertainer of the Year
Record World—Top Vocal Duet (singles)
SESAC Award—"Yesterday Will Come Again Tonight"
SESAC Award—"We'll Never Change"
(with Ernest Tubb)
SESAC Award—"Touch and Go" (with Ernest Tubb)
SESAC Award—"She Needs Someone to Hold Her"
TNN/*Music City News*—Country Vocal Duet of the Year
(with Conway Twitty)
TNN/*Music City News*—Country Female Artist
of the Year
Makes Gallup Poll as one of the Top Ten Most Admired
Women in the World
Appears on cover of international newsmagazine
Newsweek

1974

Academy of Country Music—Vocal Group of the Year
(with Conway Twitty)
Academy of Country Music—Female Vocalist of the Year
Billboard Country Awards—Best Duo/Albums (with
Conway Twitty)
Billboard Country Awards—Best Female Artist/LPs

BMI—Citation of Achievement for "Love Is
the Foundation"
Cash Box—Favorite Female Artist (albums), Favorite
Duet (albums), Favorite Duet (singles)
Country Music Association—Duo of the Year (with
Conway Twitty)
Pageant magazine—Country Entertainer of the Year
Record World—Top Female Vocalist, Top Vocal Duet
(singles), Top Vocal Duet (albums), Top Female Vocalist
(albums)
SESAC Award—"Yesterday Will Come Again Tonight"
SESAC Award—"She Needs Someone to Hold Her"
TNN/*Music City News*—Country Vocal Duet of the Year
(with Conway Twitty)
TNN/*Music City News*—Best Touring Road Show
TNN/*Music City News*—Country Female Artist of the
Year

1975

Academy of Country Music—Vocal Group of the Year
(with Conway Twitty)
Academy of Country Music—Female Vocalist of the Year
Academy of Country Music—Entertainer of the Year
Academy of Country Music—Album of the Year (*Feelins'*)
American Music Awards—Favorite Country Band, Duo/
Group (with Conway Twitty)
ASCAP—Award of Merit
Billboard Country Awards—Top Duo or Group (with
Conway Twitty)
Billboard Country Awards—Best Duo (with Conway
Twitty)

BMI—Citation of Achievement for "Some Kind of Woman"

Cash Box—Favorite Female Artist (albums), Favorite Duet (albums)

Country Music Association—Duo of the Year (with Conway Twitty)

Ladies Home Journal—Outstanding Woman of the Year

National Truck Driver Country Music Awards—Top Female Vocalist

National Truck Driver Country Music Awards—Top Vocal Duo (with Conway Twitty)

Receives Highest TVQ Rating for Any Female Musical Performer

Record World—Top Vocal Duet (singles), Top Vocal Duet (albums)

True Story magazine—Woman of the Year

TNN/*Music City News*—Country Vocal Duet of the Year (with Conway Twitty)

TNN/*Music City News*—Country Female Artist of the Year

1976

Academy of Country Music—Vocal Group of the Year (with Conway Twitty)

Cash Box—Favorite Female Artist (albums), Favorite Duet (albums)

The book *Coal Miner's Daughter* becomes a *New York Times* #1 Bestseller

National Truck Driver Country Music Awards—Top Female Vocalist

National Truck Driver Country Music Awards—Top Vocal Duo (with Conway Twitty)

Record World—Top Duo (with Conway Twitty)
Record World—Top Vocal Duet (singles), Top Vocal
Duet (albums)
TNN/*Music City News*—Country Female Artist of the Year
TNN/*Music City News*—Album of the Year
(*When the Tingle Becomes a Chill*)
TNN/*Music City News*—Country Vocal Duet of the Year
(with Conway Twitty)

1977

American Music Awards—Favorite Female Artist
American Music Awards—Favorite Country Band, Duo/
Group (with Conway Twitty)
Cash Box—Favorite Female Artist (singles), Favorite Duet
(singles), Favorite Duet (albums)
Country Style magazine—Top Female Vocalist
International Fan Club Organization—Tex Ritter Award
National Truck Driver Country Music Awards—Top
Female Vocalist
National Truck Driver Country Music Awards—Top
Vocal Duo (with Conway Twitty)
People's Choice Award—Favorite Female Musical Performer
Record World—Top Vocal Duet (albums)
SESAC Award—"Get It On" (with Conway Twitty)
TNN/*Music City News*—Country Vocal Duet of the Year
(with Conway Twitty)
TNN/*Music City News*—Country Female Artist of the Year

1978

American Music Awards—Favorite Female Artist
American Music Awards—Favorite Country Band,
Duo/Group (with Conway Twitty)

Cash Box—Album with the highest debut for *Honky Tonk Heroes* with Conway Twitty

National Truck Driver Country Music Awards—Top Female Vocalist

National Truck Driver Country Music Awards—Top Vocal Duo (with Conway Twitty)

SESAC—Best Country Album of the Year for *Out of My Head and Back in My Bed*

SESAC—Best Country Single of the Year for "Out of My Head and Back in My Bed"

Hollywood—Star Placed in Walkway of Stars

TNN/*Music City News*—Country Vocal Duet of the Year (with Conway Twitty)

TNN/*Music City News*—Country Female Artist of the Year

1979

Academy of Country Music—Artist of the Decade (70s)

Cash Box—Female Artist of the Decade, Duo of the Decade with Conway Twitty

1980

Becomes the first living entertainer to have major motion picture made of her life

Country Style magazine—All Around Entertainer, Top Vocal Duet with Conway Twitty

Oscar—*Coal Miner's Daughter* becomes an Oscar-winning movie

TNN/*Music City News*—Country Vocal Duet of the Year (with Conway Twitty)

TNN/*Music City News*—Country Female Artist of the Year

1981

Ladies Home Journal—Voted one of the "100 Most
Important Women"
NARAS—Best Recording for Children
Nashville Songwriters Assn.—Inducted into the
Songwriters Hall of Fame
TNN/*Music City News*—Country Vocal Duet of the Year
(with Conway Twitty)

1985

American Music Awards—Award of Merit
KRPT Radio—The Marty Robbins Lifetime Achievement
Award
State of Michigan—Executive Award of Honor

1986

American Academy of Achievement—Golden Plate Award
The Carl Sandburg Award
TNN/*Music City News*—Living Legend Award

1987

Nashville Chapter of NARAS—Star Walk

1988

Country Music Hall of Fame—Inductee
State of Illinois—Miner's Performing Arts Center
and School was dedicated to Loretta
Pollstar Readers' Poll Award
Wemberly, England—Marty Robbins Memorial Award

1990

State of Kentucky—US Hwy 23S named
Loretta Lynn Highway

1992

Country Music People International Awards—Heritage
Award

1993

WDOS Radio—Hall of Fame

1994

State of Tennessee—Hwy 13 named
Loretta Lynn Parkway

1995

Academy of Country Music—Pioneer Award
Country Weekly magazine—Favorite All-Time
Female Vocalist
Country Weekly magazine—Lifetime Achievement Award

1996

Christian Country Music Association—Living
Legend Award
Country Radio Music Awards—Legend Award
The Happy Chandler Foundation—Kentuckian
of the Year
Women in Music Hall of Fame—Inductee

1997

BCMA—Lifetime Achievement Award
Country Weekly magazine—Living Legend Award

1998

Grammy Song Hall of Fame—"Coal Miner's Daughter"
Inducted into Gospel Hall of Fame

1999

ABC Real Country Network: Favorite Legend Award
Country Music magazine: Among 12 Greatest Voices of
All Time
Entertainment Weekly—100 Greatest Entertainers 1959–
2000: Loretta, Garth Brooks, and Willie Nelson were the
only three country artists to make the list
Interstate Country News: Country Female Artist of the
Century
Modern Screen Presents 100 Years of Country Music: All-
Time Favorite Female Vocalist, Loretta ranked #2 behind
Tammy Wynette
Nashville Digest: Artist of the Century
National Public Radio Poll: 100 Most Important Musical
Works of the 20th Century: "Coal Miner's Daughter"
was one of eight songs to make the list
Rolling Stone: One of the Most Important People of the
Century
The Star—100 Greatest Stars of the Century: Loretta was
the only female country star to make the list
The Tennessean: Top 100 People with Tennessee Ties
VH-1 Greatest Women of Rock & Roll: Loretta was one
of only five female country artists to make the list

2000

Country Radio Broadcasters: Career Achievement Award
International Entertainment Buyers Association: Career
Achievement Award

2001

Official Torch Carrier for 2002 Winter Olympics

2002
Inducted into Kentucky Music Hall of Fame
Receives Honorary Doctorate in Arts from University of
Kentucky

Album Discography

DL 74457, *Loretta Lynn Sings*, December 1963

DL 74541, *Before I'm Over You*, June 1963

DL 74620, *Songs from My Heart*, February 1965

DL 74639, *Ernest Tubb and Loretta Lynn*, August 1965

DL 74665, *Blue Kentucky Girl*, August 1965

DL 74695, *Hymns*, November 1965

DL 74721, *The Wilburn Brothers Show* (includes Loretta
Lynn), February 1966

DL 74744, *I Like 'Em Country*, March 1966

DL 74783, *You Ain't Woman Enough*, September 1966

DL 74817, *A Country Christmas*, October 1966

DL 74842, *Don't Come Home a'Drinkin*,' February 1967

DL 74872, *Ernest Tubb and Loretta Lynn Singin' Again*,
June 1967

DL 74930, *Singin' with Feelin'*, October 1967

DL 74928, *Who Says God Is Dead!*, February 1968

VL 73853, *Here's Loretta Lynn*, April 1968

DL 74997, *Fist City*, April 1968

DL 75000, *Loretta Lynn's Greatest Hits* (compilation),
June 1968

DL 75084, *Your Squaw Is on the Warpath*,
February 1969

DL 75115, *If We Put Our Heads Together*
(with Ernest Tubb), June 1969

DL 75113, *Woman of the World/To Make a Man,*
June 1969

DL 75163, *Here's Loretta Singing "Wings Upon Your
Horns,"* January 1970

DL 75198, *Loretta Lynn Writes 'Em and Sings 'Em,* June
1970

DL 75253, *Coal Miner's Daughter,* December 1970

DL 75251, *We're Only Make Believe* (with
Conway Twitty), February 1971

DL 75282, *I Wanna Be Free,* May 1971

DL 75310, *You're Lookin' at Country,* September 1971

DL 75326, *Lead Me On* (with Conway Twitty), January
1972

DL 75334, *One's on the Way,* March 1972

DL 75351, *God Bless America Again,* June 1972

VL 73925, *Alone with You,* June 1972

DL 75381, *Here I Am Again,* October 1972

MCA 300, *Entertainer of the Year,* February 1973

MCA 2-4000, *The Ernest Tubb/Loretta Lynn Story,*
June 1973

MCA 335, *Louisiana Woman, Mississippi Man* (with
Conway Twitty), July 1973

MCA 355, *Love Is the Foundation,* August 1973

MCA 420, *Loretta Lynn's Greatest Hits Vol. Two*
(compilation), May 1974

MCA 427, *Country Partners* (with Conway Twitty),
June 1974

MCA 444, *They Don't Make 'Em Like My Daddy
Anymore,* September 1974

MCA 471, *Back to the Country,* February 1975

MCA 2143, *Feelins'* (with Conway Twitty), June 1975

MCA 2146, *Home,* August 1975

MCA 2179, *When the Tingle Becomes a Chill*,
February 1976

MCA 2209, *United Talent* (with Conway Twitty),
June 1976

MCA 2228, *Somebody Somewhere*, October 1976

MCA, *The Best of Loretta Lynn* (compilation), 1976

LL1001, *On the Road with Loretta and the Coal Miners*
(sold at concerts only), 1976

MCA 2265, *I Remember Patsy*, April 1977

MCA 2278, *Dynamic Duo* (with Conway Twitty),
June 1977

MCA 2330, *Out of My Head and Back in My Bed*,
February 1978

MCA 2372, *Honky Tonk Heroes* (with Conway Twitty),
June 1978

K-Tel, *Greatest Hits Live* (compilation), 1978

MCA 3073, *We've Come a Long Way, Baby*,
February 1979

FGLP 0002, *Ernest Tubb—The Legend and the Legacy*
(includes Loretta Lynn), February 1979

CL 3-3001, *Ernest Tubb—The Legend and the Legacy
Vol. 1* (includes Loretta Lynn), June 1979

MCA 3164, *The Very Best of Loretta and Conway*,
July 1979

MCA 3190, *Diamond Duet* (with Conway Twitty),
October 1979

SZ 36303, *The Fish That Saved Pittsburgh* (soundtrack)
(includes Loretta Lynn), November 1979

MSM35018, *Crisco Presents Loretta Lynn's Country
Classics*
(mail-order album), 1979

MCA 3217, *Loretta*, February 1980

MCA 5148, *Lookin' Good*, October 1980

MCA 5178, *Two's a Party* (duet with Conway Twitty), 1981

MCA 5293, *I Lie*, February 1982

MCA 5354, *Making Love from Memory*, September 1982

MCA 5426, *Lyin', Cheatin', Woman Chasin', Honky Tonkin', Whiskey Drinkin' You*, 1983

MCA 5613, *Just a Woman*, July 1985

HL-1059160, *The Best of Conway and Loretta*, December 1987

MCAD-5975, *Conway Twitty and Loretta Lynn 20 Greatest Hits* (compilation CD), 1987

MC-42216, *Making Believe* (with Conway Twitty), 1988

MCA 42174, *Who Was That Stranger*, May 1988

MCA, *20 Greatest Hits* (compilation), 1988

MCA, *The Very Best of Loretta Lynn* (compilation), 1988

MCA, *I'll Just Call You Darlin'*, 1989

MCA 10083, *Country Music Hall of Fame Series* (compilation), February 1990

MCA, *Peace in the Valley*, 1990

MCA, *The Old Rugged Cross*, 1992

MCA Special, *Loretta Lynn Sings Patsy Cline's Favorites*, 1992

CO 53414, *Honky Tonk Angels* (with Dolly Parton & Tammy Wynette), October 1993

MCA Special, *Hey Good Lookin'*, 1993

WMT-32194, *Making More Memories*, 1994

MCAD3-11070, *Honky Tonk Girl—The Loretta Lynn Collection* (compilation), 1994

Pair, *Country's Favorite Daughter*, 1994

Musketeer, *An Evening with Loretta Lynn*, 1995

MSD 35681, *The Country Music Hall of Fame Presents
Loretta Lynn* (compilation CD), 1995

MCA Special, *On Tour, Vol. 1 Live*, 1996

MCA Special, *On Tour, Vol. 2 Live*, 1996

Columbia River, *Loretta Lynn* (compilation), 1997

Half Moon, *The Very Best of Loretta Lynn* (compilation),
1998

Madacy, *All-Time Gospel Favorites*, 1998

Fed-CD-6542, *Best of the Best Ernest Tubb & Loretta
Lynn* (compilation CD), 1999

#MCAD-70106, *The Best of Loretta Lynn: 20th-Century
Masters* (compilation CD), 1999

Audium/Koch, *Still Country*, 2000

#088112251-2, *The Best of Conway Twitty & Loretta
Lynn: 20th-Century Masters* (compilation CD), 2000

#088170215-2, *The Best of Loretta Lynn: 20th-Century
Masters, Vol. 2* (compilation CD), 2001

#WIL336792, *The Gift* (music from the motion picture,
includes two cuts by Loretta), 2001

Singles Discography

1960

"I'm a Honky Tonk Girl" b/w "Whispering Sea," Zero

"New Rainbow" b/w "Heartaches Meet Mr. Blues," Zero

"The Darkest Day" b/w "I'm Gonna Pack My Troubles,"
Zero

1961

"I Walked Away from the Wreck" b/w "The Girl That I
Am Now," Decca

1962

"Success," b/w "Hundred-Proof Heartache," Decca
"World of Forgotten People" b/w "Get Set for a
Heartache," Decca

1963

"The Other Woman" b/w "Who'll Help Me Get
Over You," Decca
"Before I'm Over You" b/w "Where Were You?" Decca

1964

"Wine Women and Song" b/w "This Haunted
House," Decca
"Mr. and Mrs. Used to Be" b/w "Love Was Right Here
All the Time" (with Ernest Tubb), Decca
"Happy Birthday" b/w "When Lonely Hits Your
Heart," Decca

1965

"Blue Kentucky Girl" b/w "Two Steps Forward," Decca
"We're Not Kids Anymore" b/w "Our Hearts Are
Holding Hands" (with Ernest Tubb), Decca
"The Home You're Tearin' Down" b/w "Father
to Go," Decca

1966

"Dear Uncle Sam" b/w "Hurtin' for Certain," Decca
"You Ain't Woman Enough" b/w "God Gave
Me a Heart to Forgive," Decca
"Don't Come Home a'Drinkin' (with Lovin'
on Your Mind)" b/w "Saint to a Sinner," Decca

1967

"Sweet Thang" b/w "Beautiful, Unhappy Home"
(with Ernest Tubb), Decca
"If You're Not Gone Too Long" b/w "A Man I Hardly
Know," Decca
"What Kind of Girl (Do You Think I Am?)" b/w
"Bargain Basement Dress," Decca

1968

"Fist City" b/w "Slowly Killing Me," Decca
"You've Just Stepped In (from Stepping Out on Me)" b/w
"(This Bottle Is) Taking the Place of My Man," Decca
"Your Squaw Is on the Warpath," Decca

1969

"Woman of the World (Leave My Man Alone)," Decca
"Who's Gonna Take the Garbage Out" (with Ernest
Tubb)
"To Make a Man (Feel Like a Man)," Decca
"Wings Upon Your Horns," Decca

1970

"I Know How" b/w "Journey to the End of My World,"
Decca
"You Wanna Give Me a Lift" b/w "What's the Bottle
Done to My Baby," Decca
"Coal Miner's Daughter" b/w "The Man of the House,"
Decca

1971

"After the Fire Is Gone" b/w "The One I Can't Live
Without" (with Conway Twitty), Decca

"I Wanna Be Free" b/w "If I Never Love Again," Decca
"You're Lookin' at Country" b/w "When You're Poor,"
Decca
"Lead Me On" b/w "Four Glass Walls" (with Conway
Twitty), Decca
"Here in Topeka" b/w "Kinfolks Holler," Decca
"One's on the Way" b/w "Kinfolks Holler," Decca

1972

"Here I Am Again" b/w "My Kind of Man," Decca
"Rated 'X' " b/w " 'Til the Pain Outwears the Shame,"
Decca

1973

"Love Is the Foundation" b/w "What Sundown Does to
You," MCA
"Louisiana Woman, Mississippi Man" (with Conway
Twitty), MCA
"Hey Loretta" b/w "Turn Me Anyway but Loose," MCA

1974

"They Don't Make 'Em Like My Daddy Anymore" b/w
"Nothin,' " MCA
"As Soon As I Hang Up the Phone" b/w "A Lifetime
Before" (with Conway Twitty), MCA
"Trouble in Paradise" b/w "Don't Leave Me Where You
Found Me," MCA

1975

"The Pill" b/w "Will You Be There?" MCA
"Feelins' " b/w "You Done Lost Your Baby" (with
Conway Twitty), MCA

"Home" b/w "You Take Me to Heaven Every Night,"
MCA
"When the Tingle Becomes a Chill" b/w "All I Want
from You Is Away," MCA

1976

"Red, White and Blue" b/w "Sounds of a New Love,"
MCA
"The Letter" b/w "God Bless America Again" (with
Conway Twitty), MCA
"Somebody Somewhere (Don't Know What He's Missin'
Tonight)" b/w "Sundown Tavern," MCA
"Out of My Head and Back in My Bed" b/w "The Ole
Rooster," MCA

1977

"She's Got You" b/w "The Lady That Lived Here
Before," MCA
"I Can't Love You Enough" b/w "The Bed I'm Dreaming
On," MCA
"Why Can't He Be You" b/w "I Keep on Puttin' On,"
MCA

1978

"Spring Fever" b/w "God Bless the Children," MCA
"From Seven till Ten" b/w "You're the Reason Our Kids
Are Ugly" (with Conway Twitty), MCA
"We've Come a Long Way, Baby" b/w "I Can't Feel You
Anymore," MCA

1979

"I Can't Feel You Anymore" b/w "True Love Needs to
Keep in Touch," MCA

"I've Got a Picture of Us on My Mind" b/w "I Don't
Feel Like a Movie Tonight," MCA
"You Know Just What I'd Do" b/w "The Sadness of It
All" (with Conway Twitty), MCA

1980
"Pregnant Again," MCA
"It's True Love" (with Conway Twitty), MCA
"Naked in the Rain," MCA
"Cheatin' on a Cheater," MCA

1981
"Lovin' What Your Lovin' Does to Me" (with Conway
Twitty), MCA
"Somebody Led Me Away," MCA
"I Still Believe in Waltzes" (with Conway Twitty), MCA

1982
"I Lie," MCA
"Making Love from Memory," MCA

1983
"Breakin' It," MCA
"Lyin', Cheatin', Woman Chasin', Honky Tonkin',
Whiskey Drinkin' You," MCA
"Walking with My Memories," MCA

1985
"Heart Don't Do This to Me," MCA
"Wouldn't It Be Great," MCA

1986
"Just a Woman," MCA

1988
"Making Believe" (with Conway Twitty), MCA
"Who Was That Stranger," MCA

1993
"Silver Threads and Golden Needles" (with Dolly Parton
and Tammy Wynette), Columbia

1994
"We Need to Make More Memories"

2000
"Country in My Genes/I'm a Honky Tonk Girl"
(released to radio stations only, not for retail sale)

2001
"I Can't Hear the Music"
(released to radio stations only, not for retail sale)
"Table for Two"
(released to radio stations only, not for retail sale)